FAMINE WORLDS

Famine Worlds

LIFE AT THE EDGE OF SUFFERING
IN LEBANON'S GREAT WAR

Tylor Brand

STANFORD UNIVERSITY PRESS
Stanford, California

Stanford University Press
Stanford, California

© 2023 by Tylor Brand. All rights reserved.

No part of this book may be reproduced or transmitted in any form or by any means, electronic or mechanical, including photocopying and recording, or in any information storage or retrieval system, without the prior written permission of Stanford University Press.

Printed in the United States of America on acid-free, archival-quality paper

Library of Congress Cataloging-in-Publication Data
Names: Brand, Tylor, author.
Title: Famine worlds : life at the edge of suffering in Lebanon's Great War / Tylor Brand.
Description: Stanford, California : Stanford University Press, [2023] | Includes bibliographical references and index
Identifiers: LCCN 2022048604 (print) | LCCN 2022048605 (ebook) | ISBN 9781503633247 (cloth) | ISBN 9781503636163 (paperback) | ISBN 9781503636170 (ebook)
Subjects: LCSH: World War, 1914–1918—Social aspects—Lebanon. | Famines—Lebanon—History—20th century. | Lebanon—Social conditions—1516–1918.
Classification: LCC D524.7.L4 B73 2023 (print) | LCC D524.7.L4 (ebook) | DDC 940.35692—dc23/eng/20221011
LC record available at https://lccn.loc.gov/2022048604
LC ebook record available at https://lccn.loc.gov/2022048605

Cover design and illustration: David Drummond

Typeset by Elliott Beard in Adobe Caslon Pro 10/14.75

For Abed

Contents

	A Note on Translation, Transliteration, Abbreviations, and Anachronisms	ix
	Preface	xi
	Map	xvii
	INTRODUCTION Four Years of War	1
1	Some "Sufficed"; Others Died	17
2	Death and the Famished Body	38
3	Staying Alive	61
4	Trauma and Time	83
5	A World in Decline	105
6	The Unwashed and Unwell	127
7	The Sheep and the Goats	147
	CONCLUSION An Uncomfortable Memory	173
	Acknowledgments	191
	Notes	193
	Bibliography	223
	Index	243

A Note on Translation, Transliteration, Abbreviations, and Anachronisms

This book is aimed at a broad audience of both specialists and novices, which has required me to sacrifice some specificity in the service of accessibility. Throughout the text I anachronistically refer to the area that fell into the boundaries of Greater Lebanon after World War I as "Lebanon," both for simplicity and because the famine has special importance in the Lebanese national historical narrative. Where specificity is necessary, I refer to the *mutasarrifiyya* of Mount Lebanon as such or as "the mountain" in the text. For similar reasons, terms like the Turkish *vilayet* and Arabic *wilaya* are rendered as "province" for the sake of nonspecialists, and the smaller geographical division *qadha'* is termed "district." Apart from in citations and a few particularly evocative terms and exclamations, I have translated instead of transliterated quoted passages. When non-English terms are necessary, the book uses a simplified transliteration style that is light on diacritics and favors common spellings whenever possible. Deferring to common use, the letter *shiin* is represented by both "ch" and "sh." The only diacritics used are the ' for the *'ayn* and the ' for the *hamza*, but apart from using "ou" rather than "u" for the long vowel *waw*, neither long vowels nor emphatic consonants are otherwise distinguished. I have rendered the *nisba* as -*iyy* in most terms (an exception is the use of familiar spellings such as "Nabatieh" over "Nabatiyya"). I indicate the presence of a feminine *idafa* with a *-t* in transliteration but otherwise do not add extra letters beyond the *a* to denote the *taa marbuuta*. Within the text, I choose common or preferred spellings for names and proper nouns, such as Beirut instead of "Bayrut," and use anglicized versions of well-known names, such as Sidon instead of "Sayda." I have attempted to limit the use of abbreviations and acronyms, except in the citations, in which I use PHS for the Presbyterian Historical Society and AUB for the American University of Beirut. I hope that these choices make for a more pleasant reading experience without sacrificing meaning in the process.

Preface

This book is about a crisis in the past, but it has been tragically connected to crises of the present from start to finish. When I first began my research on the Lebanese famine of World War I while at the American University of Beirut, the consequences of the rapidly unraveling Arab Spring had just begun to show in neighboring Syria. Initially I had watched the distant protests with muted optimism, but hope gradually faded when demonstrators faced repression and eventually violence as the country tipped toward civil war. With the conflict next door intensifying, the streets of Beirut began to fill with people fleeing the chaos and blind violence that had spilled into their lives in Syria. My work and the growing crisis progressed separately, but as the years passed, they began to converge in unexpected ways.

In the first year of the crisis, the Syrians in our midst were met with sympathy from many in Lebanon, which had itself been under the direct or indirect sway of the Syrian regime since the 1970s. But this initial sentiment was fleeting. As time passed and their numbers swelled, our guests gradually ceased to be objects of sympathy and increasingly became targets of derision and frustration. None were immune. While wealthy Syrians were scorned for driving up rents, the middle and lower classes felt resentment for occupying jobs at often exploitative wages, and the refugees on the streets were reviled as rough living and begging became common sights at various high-visibility points around the city. As their suffering grew, the collective and individual will to alleviate it faltered. It was at this point that I began to notice peculiar parallels between those who lived the wartime famine and those occupying the crisis in my own world. The rationalizations of suffering and moralizations of poverty I heard in my own life were buried thinly under sympathetic platitudes in books and reports written a century before. Like in the past, the child beggars on the streets earned sympathy as well as scorn for their parents. Just as my sources dwelled on the refugees' contribution to a deadly typhus epidemic in World War I, we in the present fretted about the risk of polio, tuberculosis, and waterborne diseases in refugee communities. While my sources complained of the filth and smell of those struggling to survive on the streets of 1917, we in the present complained of aggressive beggars, the threat of crime, and the human effluent and litter flowing from the informal camps scattered about the country. In the present, like in the past, the marginalized members of society were revictimized by our perception of them and their place in a crisis they had to endure just to survive.

The historical parallels began to open my eyes to my own deficiencies as a participant observer in the present crisis. Alarmingly, I first recognized my own compassion fatigue when I read it in the words of writers from a century before. I saw their avoidance strategies in my own rerouted journeys through the city, which over time began to favor streets where I would be less likely to encounter certain persistent child beggars and shoe-shine boys. The writers voiced the same sense of guilt that I felt in my desire to help, the same slow souring into resignation that I could not help, and eventually the same tacit admission that I would choose not to overburden myself with other peoples' unsolvable problems—even when a scrap of kindness would have been better than nothing. Though I made a conscious effort to change my behavior once I realized this, like many who lived through the famine, my initial response still haunts me to this day.

To some extent, the parallels that I saw were simply flashes of apophenia—I found patterns where I perceived them to exist. While I sought to keep a firm boundary between the past and present when I began to work on the wartime famine, I can attest that my own experience on the edge of suffering did influence my work in the sense that it revealed what was most important about the crisis of the past in the first place: the people within it. At that point, my work shifted from a social and environmental history of the war into an investigation of how people experienced the crisis. Rather than chasing the tails of historiographical debates over causality and politics, I instead became far more fascinated with how people understood their own personal crisis and how they dealt with its intrusions into their lives.

While I remained interested in the ways that people experiencing the famine adapted to survive, I also began to wonder about those like myself: people whose daily realities were not filled with direct suffering but who constantly brushed against it as they went about their lives. I saw my own petty plights in their words. Like them, the crisis in the streets was a part of my world that I could not escape when I walked within it, but it practically disappeared when I closed my door—except perhaps for the conflicted emotions that I felt about my own peripheral role in the lives of those around me. I also began to ponder my own relationship with the refugee crisis. Though all of us in Beirut lived amid the same situation, it affected all of us differently. The refugees I saw on the streets lived their worlds, and I lived my own. The same held for everyone in society, from the nine-year-old boy who told me how he shined shoes to support his mother and younger siblings back in Syria, to my Lebanese neighbors and colleagues, to the erudite Syrian English literature students who served us coffee and the talented musician who sold us pirated DVDs, to their exploitive Lebanese bosses who abused them because of their passports—all the way up to my wealthy Syrian acquaintance and his peers, who lived out the war in gilded exile. I found that our different vantage points, our different levels of self-awareness, our different coping mechanisms, and our different politics and values led each of us to interpret the crisis in a slightly different way. Ultimately, those perceptions influenced how we acted and how we treated each other.

This book is largely a product of that realization. While many of the books written on the period have aimed to understand what happened during the war and why, I try to answer the question, How did it *feel* to live the famine? This question offers up far more specific, and far more diverse, sets of answers than the question of what happened during the famine, and its implications for our understanding of the disaster's place in history is no less important. I am much more concerned with the lived context that existed nebulously behind the major events on the timeline than with those events themselves. Like in any crisis, we can talk of the wartime famine as a cohesive event. However, that event was itself something of a "metacrisis" in which thousands of individual stories played out. Each of those people experienced a slightly different war and a slightly different famine. These varied experiences in turn influenced the ways that people conceptualized the crisis and how they conveyed what they experienced to others. To try to access these subjective experiences, this book approaches the famine thematically rather than chronologically and explores the experience of famine on a more personal rather than structural level. Overall, I have sought to consider big ideas through the narrow scope of microhistory, and when analyzing the famine as a whole, I have tried to show the texture of the crisis and its effects on the social, local, and individual levels. I try to indicate patterns where they exist, but I am cautious about inferring universality from particular cases: their particularity is the point.

This book does not claim to address every question about the famine era, nor does it make use of every possible source. I have intentionally skirted certain sources and topics to avoid excessively overlapping with the excellent work of my colleagues, who have happily grown in number in the wake of the war's centennial. Where I do touch on similar topics, I have sought to ask different questions to augment the analysis that has come before me or to expand on areas that needed additional coverage. In any case, sourcing such a history of the famine is more difficult than simply narrating the wartime period as a single event. Many contemporaneous overviews of the war are overly broad and rarely extend beyond summaries of major events or catalogs of woes revolving around the unforgettable triad of the locusts, the famine, and the reviled Ottoman regional commander Jamal Pasha and his affiliates. Many typical sources for such research are not particularly useful for my ends. Much of the Ottoman and Entente archival material is too distant from daily life and too concerned with the war to be useful. Ottoman journalistic sources from the war (like wartime sources across the globe) are hamstrung by press closures and the strict wartime censorship that limited what could be reported and how. Reports from outside Ottoman territories like those in Egypt or the publications in the American diaspora enjoyed fewer limitations than those within the empire, but many who took a special interest in the famine situation from abroad either lacked immediate knowledge of the famine or published with clear motivations—perhaps to encourage a French invasion or to generate sympathy or anger in their audience. While a number of historians have done excellent work with the truncated journalistic archives, the questions that such sources can answer are ultimately not the ones I am asking.

To access more detailed, direct experiences of the famine and how it was narrated, I focused heavily on memoirs, letters, diaries, overviews, and reports as primary sources. Each type of source has both advantages and flaws. The most useful sources were those that described life in the crisis while it was taking place, occasionally offering either deliberate or unintentional commentary on the personal tolls that the famine took and the ambivalence that many felt about life within it. This insight is present in certain war-centric memoirs, personal diaries, family and local histories, and archival materials—including reports and letters from the American college and missionary employees who remained in the region during the war. Such sources have been particularly valuable as windows on contemporary attitudes due to their proximity to the famine and the occasional slip of self-consciousness, which can provide somewhat honest glimpses into the subjective internal worlds of those who lived the era, often without the filter of retrospection that we find in memoirs.

All of these documents need to be read with a sense of their limitations. Despite the deceptively omniscient narration they so often provide, their perspectives are hardly objective. As might be expected in an era when literacy rates were low and publishing was beyond the reach of all but the privileged few, most of the written records were left by members of the social and intellectual elite or by foreign observers who were present during the war. For the prominent individuals who were blessed enough to be able to leave us their memoirs, the war and its suffering were often depicted as just another waypoint to episodically pass as they moved from one phase of their lives into another.[1] Many of those works were published years after the war and often exhibited a keen eye for their historical legacy. This elite perspective can be a limitation, but it is also an opportunity. Although I have sought as much as possible to find the voices of those who endured the famine from within, I have deliberately included the experiences of nonsuffering interlocutors as well—it was their disaster too, after all. Not everyone suffered equally, so it is important to show what that might have meant both within the famine and for how we remember it. Though this book is not particularly interested in renarrating the wartime period, it is quite concerned with how the famine *was* narrated by its contemporaries and with the character of those depictions. For this purpose, such elite sources can be invaluable, since they demonstrate how calamity intensifies social identities and relations of power, whether they intend to do so or not (usually not).

The primary focus of this book is the famine of World War I in the area that would later become the Republic of Lebanon, but it aims to be relevant to more than simply that fragment of space and time. Now is a time of disasters, individual and collective. While this book began within one social crisis (that is ongoing still), it has been completed in the midst or wake of several others, including a global pandemic and an economic collapse in Lebanon that has drawn ominous comparisons to the wartime famine—all with the specter of global climatic catastrophe looming dreadfully. Just as the crisis of the present brought clarity to my understanding of the past, I hope that this analysis of the past might bring similar insight into our understanding of our present and our future calamities—and above all into our understanding of humanity in times of crisis. This is not to say that those lessons will be direct or easy. Drawing holistic conclusions about disparate events is inadvisable and becomes even more so as the gulf of time separating the events widens. Different contexts lead to different processes that produce different outcomes, so no matter how similar two cases may be, they will never be identical. However, many of the same challenges that individuals and their societies faced during the famine of World War I have obvious correlates in other contexts. If the particular lives and contexts explored in this book can help us to better understand patterns of life in crisis in general, then in my eyes this book will have succeeded. It is apparent that we need all the help we can get.

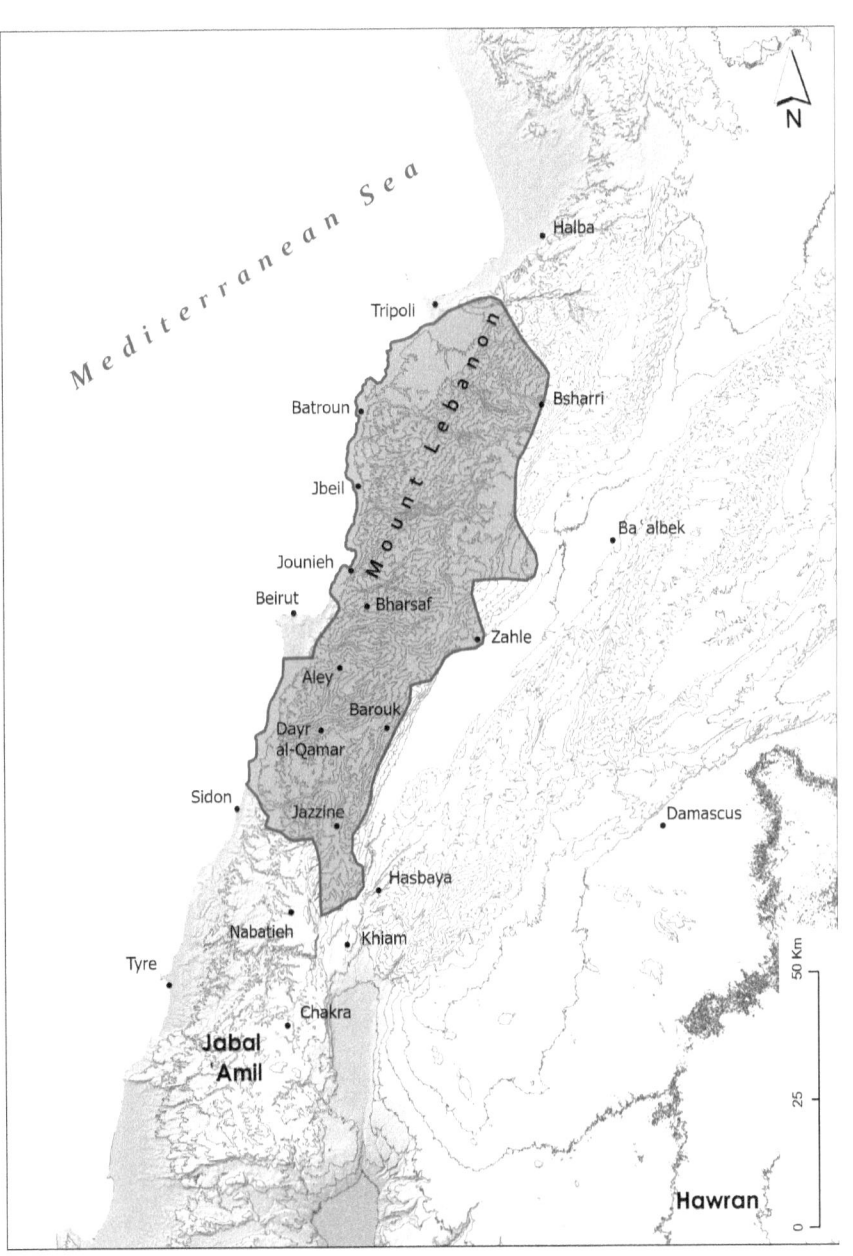

FAMINE WORLDS

INTRODUCTION

Four Years of War

> Shame on you who do not record for us the scandal, the disgrace, so that we can fight against the oppressors and blacken the pages of the lives of those greedy ones from among the sons of this miserable nation.
> —ANTUN YAMMINE

THAT 1914 WAS A WAR year would not have been particularly surprising for the residents of the Ottoman eastern Mediterranean, for whom every year since 1911 had been a war year without much obvious war. Apart from the shelling of Beirut's customs house by an Italian naval cruiser in 1912, the events that shook battlefronts and transformed politics in the imperial capital had only tangential impacts on those living in the empire's Arab periphery. If they suffered, it was from an uptick in conscription, increased taxation, inflation, and a growing sense of urgency among partisans.[1] Though the list of participants in the war of 1914 was from the outset far more impressive and carried far greater stakes for the Ottoman imperial center, there were few in the area that would become "Greater Lebanon" after the war who seemed to suspect that the broader effects of this conflict would be any different from those of the last ones. In his literary memoir *Qabl an ansa*,[2] the cultural and linguistic scholar Anis Furayha recalled a childhood scene soon after the war's announcement that spoke to this innocent indeterminacy. In it, a cluster of men in the mountain village of Ras al-Matn clamored eagerly to hear news of its progress—arousing the disdain of one observer who dryly quipped, "Why, *ya 'ammi*, are you all so concerned? Hopefully they will all kill each other." In the moment, this aside was clever cynicism, but read retrospectively, it was foreshadowing at its grimmest. As Furayha went on to observe, "No one knew that the war would bring Lebanon hunger, sickness, and death."[3]

And certainly, the innocence of those early months did not last. Within months, the long fingers of the conflict began to touch intimate aspects of life across the region. Soon it became apparent that what we now know as World War I would be very different from the comparatively compartmentalized spats with Italy and the Balkan states that had preceded it. While fortune would once again spare the region that would become Lebanon and Syria from the horrors of the trenches, it would be impossible to evade the broader impacts of a conflict as profound and as pervasive as the Great War.

For the home front, the first hints of war came with the anticipatory logistic moves that the Ottoman administration began in August 1914. Though the army had only demobilized its troops from its last disastrous campaign in the Balkans months before, the fresh existential threat presented by war among European imperial states prompted an unprecedented remobilization campaign whose Turkish name, *safar barlik*, would soon become notorious across Greater Syria.[4] In the months that followed, recruiters swept the nation's men from cities and countryside alike, cobbling together an army in the likely event that the empire's bid for neutrality would fail. As state agents plied villages for bodies to fill their quotas, hundreds of thousands of men, young and old, were sucked into the war machine. The push to engage the nation as a whole meant that more of the empire's Arab and Christian citizenry were caught in the efforts than in previous conflicts. Although the fact that such recruits were disproportionately relegated to lowly labor battalions or backline positions might appear fortuitous, their posting did not grant immunity to death from disease or combat, nor did it prevent their home villages from suffering from their absence.[5]

And the state was not just after men. Implementing the Law of the Method of Imposition of War Taxes and the Law on the Acquisition of Military Transport Vehicles allowed agents to harvest commodities, useful goods, vehicles, animals, and even personal belongings from homes to provision an army that could not even feed or clothe its conscripts as they mustered.[6] Those who could not afford to buy exemptions were required to supply both uniforms and five days of rations to sustain themselves on the way to their units.[7] For the residents of rural regions, this mass-requisitioning was particularly ill timed, since it disrupted agricultural cycles and deprived families of food reserves that had been collected for the winter.

Events accelerated after October 29, 1914, when an Ottoman naval bombardment of Russia's Crimean ports officially catapulted the reluctant empire into the war and set events into motion that would have devastating consequences for its populations.[8] Though no home front escaped the war unscathed, the social impacts were especially profound for the inhabitants of Greater Syria, which almost immediately found itself politically and economically impacted by the might of both sides of the conflict. Soon after joining the war, Istanbul subordinated the civilian authorities of the region to the political control of nationalist triumvir and commander of the Ottoman Fourth Army, Ahmed Jamal Pasha, whose unyielding authoritarianism and merciless demeanor during the war would brand him as the greatest monster of the era in local memory.[9] Strategically, Jamal sought to consolidate power with the central authorities and maintain stability, which included suppressing fifth columnists, real or potential.[10] For the citizens of Syria, Jamal's wartime rule meant a significant loss of local autonomy across the region (particularly in the semi-independent district of Mount Lebanon), political terror, and decisive—if often ineffective—centralizing policies. To make matters worse, Entente naval supremacy began to stifle the coastal region with a blockade soon after the war began. Trade nearly ceased after Jamal Pasha's closure of Syrian ports in February 1915, and hope of normalcy evaporated when Britain instituted a full trade embargo in June 1915.[11] Once the official cordon descended and the final ships departed, the ports of the empire remained sealed to civilian vessels until the Entente occupation of the region in late 1918.[12] The embargo was unequivocally a tool of war that sought to collectively punish a civilian population into revolting against its Turkish overlords,[13] but amid Jamal Pasha's political repression and the enervating effects of social crisis, the Syrian revolt never came. The blockade only succeeded in inflaming the crisis and making it nearly impossible to leave when the famine began.

Trapped between feuding imperial interests, the region soon began to suffer. The excision from global markets devastated the merchant economy of Beirut and other coastal towns, which were now cut off from the shipping, finance, and service sectors that fueled the region's vibrant economic growth in decades prior. In Mount Lebanon this meant the loss of the silk industry and tourism sectors, which together contributed to countless jobs and roughly 47 percent of the mountain's estimated prewar GDP.[14] Ottoman precautionary policies only deepened the crisis. Soon after the war began, regional grain production and its distribution networks were commandeered by a military government that had no idea how long the conflict would last and whose priorities thus favored the immediate demands of the army over the needs of society. To be fair, at the time, there was no indication that the region would face a famine—after all, Syria and Palestine were regional breadbaskets. But such policies extended to other administrative areas as well. For instance, in anticipation of capital flight if Britain and France called in the country's debt (they did, after all, control the Ottoman Bank), the Ottoman state froze the transfer of funds into and out of the region through Entente clearinghouses and financial institutions.[15] This may have saved the treasury, but for those across the region who depended on remittances from the vast Syrian and Lebanese diaspora, this meant an immediate loss of income and a far more precarious future than they faced in July 1914.

The first real warning signs of crisis appeared in November of 1914, when flour shortages along the coasts and in the mountains prompted general discontent punctuated by sporadic protests. In February 1915, weak rainfall and fears of famine in the Syrian hinterlands led the Damascene municipal council to suspend shipments of flour to Beirut, Mount Lebanon, and Palestine.[16] Both coastal areas and Mount Lebanon were left particularly vulnerable to such decisions. These were variously lands of mulberry groves and vineyards, olive trees and fruit orchards—not of rolling grain fields that would allow them to feed their own populations. Mount Lebanon's annual local production accounted for less than a tenth of the of the 23.5 million kilograms of wheat that it consumed.[17] Normally, the shortfall would be addressed by cash purchases from regional suppliers, but this option was negated by the blockade and Ottoman anti-smuggling policies. Worse, the state's attempts to prevent wartime grain profiteering actually encouraged corruption, speculation, and transportation inefficiencies that made a growing crisis even bleaker. The state's solution to flour shortages in the city of Beirut was a political one: to create a private-public flour cartel in conjunction with local elites like the Sursuq family (a plan that was later imitated by the district governor of Mount Lebanon, 'Ali Munif Bey).[18] While such official conduits eased the flow of food, the cartels almost immediately became hotbeds of corruption.

Even early on, the war left uneven footprints across the region. This was in part due to Lebanon's geographical layout, around which local economies and societies were molded. Large population centers dotted the coastline, concentrated around the sprawling nexus of Beirut. The region was dependent upon the influx of goods and capital from Europe and the outflow of cash crops like citrus, soap, olive oil, tobacco, and especially silk cocoons toward Europe. In an age of steam travel, the coast was well positioned to benefit from the transit of consumer goods from the coastal ports to the old wealth of the Syrian interior. From the coastal littoral rose the foothills and the peaks of the independent district of Mount Lebanon, where communities big and small nestled along garden terraces amid the parasol pines and the ubiquitous mulberry trees that fed the mountain's silk industry. On its fringes, the mountain fell away to agrarian hinterlands—the fertile hills and plains of 'Akkar in the north, the Biqa' Valley in the east, and the rolling hills of the Jabal 'Amil in the south. Each area faced different challenges in the war. While rural areas struggled to find necessary hands due to conscription and the requisitioning of vehicles and beasts,[19] the loss of coastal trade and its related industries threw thousands of workers in Mount Lebanon and the coast into desperate circumstances. By early 1915, the cities and the mountain began to fill with unemployed men seeking some way of sustaining themselves and their families. Incomes collapsed, and life grew precarious for people across the region long before prices rose in late 1915. And when they rose, things went from bad to worse.

As difficult as the early months of the war seemed, the situation dramatically worsened when locust swarms vast enough to blot out the sun descended on the region in April 1915. The insects progressively denuded fields and orchards from the Hijaz region in western Arabia to southern Anatolia. Their devastation came in waves: after the adults devoured the nearby greenery, they bred and laid eggs, which soon led to hatchlings and then nymph hoppers. In each stage, the creatures ravenously consumed whatever they could find to fuel their rapid metamorphosis. Communities toiled in their wake to save the harvest, but it was mostly in vain. "The year of the locust" would foreshadow harsh times to come. In one reckoning, the region lost 536,000 tons of production in 1915 alone, and the all-important wheat harvest of 1915 fell to 942,319 tons—over 30 percent lower than in 1913.[20] Monetary losses from the plague were estimated by one observer at one hundred million francs,[21] but it would be impossible to tally the intangible costs that this disaster imposed on farmers and their communities or for local grain markets that were thrown asunder by the disaster (except perhaps for the profits pocketed by speculators amid the volatility).

Even with the locust plague, the Ottomans entered the war with a two-year grain reserve in Syria, but its benefit was largely canceled out by policy and technical failures. The wartime transportation crisis was a prime example of this. The limited regional rail infrastructure was entirely controlled by the military administration, which could redirect loads of grain at will. A fuel shortage only added to this problem. Beirut had exhausted its coal supply before the war had even begun, and the prospect of replenishing its stores was dim, since the empire had declared war against the source of 90 percent of its coal imports, Great Britain.[22] In their desperation for fuel, the regional authorities denuded stretches of Mount Lebanon to make charcoal. Unfortunately, this replacement was far less efficient than burning mineral coal—so much so that stories emerged of Beiruti conscripts deserting simply by walking off the trains as they wheezed up the mountains toward Damascus. Between the militarization of the railway and the overzealous requisitioning of pack animals and vehicles, transportation became a logistic nightmare for a region that still heavily relied on camel and mule caravans to move food and goods.[23]

Policy failures and environmental calamities from the war's first year further catalyzed an economic crisis that began to spiral out of control by late 1915. The shock of the locusts placed further stress on a grain market that was already wavering under the pressure of profiteering, consumer demand, and the voracious appetite of the war. Local merchant capitalists did much to exacerbate these problems. Because normal opportunities for commerce had been upended by the war, many with liquid capital turned to speculation or lending.[24] The social influence of such wealthy profiteers ensured that corruption plagued supply chains from the points of production to transportation to warehousing to the eventual distribution of whatever grain reached the market for civilians. Though the state tried fixing prices and implementing transportation control measures to prevent hoarding, private speculators were undeterred—in no small part because many of the worst offenders were local elites with close ties to the Ottoman authorities.[25]

Introducing a new paper currency in 1915 also inadvertently dropped a ticking time bomb into the Ottoman economy. Initially fixed at a value of 108 piasters to the gold lira, the paper note remained valued on par for only two months before it began to float against Ottoman metal coins, which grew increasingly scarce as the state began to withdraw them from circulation to pay for the war. The government eventually attempted to fix the lira at a straight exchange rate of 100 piasters to the lira and implemented harsh penalties for those who refused to accept it at face value, but this did little to deter black marketeers. Even in the absence of foreign currency exchanges, the paper note's value began to collapse as people began hoarding specie and demanding different rates for paper and coin.[26] As the value of paper collapsed, it became far harder and much pricier to buy necessities without specie. Between July 1915 and July 1916, the value of the paper currency declined from 100 piasters to the gold lira to 121 piasters to the gold lira in Istanbul exchanges. After mid-1916, the bottom dropped out and the value of the piaster fell to 183:1 in December, 381:1 in July of 1917, and finally to its low in September of 1918 when it was worth a mere 18 percent of its face value.[27] Exchange rates were even worse outside of major cities and in areas like Mount Lebanon. Along with the impacts that this had on the cost of living, the currency collapse contributed to the already vigorous crisis of confidence in the Ottoman state and to rampant wartime corruption as civil servants scrambled to survive on increasingly worthless salaries.[28]

To some extent, a crisis as large and complicated as the famine would have also been beyond the control of even a far more focused and competent administration than the Ottoman wartime authorities proved to be. However, the government's emphasis on the war and on maintaining its public image led it to stumble at times when positive action was needed. The state under Jamal Pasha did not entirely neglect the crisis, nor did it deliberately stoke it, as was rumored, but its wartime actions were often misguided or counterproductive. Despite its efforts to preserve morale, administrators persistently failed optics tests, like when Beirut's new governor 'Azmi Bey banned the relief work that was already underway in the city when he assumed his post in 1915. Though his move aimed to consolidate state power and deflect the appearance of competition from foreign humanitarians as he implemented his own public works projects, he did little more than earn the enmity of his community.[29]

The state's proactive moves were on the whole too little and too late and were plagued by mismanagement, conceptual failures, and the effects of wishfully delegating responsibility to incompetent allies and bad actors. Many moves were inconsistent with local realities. When the administration fixed grain prices in shops, the most immediate effect was to drive necessities like flour from the shelves and into the black market. Merchants who had paid market rates for their goods were not going to sell at a loss, so they pulled their products and passed them under the table at the going rate.[30] Ongoing supply shortfalls only encouraged speculation and hoarding, which drove prices to previously unseen heights in 1917 and 1918.[31] Similar problems plagued the state's production and distribution controls, which disrupted preexisting networks and disincentivized honest dealings with the government and its agents. The effect was hidden stockpiles and illicit demands for payment in gold by agrarian elites like the Druze shaykhs of the Syrian Hawran region.[32] The rise in speculation prompted by the initial crisis and the loss of agricultural workers to the war further hindered the grain market's ability to correct itself after the systemic shocks of 1915.

Unchecked and catalyzed by the war, such social, economic, and political factors gradually pulled the region into a destructive cycle. The crisis developed unevenly, but it gradually worsened as time passed. Life grew more difficult in 1915 due to the labor crisis and falling incomes, and telltale signs of famine began to show in early 1916. Ibrahim Khalil 'Awad, who was a child at the time of the war, described the transition that his family faced in the central Lebanese village of Bharsaf: "It was the beginning of poverty and the intensification of dearness, and the people took to dying of hunger."[33] Nearly all historians have dated the start of the famine to mid to late 1915, when a rise in visible poverty and mass migration made the presence of famine undeniable to local observers. However, the increase in malnutrition and mortality that announced the famine in 1916 was well on its way by the end of 1914. Many who lived in or on the verge of poverty faced immense risk soon after the war began, and many in the middle class gradually fell into poverty as soaring prices and joblessness led to precarity and migration. As poverty spread and desperation grew, preexisting social structures began to crumble. By 1916, food-access failures abounded, and the streets and towns of the region began to feature the skeletal bodies of the starving with alarming regularity. Worsening social conditions and migration amplified the spread of terrifying pathogens like typhus and tuberculosis, and under the pressure of poverty and persistent malnutrition, even relatively pedestrian afflictions like dysentery and malaria became uncharacteristically deadly. When good food grew rare and prices rose, even well-to-do families were forced to exchange such wartime luxuries as white bread and meat for adulterated bran loaves, pulses, seeds, and other often unsafe alternatives.

We tend to associate famine with starvation in the streets and widespread death, but the first stages of famine were far subtler and its effects far more diffuse.[34] Though retrospectively the famine appeared to be a single event, the different ways that wartime circumstances affected the region produced what was essentially three overlapping subfamines that existed within the broader, regional crisis: a famine of the mountain, a famine of the cities, and a famine of the countryside. Each subcrisis was shaped by the unique economic and social factors of its situation, as well as the variable effects of catalysts and the effects of the war. Some areas were more vulnerable to the crisis, and others were better suited to weather it. Rural areas were deeply disadvantaged by Ottoman military policy and were hampered by unequal social structures and natural disaster. Famine in the mountain, on the other hand, was mainly driven by the cessation of overseas trade, the elimination of remittance money, and failures of Ottoman policy. The mountain's unusually internationalized economy made it vulnerable to the blockade, but Mount Lebanon also contended with a disastrous Ottoman anti-smuggling cordon that made moving food into the region nearly impossible for the average family (at least by legal means). Locally known as the "blockade of the mountain" this policy contributed to even higher prices and local shortages. Coastal urban areas were similarly affected by the loss of foreign markets, but they also suffered the side effects of famine in rural and mountain areas, mainly in the form of in-migration. Though each area's problems were rooted in the same basic structural issues that came from the war itself, these differences meant that enduring the famine in Beirut was very different from living it in the agrarian market town of Baʿalbek or in the mountain village of Barouk.

Famine conditions may have fluctuated by season and in response to various internal dynamics, but the social and individual impacts were cumulative and often horrific. Poverty surged, and with it came suffering, emotional misery, sickness, and starvation. The famine was inescapably public and emotionally traumatic. Even those whose lot was merely to sit and watch as their world dissolved in front of their eyes were appalled by its transformations. As the crisis grew, waves of people poured from the mountains into both coastal and inland market towns. The first influx included wealthy elites seeking safety in cities or unemployed laborers seeking work, but later waves included whole families, widowed women, and orphaned children who came seeking a chance at life when survival in their home villages was unsure. Social judgment and acts of desperation litter the sources from this era, as observers grew increasingly appalled by the degeneration that they saw in the behaviors and even in the very bodies of their starving peers. For untold thousands, death was the unavoidable result, but many more continued to struggle, to strive, and to adapt to survive those "years of horror."

From the onset of hostilities until the Armistice of Mudros on October 30, 1918, life in the region was defined by the pressures of the war and the omnipresent suffering of the famine. Though the entire Ottoman home front suffered,[35] the brunt of the crisis fell on the province of Beirut and especially the district of Mount Lebanon.[36] Widespread starvation and the increasingly despotic behavior of Jamal Pasha's military administration convinced many contemporaries that the Ottomans were deliberately targeting the mostly Christian populations of the mountain because of their close ties with France and their contentious politics in the decades prior to the war. Some contemporaries even saw the famine as a deliberate extermination campaign, using food as its weapon in a way that mirrored genocide and ethnic cleansing against the Armenians, Assyrians, and Greeks of Anatolia.[37] As more detailed historical analysis has been conducted in recent decades, this speculation has been shown to be inaccurate, but it is readily apparent that the state's disaster response was no less a disaster itself.

With the arrival of Faysal ibn Husayn's fabled Arab Revolt in 1918 (with the Entente occupying force on its heels in support), the Ottoman administrators retreated, and the empire's policies evaporated. Soon after, the blockade lifted, and normalization mercifully began to commence. Speculators who had been hoarding grain for years released their inventories in a single wave, causing a sudden collapse in food prices. This alleviated some immediate suffering, though inflation remained for some time.[38] The lifting of Ottoman banking restrictions and the embargo brought an influx of bank transfers and family members who had been prevented from coming home to relieve their loved ones. As ports once again opened to the outside world, aid poured in through private donors like Near East Relief and through French agents seeking to burnish France's prospective imperial reputation as it awaited the results of the Paris Peace Conference.[39] Within months, a muted postfamine normalcy gradually descended while politicians and imperialists began to reimagine the region's future in Sevres and San Remo.[40] Though the end of the war brought the nominal end of the famine, its effects would reverberate through society for years to come.[41]

Tracing the War through History

That is the story of the home front in the territories that would become Lebanon after the war, or at least a basic sketch of it. Like any complex historical process, such a narrative is necessarily limited by scope, scale, and framing. Indeed, this triad has frustrated efforts to situate the wartime crisis in the Great War's broader historiography for over a century now. Each nation has its own mythologies, and for general audiences, the wartime suffering of a tiny fragment of a peripheral region in the Middle East has difficulty competing with the familiar horrors of the trenches and the fables that they produced, no matter how intense that suffering may have been. Even if we neglect the general Eurocentrism of the wartime historiography (and no, we should not neglect it), the tragedies of the Ottoman home front hardly matched the sheer scale of the carnage in Europe. How does one justify the importance of a localized calamity when twice as many men perished in the Battle of the Somme than in all of the nearly four years of famine across western Syria?

Even within the region, the famine suffers challenges of framing. The war was an unequivocal watershed event in the regional history of the Middle East. Not only did it mark the end of the two great remaining empires in the region, those of the Ottomans and the Qajars, but their dissolution launched their former imperial subjects unevenly into eras of imperialism and nationalism, which in turn laid the foundations for many of the political realities of today. Juxtaposed with these profound events, the general neglect of the home fronts in wartime historiography is somewhat understandable, if not entirely justifiable. When the famine has been studied, its historical importance has often been seen as a hinge event that linked the era of Ottoman imperial rule to one of European imperial domination[42] or to the admittedly important topic of national creation.[43] Until recently, the war has rarely been granted real value as a self-contained historical event.

Changing historical trends have amended this, but slowly. Like the often competing historiographies of the European fronts, language and identity initially cleaved Ottoman wartime experience into distinctly Turkish, Armenian, Greek, and Arab (primarily Lebanese) proprietary traumas, which have only recently begun to be critically analyzed or integrated into a collective whole.[44] Recent inquiry into the war in the Middle East has begun to shade away from political and diplomatic history in favor of a more comprehensive social history,[45] offering distinct niches for the study of the crisis, disease, famine, and genocide that devastated the region during the war.[46] Much of this attention has centered on the "Lebanese" famine of the war (indeed, it is the focus of this book).[47] Though the area that would become the Republic of Lebanon after the war was not the only place in the empire that experienced famine,[48] the appalling suffering of Mount Lebanon has given the famine special meaning for the country's Maronite Catholic community in particular and, by later extension, to the Lebanese nation as a whole.

Thanks to retrospectives, diaries, and archival sources, it has not been particularly difficult to trace a narrative arc for the history of the wartime famine in the area that would become the Lebanese Republic. However, this narrative can be deceptive. Many of the most read accounts were rife with tales of oppression, backroom conspiracies, clashes of personality, and the usual heroics, histrionics, failures, and follies that are so often included to sweeten the plot.[49] As such, historians have struggled with the veracity of many of the sources and their claims. This has been complicated by the politics of the famine in the postwar era. Though early accounts after the famine literature were often framed as scathing class critiques depicting common suffering under a savage imperial heel, the famine was rapidly weaponized by postwar sectarian politics, particularly after Maronite patriarch Elias Huwayek cited the disaster to justify a Christian-dominated state under French protection after the war.[50]

Many studies of the famine in Lebanon and the province of Beirut have naturally pondered over why the famine took place and what happened during the era. In its most basic sense, the answer to the causality question typically follows one of two general themes: one focusing on Ottoman oppression and Lebanese victimhood (often with local elite complicity)[51] and another placing the blame for the famine at the feet of the Entente powers, specifically their wartime blockade. Recent critical analysis has also blamed locust plagues[52] or silk monoculture and Lebanon's overreliance on foreign imports and capital.[53] Admittedly, it is almost impossible to analyze an event as devastating and vast as the famine of World War I without either rounding off the edges or focusing on a central, narratable theme—but by framing it, the messier, more personal aspects of life in the famine are often lost.

Living the Famine

This book seeks to rediscover the complexity of life in the famine. Though the events that took place within the macrofamine were objectively important (and will be dealt with thematically within this book), the subjective, experiential aspects of the famine are undoubtedly just as vital if we wish to understand the era as a lived context. This book proceeds from the basic premise that if we randomly examined the lives of a dozen people who lived the Lebanese famine of World War I, we would find a dozen different ways of understanding both the famine and life within it. Though many of those explanations would have been united by common themes and shared experiences, we would inevitably find differences in experience due to varying social circumstances, vulnerabilities, status, power, wealth, access to capital, physical location, proximity to hazards, and resilience in the face of change. All of those factors and more affected how much an individual suffered, or if they even suffered at all during the wartime crisis. In turn, each of those individuals would have interpreted the challenges that they faced through their own unique set of experiences and perspectives. While one person might have defined the era through fear, pain, and trauma, another might have spent the four years of the war bored, disgusted, and perhaps even a bit irritated at how difficult it was to acquire the little luxuries of their prefamine life. Another may have survived easily but suffered vicarious traumatization from the tragedies that surrounded them. For others the era may have been defined by the loss of loved ones, livelihoods, a home, or a future. Statistically speaking, around two of those people would have died. To access these experiences, this book focuses on tiny slivers of life in the crisis that speak to the subtle impacts of social calamity.

As a result, much of my analysis about the wartime famine in Lebanon will differ from traditional famine analysis by economists and social historians, and not every example might be immediately recognizable as a famine story. Take the following anecdote, which was passed down through generations of one family in the central mountain village of Barouk. It is not clear exactly which year this story took place—what matters is that at the time, suffering was intense, and life was hard in the mountain. The story centers on two brothers who had set out on a smuggling expedition to purchase grain from their Druze coreligionists in the fertile plains of the Hawran. With prices high and legal avenues for resupply slim, the brothers' journey was an expression of hope. If successful, they could sustain their families and perhaps even earn some extra money by selling their surplus. If they failed . . . well, it was best not to consider that. When they stopped to rest along the hidden trails of the eastern mountain foothills, one brother, named Jammul, pulled out a half loaf of bread, some olives, and an onion, which he broke on a rock, intoning, "Al-hamdulillah ʿala hadhihi al-naʿma" (Praise God for this blessing). While this little invocation may have been as much a matter of habit as anything, hearing such praise as people starved all around them irritated his brother-in-law, who snapped that Jammul should not be so liberal with his praises. Since God was so clearly taking them for granted, perhaps they should make *him* earn their gratitude.[54]

Superficially, this scenario is not necessarily interesting as a source of historical content. There is no reason to doubt that it happened, but its details are unverifiable. Even assuming its accuracy, the exchange took place between two obscure historical actors far from the suffering and starvation that we might consider the titillating bits of the disaster. A literary critic might point out that the action had no overt consequences. Nobody dies, and the only violence in the story is committed against an onion. Nevertheless, this brief moment between Jammul and his brother in that hidden corner of the famine is just as rich in historical meaning as more recognizable wartime scenes like the locust plague or the sight of dissidents swaying lifelessly in the squares of Damascus and Beirut. Within this flash of famine life, we find themes of survival and perseverance and even a hint of the emotional complexity that was an inevitable product of existing amid the traumas of the famine. The story is authentically human—perhaps even more so by virtue of not being very sensational.

These are the stories that are most important for this text. This book holds that life in the Lebanese famine of World War I was not just a montage of sorrow and woe centered on the wartime triumvirate of locusts, starvation, and the villainous Jamal Pasha. Nor was it simply a transitional point between the dying of the Ottoman age and the birth of the nation. The famine was a lived experience. It was a dynamic, four-year-long process of destruction and change that dramatically remade the lives of everyone who lived it. It was physically, socially, practically, and emotionally transformative. It forced people to adapt their behaviors, their habits, their diets, and the ways that they approached their presents and their futures. It shattered social orders and reshaped communities. From within, the famine was unpredictable, overwhelming, and unsolvable. It was, as a contemporary described it, like going up against "adamant."[55] It was "affective,"[56] it was challenging, and it was traumatic. It was the evolving milieu in which people acted, lived, survived, and struggled—for some, until they were physically incapable of struggling any longer. People experienced the famine inside their homes and encountered it when they opened their doors. They saw it, heard, it, and smelled it in the markets and on the streets. It haunted their minds in times of quiet contemplation and they felt it in the pits of their stomachs. As it filled streets with misery and warped the bodies of the starving, it even redefined the shared social constructs that shaped how people understood the world they saw and their place within it. It framed their worldviews and constricted the range of choices that they could make as they sought to survive, or even simply to endure as the days, months, and years passed.

I argue that living within the famine was not just to namelessly take part in one broad, impersonal calamity—it was to be the protagonist of one's own story, with a specific setting, a unique cast of coactors, and personal subplots that developed from one's own subjective experiences of the war and its ineffable calamity. In short, it was to occupy one's own personal famine world embedded within the broader crisis. Accessing those individual worlds is of vital importance if we wish to understand how people negotiated the uncertainty of life while their world fell apart around them.

I

Some "Sufficed"; Others Died

"Thanks be to God," the teacher, Bou Najm, would say. With the tanning and with what we could exploit from our land, we sufficed. Others of us died. Thanks be to God.

—ANIS FURAYHA

HISTORIANS HAVE SPENT YEARS DEBATING why the famine happened.[1] While questions of causality are admittedly important, an equally important question is *how* the famine happened. As tempting as it is to overgeneralize about famine suffering or, worse, to fall back on old famine truisms like "the rich get richer and the poor starve," predicting what happens to whom in a famine (and why) is surprisingly complicated. Although certain broad social patterns tend to be common across such catastrophes,[2] there was no single uniform famine experience. For some, the famine was simply a decline in the quality or quantity of food they could afford. For others, it was the unbearable strain of helplessly watching neighbors and loved ones wither and die. For many, it was hunger, sickness, and the terror of an uncertain future. For yet others, it was a slow, terrible death—or a rapid one from an opportunistic infection. While one individual lay dying in the streets, another labored in a workhouse to feed her family; while one fled his village, seeking work (and often failing to find it), another was ensconced in the cocoon of family wealth and social privilege. One man spent years in hiding after deserting from the army, while another died anonymously on some distant battlefield. As one person locked herself away in her home to escape the prying eyes and outstretched hands of the poor, another lived comfortably until an unsuspecting drink from the wrong fountain fatally infected him with cholera. While one shopkeeper struggled to maintain the profitability of his store amid soaring prices and government controls, another merchant grew wealthy on speculation and usury. Still another lent money to neighbors, then starved when the loans died with his borrowers.[3] This diversity of experience was ultimately a product of the "how" question. Within the broader causal chain of the famine, different regions and different social groups experienced different crises at different times. Sometimes those variations were subtle and other times they were stark, but the patterns that we can observe in those differences offer significant insight into the nature of life in the famine.

Sometimes a person's plight was simply due to dumb luck. A good investment turned bad, or even a chance encounter with an infected louse could change a one's outlook with alarming speed. However, generally speaking, the way that an individual or a group experienced the famine was a reflection of how their social assets and their social vulnerabilities balanced each other and how their responses to developments of the famine either muted or amplified their risk levels. Within the structural context of the famine, vulnerability added risk, assets diminished risk, and adaptability allowed people to cope with threats when they arose. Such an equation could not necessarily predict survival, but it can explain the surprising social complexity of the wartime crisis.

Each person alive at the declaration of World War I brought a unique set of personal assets and traits into the wartime situation that to some extent shaped how they would experience the crisis. Some of these, like their sex or their family name, were fixed. Others, like their profession or social status, were subject to change as the famine progressed. As the crisis coalesced and evolved, new vulnerabilities formed, and the relevance of old vulnerabilities changed. While such challenges were offset at times by adaptations or by social assets, the severe and ongoing shocks to the system and the complexity of adapting to those developments left more and more people in positions of precarity with a far slimmer margin of error as time went on. As the famine shifted, the value of social assets waxed and waned—and some even became new vulnerabilities. By the time the famine had gained its grim momentum, one's circumstances were often as closely tied to the new social realities of the famine as they were to one's intrinsic vulnerabilities alone.

Vulnerability and Resiliency

Despite some inevitable thematic similarities, no two famines are entirely alike. There may be parallels between crises, but each famine is ultimately unique in how and why it evolves the way it does. Each famine occurs in its own time and context, and how it develops depends on variables like location, the types of pressures and disruptions that prompt it, social and economic structures, political factors, and intangible factors like local resiliency and culture.[4] As this suggests, famines are not static events—they ebb and flow in response to catalysts, pressure releases, and synergies that develop over the course of the disaster. At the start, disruptions to food supply or food access, like the blockade and locust invasion, shock the system, inflaming both personal and systemic vulnerabilities. A resilient system might shrug this off, but if those disruptions are powerful or numerous, it becomes hard to alleviate this pressure or to cope. This pressure can also continue to build due to holds placed on the system, like wartime demand, the blockade, or administrative failures, which prevent it from resetting itself. As pressure builds, it produces a self-reinforcing feedback loop in which people and society begin to reorganize around the crisis. People cope by hoarding, selling goods, breaking laws, or migrating, and others engage in profiteering to exploit new crisis niches. As society turns inward, social breakdowns accelerate, and physical suffering begins to deepen and spread. If nothing intervenes to stop it, the crisis can reach a tipping point that propels it into a runaway "famine system." Collapses within the system produce new, usually bad, synergies—like the one between migration, poverty, and disease. Not all potential famines make it to this point, but once they do, the odds of a good outcome drop precipitously. The vulnerable face disease, starvation, and death; others profit handsomely; and still others eke by. Eventually, the system rebalances as sources of pressure—in this case, the war—are lifted and society can normalize.[5]

Likewise, the social effects of famine are often terrible, but they are never universal. Based on his own taste of famine in Russia after the Great War, the sociologist Pitirim Sorokin has argued that "the effects of a given calamity are not identical—indeed often are opposite—for different individuals and groups of the society concerned, since individuals and groups differ from one another biologically and psychosocially."[6] While some universal factors touched everyone in the region in some way, maybe by an increase in food prices or transportation difficulties or the effects of political policies or the loss of purchasing power due to the currency collapse, those general social trends had very specific effects at the local and individual levels. Different people and different regions were affected at different times and in different ways. The rich experienced famine differently from the middle or poor classes, and urban residents faced an entirely different famine than rural ones. Because of this, some individuals could live through the crisis relatively unscathed, even as thousands of others around them suffered deprivation, poverty, starvation, and in worst-case scenarios, horrific and painful death. Others *benefited* from the situation.

Though some famine vulnerabilities like poverty are structural, others are variable, or at least context-specific in the sense that they can be worsened (or lessened) after the crisis begins. A tremendous systemic shock can shatter even stable systems, but the effect of a shock can also vary based on how well a community's economy and society are able to absorb it. If we view a famine retrospectively, it is easy to imagine that preexisting vulnerabilities are immutable, but it is important to remember that famines happen to people, and people are flexible. This is especially the case when people have faced similar challenges before: Lebanon had dealt with famine or dearth several times between the 1870s and 1914 alone. Over time, social systems adapt, and the lessons of persistent poverty or past disasters become embedded in cultural practices and social memory, providing a sort of crisis software to help people counteract calamity when it threatens. Paradoxically, because of this, people who constantly deal with poverty can actually be better suited to respond to crisis despite the vulnerability that poverty adds to their situation.[7] In effect, their resiliency counterbalances their vulnerability.

In the Lebanese famine of World War I, vulnerabilities could be latent, acquired, or entirely unique to the wartime context. While no one factor was entirely predictive of a person's famine outcome, undoubtedly the greatest vulnerability in the famine was poverty—and it was one that affected the most people. Many entered the famine in a state of poverty, and economic collapse dropped thousands from the middle class into precarity when their resources ran out. Though even poverty was a complex concept that differed between rural and urban areas and by the social circumstances in which people lived, we can make a few general statements about what poverty meant for people in the famine. In the most basic sense, those individuals or regions that suffered the most often came into the famine with high economic vulnerability and little social power, which made coping harder when prices rose. To be impoverished in the famine meant having fewer material and social assets to spend to sustain oneself and also fewer options when problems arose. It meant less influence (*wasta*) to manipulate patronage networks or overcome political barriers.[8] It often meant poorer land and less control over it, inadequate housing, insufficient and often dangerous food, and contaminated water—which entailed a greater risk of disease. When one's assets and social credit became exhausted by the famine, one could choose to stay and hope for a resolution, but many chose migration. This meant leaving support networks and known risks for unknown ones, often with tragic consequences.

Famine poverty clearly meant more than just hunger; it meant poor living conditions and increased vulnerability to a range of other secondary famine risks as well.[9] Inadequate housing left people exposed to disease and the effects of extreme weather, especially for those whose clothing had been reduced to tatters by years of wear. In winter, the normally temperate Mediterranean coast saw temperatures approach freezing,[10] and in the icy reaches of the mountains, the drop in temperature and the freezing rain, snow, and biting wind could be deadly.[11] Such seasonal risks were exacerbated by two survival strategies that were employed in the famine: the sale or dismantling of property for cash, and migration. While the sale of the land or house itself was often a last resort, houses across the region were frequently stripped of sellable parts.[12] Those who migrated from their home villages faced the greatest risk of all. Flight deprived them of both safe shelter and their social networks, leaving them at the mercy of the elements with no social support to save them.

Wealth or high social status diminished all those risks by providing more assets, greater flexibility, more safe choices, greater security, and, often, less exposure to direct sources of danger. Assets could even be used to benefit one's social network or to profit from market volatility, cheap labor, and cheap goods as people sold off their belongings. Life was not necessarily good for the secure, but it was certainly less immediately threatening.

Poverty may have increased the risk of suffering, but it was not necessarily a death sentence per se. In famine situations not accompanied by an absolute absence of food, as in wartime Lebanon, starvation does not immediately occur; it develops gradually as good food or enough food becomes harder to acquire.[13] Starvation could be a long, excruciating process. Diminishing resources often dragged vulnerable individuals from a normal economic status into extreme poverty and from there into long-term semistarvation. A person can live in this state for months or even years without dying unless disease or exposure intervenes.[14] In fact, in severe famines like the wartime disaster, death is rarely caused by hunger alone, even if death among the starving was common.[15] This was evident in a chart outlining causes of death in Mount Lebanon in 1917. The chart offered a range of causes of death, including the rather nebulously defined category of "al-safalat al-fiziologiyya" (physiological baseness), which was the primary killer of individuals under the age of forty that year.[16] While the term suggests death by starvation, its vagueness indicates that it may have been a catchall term that included deaths that were not immediately attributable to specific causes but were clearly linked to extreme poverty. Certainly, nobody was performing autopsies on bodies before pitching them into mass graves.

Though such official statistics were vague, precedent would suggest that the majority of famine deaths would have been due to either epidemic disease or secondary infections, particularly among those who had been forced into dangerous living conditions.[17] One wartime report noted that "typhus, dysentery, typhoid, cholera, smallpox and malignant malaria swept the country with a very besom of suffering, woe and death."[18] The effects of disease were amplified by an oversubscribed medical system and a shortage of imported medicines like quinine due to the Entente coastal blockade.[19] The circulation of virulent diseases also had indirect effects for the poor. A sick primary breadwinner might mean no income for weeks. If a dependent fell ill, families would have to decide whether they would care for them or risk their loved one's life to prevent everyone else from starving. Even if the disease was survivable on its own, such secondary effects might not have been.

In the famine, to be poor meant worse food, and less of it. This too was a source of vulnerability. During one milder famine in 1902, Dr. Ira Harris of the Kennedy Memorial Hospital in Tripoli observed that his famine patients were very different from his normal cases, largely due to replacement foods. In his report he asked, exasperated, "How can the physician relieve a disease caused by eating food intended by the Creator for the beasts?"[20] Harris echoed this during another crisis several years later, observing that an increase in prices corresponded to an increase in women and children coming to his clinic with gastrointestinal distress.[21] Nutrient deficiencies like pellagra and scurvy were potentially deadly risks of the unbalanced and insalubrious diets of the famine poor,[22] but perhaps an even deadlier risk came with the consumption of stretching or spoiled items. Wartime reports accused authorities of adulterating bread and flour with items like wood, sand, chalk, and plaster,[23] and several writers described deadly instances of food poisoning that came from butchering and eating carrion.[24]

Sex and gender roles were also potential sources of vulnerability. Though it would seem odd to consider men to be a vulnerable group, during the war and the famine they faced significant peril due to their social roles and their physiology. The most obvious risks came from the war itself. The initial Ottoman conscription campaign alone took roughly 240,000 men between the ages of eighteen and forty-five from among the twenty-seven districts that comprised Greater Syria.[25] Whether they saw combat or not, many of those conscripted never returned, instead succumbing to typhus, typhoid, malaria, and dysentery in the labor battalions. Of the 2,873,000 Ottoman men who were conscripted into the war, 771,844 either died or disappeared—over a quarter of the total.[26]

The home front was also deadly for men. The "overwhelming" consensus in the famine literature is that famine is slightly deadlier for men than for women because men's higher basal metabolic rate requires more calories just to keep their bodies functioning.[27] The American missionary Robert Byerly adds anecdotal substantiation of this in his 1917–18 report of the Sidon Mission Station, writing that "everywhere the greatest mortality was among the men, who seemed less able to stand the lack of food and who so easily fell prey to various diseases, especially dysentery and typhus fever."[28] There are some social and environmental explanations for this vulnerability. Because more jobs were available to men, the breadwinners were the first to migrate in search of work. Migration meant leaving behind the social support of their home villages. When they arrived at their destinations, they often found strenuous labor, low wages, and poor living conditions—if they found work at all. Many died on the streets, unable to support themselves, let alone their dependents back home in the village. Men were also less likely to receive help when they needed it. One condition of military governor Jamal Pasha's sponsorship of the soup kitchen in the central mountain village of Brummana was that it would not serve men—who, after all, were expected to be dedicating themselves to the war effort.[29] There are a few estimates of the effect that conscription and crisis had on specific communities in contemporary reports. In Tyre, the ratio of unmarried women to men reached 3.5 to 1 by 1916, long before the worst of the famine hit.[30] Those in rural areas of the heavily conscripted southern region of Jabal 'Amil may have fared worse.[31]

While famine literature suggests that women generally stood a better chance at surviving famine, their gender was still a vulnerability during the crisis.[32] Between the demands of the war and the fact that men died at an "unbelievable" rate, many women became the sole providers for their households without a source of income or support.[33] In the uncertainty of the war, what few social support systems existed were unpredictable. Women who lost a husband to the war often had to fight to secure their widow's pensions. And they were the lucky ones. If a woman's husband disappeared on the front lines without proof of death, as so often happened in the carnage of modern warfare, she would be forced to prove his absence with no evidence.[34] Women who lost a husband to disease or to famine or who were separated from him because of conscription or by the blockade were often worse off. Without a solid source of income, they had to either seek the aid of family or community or to find work themselves—and suitable work was particularly scarce for women during the war.[35] In Mount Lebanon, the collapse of the silk industry eliminated positions that had been feminized over the preceding decades.[36] What jobs existed were often menial and offered pay that was significantly less than what a man would earn. Whereas male field workers might earn 3 to 4 piasters a day in 1916 and 1917 (which was still a pittance), a woman might command 1 to 1.2 piasters for the same work.[37] A lucky few were admitted into charitable workshops where they could earn their board but little else for their toil. Some chose prostitution to survive or to feed family members, though in doing so they faced social disapproval, a risk of violence, and the risk of syphilis, an incurable, fatal disease that thrived in the war.[38] Choosing to work was not without risk, and some women faced tragic choices if they had children and no one to care for their children while they toiled for pennies. In an interview, Mary Kfouri Ma'louf recalled waiting for days with only one loaf of bread to sustain her and her brothers Wadi' and Taniyus while their mother looked for work. When her mother returned from one journey, she noticed Taniyus was missing. She asked where he was, and Mary offered a one-word reply: "mat" (he died). Her other brother followed him a few weeks later.[39] Across the region, children were forced to look after each other with little to sustain themselves until their mothers returned—if they lived to return at all.[40]

The relationship between gender and vulnerability during the famine was difficult to quantify, but one source may offer some insights. In the sprawling compendium of knowledge about Mount Lebanon commissioned during the war (hereafter known as the *Mabahith*) Mount Lebanon's director of health, Husni Bey Muhieddine, recorded that during 1917, men accounted for 60 percent of the 1,518 total cases of recorded typhus cases. Certainly, we may be suspicious of the data. Not all of the cases could be counted, and various factors may have prevented women from seeking assistance in the clinics, leaving their suffering unrecorded in official records. The fact that women represented a minority of cases in all of Lebanon's recorded infectious disease categories but one (cholera) may support such skepticism.[41] However, there are social factors that can explain this disparity as well: men were more likely to migrate in search of work, which placed them at greater risk of proximity-spread diseases like typhus and tuberculosis, as well as afflictions like malaria, and even enteric diseases like typhoid and dysentery.[42]

Age was also a source of vulnerability, particularly for the very old and very young. The elderly would have been more susceptible to many of the diseases during the famine, and in certain cases they were denied assistance because of their age and their perceived inability to support themselves.[43] As Ma'louf's chilling story indicates, since children were a dependent group, they would have been at particularly high risk during the famine. Though they were far more likely to find help from both the state and from relief organizations, the effects of conscription, disease, and poverty on adults could mean that those children who suffered often did so without family to assist them. In his wartime retrospective, Syrian Protestant College professor Jirjis Khuri al-Maqdisi dedicates significant space to depictions of children suffering on the streets. He goes into some detail about their origins, noting that some of them were students before the war, some were deprived of their livelihoods by the war, some had lost parents to the crisis, and some had even been sold by their families to a military officer who later left, leaving them alone and without assistance. Many were forced to endure the physical effects of famine, including epidemic disease, starvation, skin afflictions and infected wounds, blinding trachoma, ophthalmia, exposure, and homelessness. They fell prey to marauders and criminals. Living precariously on the streets, "death swept the deceased from them each day."[44]

Interlocking Famines

Over the course his research into the famine, the historian and future CIA analyst Nicholas Ajay struggled to rationalize the conflicting oral accounts given by famine survivors, many of whom were convinced that their region suffered the worst in the crisis. Of course, they could not all be correct, and the divergence led Ajay to observe that "when it came to describing the suffering of the people . . . there was often a tendency on the part of the people from Mount Lebanon to claim that they had suffered the most while the people on the coast . . . had it easier. . . . A similar behavior was noted on the part of the people from the former Wilayah."[45] He concluded that the mountaineers undoubtedly suffered more, but he noted that most who believed this also held that the suffering was due to the Ottoman desire to punish its Christian populations.

This point is perhaps the most problematic aspect of basic questions of causality and relative suffering: the acceptable answers to such questions tend to be ones that reaffirm the stories that we tell to rationalize the horrors of the crisis. Though politics and policy certainly played a role in the famine that developed, they were only one part of the process. As with any famine, the wartime disaster was above all an economic crisis, albeit one that was deeply influenced by political, strategic, and social factors.[46] While tales of oppression gave purpose to an otherwise inconceivable calamity, better explanations are unfortunately more mundane.

It is true that the famine left uneven, even contradictory, impacts across the region. To some extent, this was due to basic social and economic differences. For instance, in the central Lebanese mountain town of Bhamdoun, the economy relied heavily on the sale of lucrative cash crops like fruit and grapes, which yielded significant profit at specific times of the year.[47] Other towns in the foothills of the mountain were dependent on international trade from silk production or export crops like tobacco, while along the coast, citrus was the most profitable export. All of these areas suffered when the war shut out the outside world, but areas like Bhamdoun, which was nominally less dependent on global trade, lost less once the ports were closed. Interior regions in Syria were similarly able to weather the crisis relatively well due to their access to local food production and the entrenched political power of local rural and urban elites. For instance, the Druze shaykhs of the Hawran benefited from high prices because they were able to parlay their status as (well-armed) landlords and their ability to hide their grain in underground cisterns to secure significant advantages during the war.[48] Not only were they able to demand payment in gold, thus sidestepping the collapse of the Ottoman currency, but they were also able to sell grain on the black market to smugglers, muleteers, and even to Faysal's Arab Revolt. Such independence immunized them against impacts of the Ottoman wartime production and distribution micromanagement by allowing them to negotiate their own prices and payment medium.[49]

Within the region, there were in effect three famines in one. The first of these subfamines afflicted rural hinterlands due to disaster, failed policies, and social inequalities—all of which were exacerbated by overzealous conscription policies. Outside of the administrative district of Mount Lebanon, the conscription of working-age men stripped many rural communities of their labor forces. As these agrarian areas depended on the availability of workers at key points in the planting and harvesting seasons, this worker shortage severely hampered local and household economies. Though rural Syria did not suffer as badly as rural Anatolia, labor depletion still had a deleterious effect across the agrarian regions.[50] Certain areas were worse affected than others. In the district of 'Akkar, one man told an interviewer that when a fox came into the village during the war, there was no one left to drive it away.[51] This sounds hyperbolic, but Ottoman surveyors of the Beirut province reportedly found only twenty to thirty young men in the 'Akkari town of Halba when they visited the district.[52] Since many of the areas most affected by conscription were already vulnerable from endemic poverty, the effects of conscription and unemployment were debilitating.

This self-defeating wartime policy begat others. In response to the locust plague and falling production, the state fixed the price of grain and only paid producers in paper currency, which impoverished farmers despite the soaring value of the food they harvested. By 1916, falling output was deemed so problematic that the Ottoman government launched a campaign to compensate for the lost male workers by retraining and employing women in the fields.[53] However, as was the case with many of the wartime stopgap measures, this policy did too little too late to revive the depressed agricultural sector, and production continued to slide as the war dragged on. Even after the shock of the locust plague had faded, the feedback loop that it and other crises had produced caused grain yields to fall year over year until they bottomed out at 38 percent below their 1914 levels in the summer of 1918.[54] An effect of this policy was to increasingly feminize the region's workforce (as had already begun before the war). It should be emphasized that this should not be viewed as having been a step toward equal economic participation. Work was exploitative and pay was low for women who toiled in the fields and factories, worked in homes, or sold goods on the streets. This trend was in every sense an extension of the disaster.

On top of the overlapping effects of conscription, centralization, and price fixing, life in rural areas was made even worse by disadvantageous land tenure arrangements and the debt traps that they produced.[55] Even things as basic as cultivation practices and loans were embedded with elements of an uneven relationship between rural elites and farmers. This relegated many to the status of tenants or even sharecroppers living in a de facto state of servitude to their landlords.[56] In the vicinity of Sidon, Tripoli, and Tyre, landlords had rights to a sixth of the produce of the land,[57] and they frequently took advantage of their position as intermediaries with the state to benefit themselves. Though the elites served their communities by engaging in political pageantry during seasonal tax assessments (essentially paying bribes to encourage collectors to underassess their yields), this form of patronage was recouped by elites, which ultimately spread the burden disproportionately across the poorer members of the community, who still had to pay the taxes afterward.[58] Because of peasant obligations and the loans that small-scale cultivators frequently took against their harvest, the agricultural crisis of 1915 and the ongoing conscription campaign delivered terrible blows to small rural communities across the region. Deprived of the right to much of their production, many farmers suffered when grain prices rose, whereas the urban speculators and the rural notables who controlled the land and financed the harvest profited. Lacking capital, many poor farmers were forced deeper into debt to survive—not surprisingly, postwar analysis found that the same rural notables who thrived as lenders before the war predictably prospered by issuing loans to desperate farmers during the famine as well.[59] Those who were unable to pay their debts were thrown into prison and had their possessions confiscated, even during the wartime crisis.[60]

Compared to the rural areas, coastal regions and Mount Lebanon faced different challenges based on entirely different sets of vulnerabilities, old and acquired. Ironically, the war even turned some assets into disadvantages. The wartime strategies of both the Entente and Ottoman state transformed the very economic specializations that had historically protected the coastal regions and the mountain from famine into mechanisms of their own destruction *by* famine. Since neither the mountains nor the coast was particularly well suited to large-scale grain production, both areas had long abandoned the futile pursuit of food self-sufficiency in favor of the more rational strategies of cash cropping and merchant trade.[61] Prior to the war, this was an effective risk-management strategy, since foreign import trade and specialized cash crops like citrus, olives, fruit, and silk cocoons were hugely profitable (most of the time). Though one could not eat silk cocoons or manufactured items, the cash that such trade generated allowed the residents of the mountain and coasts to purchase food from granary areas like inner Syria, Anatolia, Egypt, and Palestine at far cheaper prices than local production would have allowed.[62] Granted, there were a number of food crises and even minor famines in the late nineteenth century, but few resulted in much mortality. On the contrary, on the eve of the war, both Beirut and Mount Lebanon were prospering.

We cannot underestimate the role that the Entente blockade played in shaping how the crisis developed in the region, but it did so for different reasons than we often consider.[63] Though its critics have focused on the blockade's restriction on food imports, an equally terrible effect was the labor crisis that it created in areas that depended on international trade.[64] The trio of blows from the blockade, the Ottoman closure of the ports, and the cessation of foreign money transfers eliminated significant sources of income along the coast and in the mountain, and with it the jobs that such trade produced evaporated as well. Import-export businesses closed, foreign capital and local lending dried up, silk and soap factories idled, and unemployment rose both in the merchant hub of Beirut and in secondary towns with high rates of urban poverty like Tripoli, Sidon, and Tyre.[65] The wartime economic crisis in urban settings had wide effects. In addition to the blockade's obvious impacts on shipping companies and financiers, it also eliminated service sector jobs and even left porters without work. Simultaneous restrictions on both foreign remittances and the ability to withdraw funds from bank accounts further impacted middle-class residents, unskilled laborers, and artisans alike. The loss of remittances was hard across the region, but it was especially problematic in Mount Lebanon, where they made up 41 percent of its measured prewar GDP.[66] The resulting economic malaise had a knockdown effect for artisans like cobblers, tailors, masons, and other professionals, who largely languished during the war because of the rarity of materials like leather, cloth, and thread or just because there was less demand for their services since there was no money to pay for them.[67]

Though poverty alone contributed to tens of thousands of deaths in the urban areas and in the agrarian regions around the mountain, the suffering in those areas was worsened by the influx of migrants from Mount Lebanon, who suffered the worst poverty and highest mortality of any other demographic. Higher prices, inaccessibility of food due to government transportation restrictions, corruption and mismanagement, and the deleterious effects of disease and migration all decimated the region. Still, even within the mountain, the experience of the crisis varied significantly due to the district's diverse geography and complex social landscape. Postwar analysis suggests that famine in the elevated reaches of the northern districts (particularly in remote areas of the Keserwan) was worse than in the districts of the foothills that ringed Beirut. Estimates generally suggest that the southern central mountain districts like the Chouf suffered less. This was partly due to their physical accessibility, but it was undoubtedly also because their Druze residents were able to purchase food from their coreligionists in the fertile Hawran region of southern Syria when times were tough.[68]

Ultimately, an area's ability to weather the crisis depended on factors like its access to (or lack of) capital, its economy, its labor market, its degree of reliance on the outside world for funding or food, its ability to smuggle food through preexisting trade networks, its remoteness, and its ability to mobilize political support when needed. But in a crisis as encompassing as the famine, the difference was often simply a matter of degree.

Work and Wages in the War

Famine is not necessarily defined by a lack of food so much as it is by people's inability to acquire it in sufficient quantities.[69] In the wartime famine, access to food was hampered by rising prices, but it was exacerbated by unemployment, underemployment, and inadequate wages due to both currency collapse and stagnant salaries. In 1916, the Sidon-based American missionary, Reverend George Doolittle, highlighted this problem, writing, "During this year of exorbitant war-prices the income of missionaries and Syrians alike possesses hardly a seventh of its former purchasing power."[70] Unfortunately, 1916 was merely the intermediate point of the crisis—in the years that followed, wages continued to fall as prices rose even higher.

A cursory glance at economic statistics prior to the war suggests that the famine would have been statistically unsurvivable for the average Lebanese family, even if the prewar economy had continued unabated. Based on

Albert Naqqash's 1914 GDP calculations, per capita income in Mount Lebanon has generally been calculated at a mere 628 piasters per year.[71] Given the soaring price of wheat in 1918, this would only have purchased enough grain to sustain a family for a few weeks. One could hardly survive on such a sum, so mass mortality would seem a natural outcome. But as with all things famine related, we must be cautious with uncontextualized statistics. While this figure is technically correct if we assume a migration-adjusted population of 350,000, we should not assume that this represented anything like the functional income of those who lived in the region before, or even during, the war. So how did people survive the famine?

Simply put, though many people across the region lived in poverty, contemporaneous reports indicate that wages were significantly higher than the per-capita GDP figures suggest. The bottom end of Mount Lebanon's wage scale for unskilled male agricultural labor in 1914 was 840 piasters for a season (women made far less).[72] However, this accounts for only part of the year, and those earnings would have been supplemented with additional work. Other reports suggest that most annual incomes would have been higher. The Ottoman surveyors of the Beirut province, Muhammad Bahjat and Muhammad Rafiq Tamimi, recorded that the Muslim agricultural laborers in the poor region of 'Akkar averaged 7,000 to 8,000 piasters per year. This was not only significantly higher than Ajay's per-capita figure, it was a pittance compared to their Greek Orthodox neighbors, who averaged 15,000 piasters per year, which exceeded the income of some educated workers.[73] At the start of the war, a teacher at the American Mission school in the mountain town of Dayr al-Qamar earned an annual salary of $342, or roughly 8,208 piasters per year.[74] If we look at urban wages, we can see that incomes fell along a similar scale. The journalist turned sociologist Ahmed Emin Yalman recorded that before the war an average porter in Istanbul earned 36 liras per year (3,888 piasters) and that government employees could earn over 120 liras annually (12,960 piasters).[75] Pay was relatively similar in Beirut, where an unskilled laborer earned between 8 and 10 piasters per day. This was a bare-subsistence income, and if he did not supplement this by engaging in illicit activities (and many did),[76] there was little financial leeway in the prewar years and even less chance to build up savings.[77] But it would still have been far greater than 628 piasters a year.

During the war, those whose work depended on international trade suffered first and often worst. However, Ottoman civil servants were also devastated by a different aspect of the economic crisis. Although the salaries of government employees were adjusted in 1916 in response to spiraling inflation, because their pay was fixed and issued in paper currency, many public servants were driven into poverty, desperation, and corruption. Yalman's postwar observations of conditions in Istanbul suggest that the relatively minuscule bonuses and salary increases did little to compensate for the dramatic rise in the cost of living. He notes that in 1917, a monthly salary would be gone in the first week to pay for rent and food.[78] The memoirs of Yusuf al-Hakim, who *was* one of those bureaucrats working in Beirut and Mount Lebanon in the war, describe the situation in Beirut in almost identical terms. To survive as an Ottoman employee often meant engaging in corruption as a survival strategy.[79]

Not even the employees of the foreign-financed American Mission schools were safe. Because employees received fixed salaries from their schools rather than from the mission headquarters, many workers found themselves in desperate straits even while they distributed charity to others in their own community. The head of the American Mission's Lebanon Station, Paul Erdman, wrote that a teacher's salary would be hardly enough to purchase the 37.5 kilograms of wheat that he was charged with distributing to the poor in May of 1917.[80] On May 22, 1917, George Doolittle of the Sidon Station wrote a letter icily imploring American Mission Press treasurer Charles Dana to address the situation: "Now they [the employees] are really in greater need and some of them in distress that many of the lower classes who have come into the lists for aid, and these employees, if anybody, should be kept from famine and distress."[81] Closures and shortfalls sometimes meant that workers did not even receive their salaries. The school in the village of Suq al-Gharb paid its teachers in two installments, one at the start of the year and another at the end. The second payment did not materialize in 1916 after the school closed for the 1917 academic year, when it was repurposed as a soup kitchen.[82]

The effects of the crisis on agrarian employment varied from place to place, depending on how a community was integrated into the regional or global economy and into Ottoman war plans. This was most apparent in the inverted impacts that the blockade and conscription had on labor in the sericulture-heavy economy of Mount Lebanon as opposed to labor in the breadbasket regions on the mountain's northern, eastern, and southern fringes. The cessation of the silk industry in the mountain left it flush with unemployed men with few means to support their families, and between the glut of labor and the fact that many were forced to seek work outside of their specialization, the war was a buyer's market for labor.

The archive of the Hamlin Sanatorium provides several examples of such exploitation (at the hands of a missionary organization, no less). In a letter written in July 1916, nurse Affeffi Sabaʿ asked the hospital's treasurer Anna Jessup to approve the hire of a local woman whom she had employed for menial tasks and to prepare the simple burghul meals for the residents of the sanatorium. Clearly eager for any job she could get, the woman offered to work solely for a portion of the food that she cooked.[83] The sanatorium's project to extend the road leading to the hospital likewise demonstrated the willingness of even purportedly humanitarian organizations to exploit the labor glut. Although Dana had approved five liras for the construction as a charitable project, the pay was hardly enough to sustain the laborers, who Sabaʿ described as "pitiful to behold."[84] In a letter to Jessup on September 18, 1916, she suggested that another week of work and 150 piasters would be needed, though even this disconcerted her. She wrote, "Does it not seem little to pay for six workers together 150 piasters per week?"[85] At this scale, the workers were each earning a mere 2.4 piasters per day at a time when the sanatorium was paying between 17 and 19 piasters for each two-and-a-half-kilogram measure of wheat for its own uses.[86] Though the very funding of the sanatorium was tenuous after Dana declared the consumptive residents a poor investment, the parsimony of the treasurer with his hires is still quite telling, if not necessarily surprising.

While urban and professional labor suffered from a decline in job availability, rural labor markets beyond the mountain suffered a lack of labor that was only exacerbated by natural disaster, a preexisting debt crisis, and the problematic policies of the Ottoman state. Agricultural laborers were highly vulnerable in the wartime period. Not only were they conscripted at alarming rates, but debt and a loss of purchasing power left many working difficult jobs for compensation that failed to meet the rising cost of living. The pay for field work varied according to the skill level and specialization of the work, as well as the phase of the season in which it was conducted.[87] Those who were basic laborers involved in menial tasks were generally paid at a significantly lower rate than the skilled *fallaha* class. The required level of skill differed by crop, as did the pay. Wages for workers in olive groves, for example, ranged from eleven piasters per diem for experienced workers to four piasters for unskilled workers.[88] Curiously, the wage data collected during the war indicates that the dearth of workers in agricultural areas did not generate a corresponding increase in pay. The salaries of workers from 1914 to 1918 varied in absolute terms, but adjusted for inflation, wages were dramatically lower at the end of the famine than in 1914. Though the absolute value of pay began to increase in the final years of the war, the combination of a sharp increase in the cost of living and the plummeting value of the Ottoman currency meant that while workers earned a bit more money, their real income was still far less than it would have been before the war.

However, the war's effect on income affected more than just wages—merchants and investors were also sidelined by the blockade, which led to unfortunate secondary effects as they sought to mobilize their idle capital following the closure of the ports. As normal investment opportunities dwindled, many who had cash directed it into lucrative new niches created by the war and the famine. Among the most popular of these wartime investments were predatory domestic loans with exorbitant interest rates and speculation on either the soaring price of commodities or the crashing value of Ottoman currency (or both).[89] Prior connections often enhanced such investments. For instance, merchants who were linked to wholesale grain provisioning for the city or to the retailing of such commodities often had disproportionate and arbitrary control over the cost of goods in the marketplace. Their ability to command supply and control its release encouraged hoarding and worsened price swings because of market manipulation. Even rumors could produce dramatic price spikes with startling speed. Syrian Protestant College president Howard Bliss described with incredulity a grain contract that was renegotiated as it was being signed when a message arrived at the office indicating potential supply shortfalls.[90] Government attempts to stabilize food prices at reasonable levels did little to alleviate the situation because merchants responded to price controls by funneling items into the black market.[91] Attempts to mete out punishment for speculation prompted outrage among the shopkeepers, which American professor Edward Nickoley scorned as the response of "the very naughty boy who at any time deserves a whipping because of some transgression but whose indignation is roused by the fact that he is punished for some act which he just happened <u>not</u> to commit."[92] While gouging certainly happened, high retail prices were also reflective of the wholesale price of grain and the impact of currency collapse. Many shopkeepers were implicated in profiteering during the period, but part of the problem was that they were understandably unwilling to sell at a loss if it cost them their own livelihoods (or lives).

Some "Sufficed"—But Why?

Vulnerability was not merely a product of identity or place or profession, but each of these were certainly factors in the complex equation that determined what sorts of specific challenges individuals faced during the wartime period. Just as there was no universal suffering during the famine, the complexity of the crisis and the diversity of life across the region dictated that there was no quintessential famine sufferer either. The effects of the famine varied from person to person and from place to place depending on how one's personal experiences intersected with the crisis as a collective event.

Ultimately, the reasons why some suffered and some succeeded were complicated and often unpredictable. This is particularly evident in the stories that Hayat Mahmud told about her family during the war. Hayat's maternal grandfather, Shahin Ghassayni, was a Maronite member of the administrative council in Mount Lebanon and was politically prominent in the influential town of Baʿqlin. In contrast, her paternal grandfather, Jammul Mahmud (who we have already met), was a Druze muleteer, smuggler, and *shaykh shabab* of the town of Barouk— the latter was an honorific title that offered local influence but little official glory. While Shahin's ostensibly less vulnerable family was subject to deprivation and hunger during the famine period, Jammul's Druze connections in the Hawran and his less prestigious profession allowed him to acquire food to feed his family (and to sell surplus for a tidy profit). Even though he was not from a demographic that was assumed to benefit from the crisis, like the wealthy merchants of Beirut or agents affiliated with the government, Jammul leveraged his opportunities to his advantage. His ability to negotiate his circumstances not only saved his family from starvation, but it even brought him a moderate degree of prosperity in the process.[93]

As this anecdote shows, analyzing identities, vulnerabilities, and assets alone cannot necessarily predict the outcome of a crisis like the famine, but it can still help to explain the sorts of risks that individuals faced in their attempts to survive the era and why the effects were so uneven and often contradictory across the region. Consider the following: High seasonal prices dramatically increased one's risk of poverty, particularly in a remote mountain village. However, one might have profited from high prices if one's family was among those who controlled the production or distribution of food. Wealthy merchants and lowly muleteers were well placed to weather the storms of the famine—the former because of their existing capital and political power, the latter simply because they were used to smuggling. But the consequences of famine were not always so direct. Though the primary effects of the crisis may have had little impact on those who could afford the high prices, the suffering of others in their community might have inadvertently put everyone at greater risk as a secondary effect if poverty and displacement sparked epidemics in their home communities. A rise in typhus cases or the incidental contamination of a town's water supply could indirectly change everyone's risk levels for the worse.

Though the degree of suffering in the region varied, nearly everyone faced loss of some sort. Even members of the middle class who were cut off from their work or their lifelines abroad found themselves facing rising vulnerability as the war went on. However, for those who were most vulnerable—the poor, unemployed, widowed (or left on their own by conscription), disabled, or otherwise marginalized—the famine was a seismic disaster. Many migrated, many were evicted, and many fell into lives of precarity, hunger, disease, filth, and misery. As the famine deepened from the end of 1915 onward, the overt effects of the crisis became more and more prevalent, and the secondary effects permeated deeper into the lives of people across society. Whether they starved or not, those living in Mount Lebanon and western Syria found their worlds increasingly dominated by the famine and the horrific suffering that it produced. And time simply made it worse.

2

Death and the Famished Body

> Death, in its most squalid forms is on every hand.
> —EDWARD NICKOLEY, MAY 23, 1917

THE TOWN OF KHIAM BORE a heavy burden during the war. The predominately Shiʻi municipality in what is now southern Lebanon was plagued by Ottoman provisioning policies, abusive policing, forced financial contributions, and occasionally violent conscription by unsympathetic government agents.[1] Between 1914 and 1915, the town was called to sacrifice its sons, its animals, and even its transportation bags for the distant war. Like the rest of the region, rising prices impoverished a community that had already faced the confiscation of metal currency and the widespread exploitation by wealthy creditors. Though Khiam was far from the front lines, the war continually intervened in the lives of its residents throughout the period. In August 1916, the Ottoman effort to counteract chronic harvest shortfalls through retraining and forced labor dragged Khiam's women and elderly into the fields for an obligatory eight hours a day.[2] Government agents returned at the height of the famine in 1917 to demand even more men and more livestock, depriving the town of necessary resources while they fought a losing battle against social collapse. As time passed and famine mounted, typhus, malaria, and smallpox spread through the town, killing many. Deepening poverty gnawed at those who remained.[3]

As if its own problems were not enough, Khiam's size and location made it a destination for those trying to escape the effects of famine in

Mount Lebanon and nearby villages. Like the thousands across the region who fled from suffering at home, these migrants often faced harsh realities upon their arrival—if they arrived at all. One particular tale of forlorn hope deeply touched the famine-scarred psyche of the missionary humanitarian Reverend George Doolittle. In his unpublished account of the war, he made special note of one family's failed final bid for survival that ended on the outskirts of Khiam. Their arduous trek toward safety, food, and shelter may have begun with dreams of a better future, but as they trudged toward their destination, it slowly turned into a nightmare. At one point, the father stopped and laid down to rest. He never got up again. The remaining members pressed wearily on until they neared the outskirts of Khiam, where the mother also fell. Her daughter rushed into the town crying that her mother had died, and a number of the townsfolk followed her back to the body to bury her. When they reached the mother, they were surprised to find her still alive, if barely so. Since death seemed imminent, they began to dig the mother's grave as she lay next to it, occasionally opening her eyes to watch them. Then they waited. Their vigil lengthened, and over time they grew restless at her persistent survival. Still convinced that her death was close, the men were instructed to turn her from side to side to accelerate her demise. This had predictably little effect other than to make her final minutes more agonizing.

Eventually they gave up and buried her alive.[4]

Superficially, this story is not so different from any of the innumerable episodes of human misery that have been told and retold about the famine period. Doolittle's account of the war alone is a grim repository of anecdotes that he collected on his journeys throughout the famine-stricken region—but even he was left aghast by the incident. Even if we read the story charitably, it still raises a number of unsettling questions about the effects that famine had on society, the most poignant of which surround the choice that the men made at the end. They could have brought the mother into town to revive her, but they chose not to. Why? What did their decision mean? Was it simply a matter of practicality? Saving her would have meant sacrificing precious food and an investment in another hungry mouth had she lived. But the cost of care was not enough for them to drive her daughter away. What made the mother different? Did they view her as irreparably broken?

Why did they choose to bury her alive rather than simply leave her by the side of the road to die naturally? Did their act constitute murder? Or was their terrible decision motivated by a form of mercy—or at least mercy's famine-inverted twin?

Retrospectively, we can read this story as a parable of how death grew to impact life in the famine period. Even accepting the possibility that this story is fabricated (and there is little reason to think so), it reflects a common refrain in famine literature—that the crisis changed how society had begun to regard human bodies, death, and the dead. To address such themes, this chapter aims to redirect the analysis of death in the famine away from typical concerns over the number of dead to try to reach a qualitative understanding of how death and bodily degradation touched the lives of the living during the war. The sources make it clear that the most horrifying scenes of mortality became frequent and altogether unwelcome aspects of daily life for both sufferers and the secure alike. As time passed, individuals and communities began to rationalize death's presence in their worlds and to adjust how they dealt with the emotional and practical burdens that it placed on them.

However, rather than simplifying the relationship between the dead and the living, such scenes of mass mortality complicated it. Although the omnipresence of death and dead bodies was normalized over time, seeming to soften death's impact on those who constantly faced it, there were also glimmers of grief and humanity in the era that indicated that some deaths still stung. Those who died miserably in the famine may have been difficult subjects to grieve for secure observers who wrote about them, but their deaths were still an acute reminder of the difficulty of life in crisis and the shared humanity that bound even the most tragic cases to their secure counterparts.

Numbering the Dead

It may seem odd that a work on famine would not immediately address something as important as death tolls, particularly since it is practically a convention of the famine genre to measure a crisis's severity by how high it stacked its bodies.[5] However, estimated death tolls are often more trouble than they are worth. Suffering in famine does not necessarily correlate with death. In even the worst famines, the vast majority of people survive, and famines with relatively low mortality can still be filled with terrible suffering. Moreover, it would be difficult to imagine a more unreliable class of statistic than famine death tolls (at least in this era), and, since numbers convey meaning in a disaster, statistics are often used to sensationalize or shape public opinion about the crisis. As a result, we generally cannot know how many died, and we should have every reason to distrust what numbers we do have.

While we can imagine that accurate figures from the Lebanese wartime famine would be chilling, the available statistics are little more than pointed guesses or ways to denote severity. It is widely claimed that 500,000 died across Greater Syria during the war, a figure that many historians have accepted because the German sources that produced it were theoretically insulated from the influence of Lebanon's postwar famine politics.[6] Accounting for combat deaths, death from disease, normal mortality, and the excess death of the famine, this is a fair guess, though there is no reason to believe it to be particularly precise. In the more specific Lebanese-Beirut arena, where starvation, disease, and migration were felt the worst, contemporary figures vary widely. In *Quatre ans de misère*, Father Antun Yammine claimed that 100,000 had died by 1916 alone.[7] A postwar estimate by *L'Asie Française* put the regional death toll at 180,000.[8] The journal *Lisan al-Hal* estimated that 150,000 died in the mountain (amounting to 43 percent of its total population) and noted that of the over 40,000 who perished in the city of Beirut, half were Lebanese refugees.[9] In a broad analysis of Lebanon published immediately after the war, Augustus Adib Pasha conservatively guessed that "tens of thousands" had died ignominiously, "hungry and sick and naked."[10]

Death estimates in Mount Lebanon were always high due to the intensity of its suffering. As early as 1917, rumors suggested that up to 70 percent of the population had perished.[11] After the war, George Doolittle estimated that 38 percent of the central Chouf district had died and that the northern district of Keserwan (which by all accounts suffered the worst in the famine) lost 75,000 people—half of its population.[12] In 1921, the former French spy Butrus Khuwayri guessed that 170,000 had died.[13] Even

Jamal Pasha's erstwhile ally, Emir Shakib Arslan, eventually suggested that a stunning 200,000 had died in Lebanon alone (perhaps to compensate for his earlier skepticism).[14] No guess is trustworthy. Estimating numbers would have been difficult enough from on the ground, but it would have been nigh impossible from abroad, where some of these numbers originated. If we still have any doubts, the roundness of the numbers indicates guesswork—educated or otherwise.

Regionally, the tallies ranged from 180,000 to 500,000 dead, though the definition of "region" varies since the lands that would comprise the postwar entities of Lebanon, Syria, Palestine, and Transjordan overlapped significantly during the Ottoman era. The province of Beirut alone included land that would become parts of Syria, Lebanon, and Palestine, so using figures from the province as a whole would be misleading if we wish to anachronistically apply this to the Greater Lebanon formed after the war. After all, local tolls varied considerably. In one count, Palestine suffered a population decline of 50,281 during the war, or slightly less than 7 percent,[15] while contemporary estimates of the number of dead in Mount Lebanon ranged from 100,000 to an unimaginable 250,000, which would place the death toll at 28–57 percent of the population, assuming it contained around 350,000 actual residents in 1914.

The vagueness of popular estimates led many authors of historical accounts to speculate or estimate at the upper range for effect. The Syrian Protestant College professor and indefatigable humanitarian Bayard Dodge offers two excellent examples of this. In one of his reports on relief work written immediately after the war, Dodge astutely observes that "nobody knows how many people died in Lebanon and Beirut. The Government report for some months indicated that one hundred and forty thousand had disappeared, but such figures mean nothing."[16] Conversely, in the detailed history of the American University of Beirut published in 1958, Dodge vaguely estimates that by the end of the war, 300,000 had died across Mount Lebanon and the province of Beirut.[17] Which was it? And why was he so hesitant to guess in his earlier account? As a director of relief work both during the war and in conjunction with Near East Relief in its aftermath, Dodge's opinion was at least rooted in a traumatic personal and professional experience, which perhaps explains why it was among the highest of the figures offered by historians studying the period. In general, estimates varied from about 100,000 dead in Mount Lebanon to 200,000 (or from about 20 percent to over 50 percent) and from 300,000 across Greater Syria to 500,000.[18]

This wide disagreement over tallies should not be taken as a range but rather indicates the utter unreliability of contemporaneous statistics in general and the epistemological impossibility of being any more specific. The numbers are especially tricky at this point in Lebanon's history due to migration and the imprecision of the data-collection process, which often involved merely extrapolating from the number of households in an area.[19] Paradoxically, specificity may be just as problematic as vague estimates, since in the absence of actual death counts, we must rely on comparisons between prewar figures and postwar census counts to tally missing people who we then must assume to be dead. We can do this with some specificity based on official government figures but probably not with much accuracy. The French-administered census of 1921 found 652,229 residents in the new Greater Lebanon, down from prewar figures of approximately 731,870 residents.[20] This latter total can be reached by combining the migration-adjusted government estimate for the mountain, wartime government tallies for those districts in the Beirut province that were appended to Lebanon, and a contemporary estimate of the district of Baʿalbek.[21] The difference between these figures is a loss of only 79,641 people in all the territories that would become Greater Lebanon between 1914 and 1922. This falls far short of nearly all mortality estimates during the war.

The implication is that we should doubt any statistics based solely on the absence of bodies after the war. First, the prewar figure is undoubtedly imprecise because of loose counting methodologies and the fact that evading the census was proud tradition for people across the region.[22] Moreover, any prewar figures are skewed by migration, which left tens of thousands of nonresident ghosts haunting the official registers.[23] Both Mount Lebanon's agricultural director Jalal Bey and Albert Naqqash explicitly include migration when discussing the mountain's actual population in relation to the 1911 census count of 414,800 (a number listed by census director Salim Baylan in his chapter of the *Mabahith* and frequently cited in the wartime historiography).[24] Jalal estimates that 120,000 people had migrated from Lebanon prior to 1914, while Naqqash ignores the census data altogether, instead offering an unofficial estimate of 350,000 *actual* residents in the region at the time of the war. Both figures would also roughly account for the thousands of registered Lebanese who had left the mountain for Beirut after the 1860 civil war and the tens of thousands who migrated abroad, most never to return.[25] But as the roundness of the figures would suggest, they are guesses. If that is not vexing enough, the far more specific figure from the French authorities that I used to estimate the number of missing is clearly incorrect too. In their tally, the French census takers included an indeterminate number of (mostly Christian) Lebanese living in the diaspora while also missing a significant segment of the Sunni population who chose to boycott the census to protest the new imperial government.[26] It is hard to determine whether this skews the number lower or higher, even when we compare it against the expected jump in the Muslim population in the also-flawed 1932 census. All we know is that it was wrong. Even if we arbitrarily adjust for migration, it is still impossible to determine whether either census number reflects actual people who were living in the region during the war and how population dynamics between the reopening of the ports in October 1918 and the census in 1921 skewed the totals. It is, to put it bluntly, a mess.

Moreover, even if the absent were dead, we cannot truly know how many deaths were actual "famine deaths." For instance, because it would be important to differentiate between famine deaths and general wartime deaths if we wish to measure the effect of the crisis itself, we would need to understand how soldiers skewed the statistics. Fighters died in droves in the trenches, and even conscripts who survived battle still faced deadly peril from hunger, disease, and exposure. Between 460,000 and 501,091 out of the roughly 2.8 million Ottoman wartime recruits died or disappeared in the war.[27] Undoubtedly, many of those were from Lebanon and Syria, but how many were there, and how many were factored into famine death tolls? (Of course, for those who lost sons and husbands on the battlefields, the distinction was meaningless. A dead loved one was a dead loved one).

Using missing persons to estimate famine death tolls also requires us to account for normal population dynamics. Not all who died in the famine died "of" famine, though the famine situation undoubtedly contributed to the premature mortality of most of those who passed. Statistics from Lebanese director of health Husni Bey Muhieddine remind us that a nontrivial number of the recorded deaths in Mount Lebanon during the terrible year of 1917 were from superficially unrelated causes like violence, heart disease, and cancer.[28] Likewise, while births dipped, they did continue to take place in the famine. Health officials in Mount Lebanon recorded 641 births and an underestimated 1,708 deaths in the short year of 1917. If we naively estimate the deaths from the famine during that year solely by absence, we would mistakenly believe that 1,067 had died instead of 1,708, the recorded death toll.[29] Similarly, if a typical postfamine baby boom took place between 1919 and the census in 1921, the number of famine deaths would appear smaller because of the new additions to the rolls. We also do not know if those figures would be skewed in the opposite direction by the waves of immigration that followed the war. There is quite a bit that we do not know, and this should inspire caution.

Immediate mortality is also not the only effect that famine can have on a population. Famine conditions produced subtle long-term morbidities that carried the era's effects far into the future. This was evident in the case of tuberculosis, which spread widely during the war but often killed only after its end. Even Howard Bliss, the venerable president of the Syrian Protestant College, died in March 1920 from complications of a tuberculosis infection that he contracted during the war. If we interpret effects broadly, we can ask if malnutrition contributed to greater instances of birth complications and miscarriage in the war and its aftermath,[30] or if some of the apparently innocuous heart conditions were caused by acute malnutrition,[31] or if the physiological effects of the famine might have led to poor health for survivors years later.[32] Of course, we have no answers to these questions, but they palpably diminish the validity of simple absenteeism as a measure of famine severity.

However, skepticism about death tolls should not minimize the very real severity of the crisis. The famine that struck the region during the war was not a classic Mediterranean subsistence crisis. It was a prolonged systemic collapse tied to political and economic failures catalyzed by factors like natural disaster, migration, social breakdowns, and epidemic disease—all of which unevenly overlapped within the context of an unprecedented global war. Given the extraordinary duration of the famine, the small size and broken geography of the area in question, and the severe confluence of compounding factors, it is very likely that the region lost a far greater proportion of its population than the 5–10 percent that has been seen in other severe famines.[33] Indeed, a detailed analysis of village death tolls in the famine suggests that a population loss of 20–30 percent due to a combination of mortality and migration was not implausible, nor even uncommon, in parts of Mount Lebanon.[34] However, not every community lost nearly a third of its population. Some were relatively insulated from the famine. Other communities nearly disappeared. A few *did* disappear. If we can make any definitive statement about death tolls it is this: not only are accurate figures incalculable in a crisis of such a scale, but they are literally inconceivable. Lacking context or comparative reference, one hundred thousand deaths is as incomprehensible as two hundred thousand deaths, just as 20 percent overall mortality is as incomprehensible as 40 percent. Applied to the patchwork of communities that stretched from the mountains of the Anti-Lebanon to the Mediterranean coast during the war, even the lower number would, on a per capita basis, exceed some of the grisliest disasters in history.

The Ungrievable

Like its companion horsemen of the apocalypse—war, plague, and starvation—death was an unavoidable part of life in the wartime crisis. In a passage filled with pathos, Antun Yammine observes that death developed "in a terrifying manner," writing that "the roads were littered with cadavers, and the forests where the unfortunate Lebanese went to seek wild herbs for nourishment were filled with rotting bodies."[35] Doolittle concurred in one of his reports on the Sidon Station, writing, "Whole villages have been laid low by famine, sickness and disease; the dead have often remained unburied for lack of those to dig a grave or carry the body."[36] Dodge wrote that every Syrian could name ten to twelve family members who had died,[37] to say nothing of the death of neighbors and the frequent sight of anonymous bodies in the streets. Death marked a stark end of the famine saga for those who perished. But for their survivors, the loss of loved ones, the fear of their own death, and the constant intrusion of anonymous mortality in their lives were not things that could be passively experienced. The superlative nature of death demanded that people devise ways to cope with it—because it was not going anywhere while the famine persisted.

Not all deaths lost value during the famine, but the effects of time and volume eventually shifted how certain deaths were perceived and portrayed by contemporaries. The impact that death had on observers varied by case and often by the identity of the deceased. The prominent and famous were still publicly mourned as usual, and writers often attached extra significance to the deaths of those who were not expected to die in famine, like the wealthy merchants and doctors who fell victim to the waves of epidemics that swept the region. Harriet LaGrange of the Tripoli Girl's School specifically differentiated the surprise cases of "citizens, men of influence, many Moslems [*sic*]" who were "carried away" by the typhus epidemic.[38] Conversely, while the risk of one's own death and the deaths of loved ones could still be emotionally devastating, the deaths of strangers and social out-groups were easier to ignore. In general, dead innocents like children or mothers were portrayed with greater sympathy than dead men, though in certain cases the portrayals of male mortality were given additional value by virtue of the suffering that it caused the loved ones they left behind.

Like suffering, death was understood differently in the first years of the famine than in the final weary months. Faced with the emotional weight of mass mortality, many people began to normalize death as a way to cope. The sheer volume of death made it especially easy to view it in the abstract, particularly when the dead were poor, starving, migrants, or sick. For those groups, death was not unexpected, and as long as mortality conformed to this particular famine logic it remained ghastly and disturbing but not necessarily out of character for the crisis. Indeed, the starving were *meant* to die—for some it was even apparently inevitable. Deaths within such famine out-groups were often depicted as anonymous. This was partially because of the social distinctions that arose between the suffering and the secure but also because many of the dead were like the family mentioned at the start of the chapter: impoverished outsiders migrating to nearby communities. As strangers, they very literally had no known identities and were thus easily depersonalized. For observers, such individuals were identified with their need, their suffering, and eventually their corpses—not their names, their personhood, or their life histories. We need only think back to Doolittle's story: despite all the detail that he provided about the mother's process of dying, we never learned her name.

Anonymizing the death of the poor was made easier by the physical grotesqueness of those in the grip of long-term semistarvation. Though perishing by hunger may seem poignant in theory, it is not easy to romanticize famine death when one has to see it up close and in person. As the professor and famine witness Jirjis Khuri al-Maqdisi wrote, "There was no type of death more gruesome than the evil death that was seen from hunger." In his postwar account, al-Maqdisi contrasted the anonymous soldiers, who were "bathed in honor and self-respect," with the poor of the famine, who "perished decayed and downtrodden."[39] Indeed, the "decayed" body that had been emaciated by starvation and disease was frequently portrayed as a source of horror or pity rather than one of sympathy. As years of famine gradually disconnected the poor from those who wrote about them, their deaths began to lose the usual sense of tragedy.

The social theorist Judith Butler has referred to such cases as "ungrievable"—lives and deaths whose value has been denied or stripped by their very identity and how the world perceives them. One cannot mourn the death of such individuals, because death is essentially redundant for someone who was not truly socially alive.[40] Though Butler's theory primarily shows how we value one's life differently during times of war because of where one is born, this observation also holds true in cases of contingent precarity like in the wartime famine, when the physical and social effects of the calamity transformed normal people into abject unsympathetic objects in the eyes of observers.[41] This went beyond simple distaste or an aversion to the horrors of starvation—it was a conceptual "reframing" of the value that was attached to the poor. Instead of individuals in need of support, they became sources of distaste and disease. This made them doubly problematic for secure members of society because their presence was both unsettling and dangerous. Their deaths were not only "ungrievable" due to the horror or guilt that they invoked in those who viewed them, but in a "twisted logic," their deaths were a benefit, because their passing protected the secure from the threat that the very existence of their bodies represented.[42]

Perceptions of death seem to have changed even among the sufferers themselves after years of fear and loss. In his 1916 report on the Sidon Mission, George Doolittle observed that "everywhere the overburdened women are disheartened, and in many places indifferent. Children are dying of starvation before their mothers' eyes." Doolittle recorded the story of a pastor who encountered silence and solemn acceptance rather than weeping and grieving when he visited a family whose only infant son had died.[43] In another example, resident scholar and physician with the Palestine Exploration Fund, E. W. G. Masterman, wrote that among Palestinian women who commonly faced stunning infant and child mortality rates, sickness was seen as a time for mourning, but the arrival of death required stoicism. Children's deaths were so frequent that mothers were conditioned to not display emotion when they passed—theirs was a "death without weeping."[44] Still, we may be forgiven for exercising some skepticism about these examples. While child mortality was certainly high among the poor before the war,[45] the systemic effects of poverty do not necessarily translate to the unique sorts of risk that were elevated by the famine, which forced even those who were less accustomed to death to confront it far more frequently. Moreover, one might doubt external observers' ability to divine the actual thoughts and feelings of the silently aggrieved, particularly since scholars have habitually misread Arabic linguistic conventions regarding death and pestilence as pious fatalism. As a longtime resident of the region, Doolittle was no stranger to the culture of his adopted home, which lends some credibility to his observations. However, he was also writing for an unfamiliar audience back in America whose feelings and opinions would be swayed by such a tragic case. As we will see below, there are many examples that indicate that intimate death still carried great meaning on an individual level, even when it happened to the poor and sick.

To some extent, the social response to death in the famine was a paradox. The powerful impact that death had on many of those who observed it seemed to overwhelm their emotional capacity to cope with it. Some responded to this overload by normalizing death—to make it simply another thing that happened in the new world of the famine. Since most of those who died were already in a group that had been depatterned from society—the starving, migrants, and the sick—their deaths were grotesque and pitiful, but they were also expected. Ultimately, the suffering poor, unsympathetic in life, became even less grievable when their lives came to an end.

Dealing with the Dead

In normal times, death's finality attaches extra significance to the ways we view and treat the dead body once its owner vacates it. Funerary practices are essentially rites of passage that both usher the dead into the afterlife and provide a sense of resolution for those left behind.[46] Because they offer the community a chance to process grief, such commemorations are usually social events filled with customary rituals and obligatory gestures that show communal solidarity and provide support for both the deceased and their living relatives. This support often includes assistance to the spirit itself through religious services and pious invocations for God to have mercy on their soul.[47] Since they are usually performed by those closest to the deceased, such rites carry significant personal and cultural value.[48] However, the famine was not a normal time, and even those practices that related to death and dying were altered by its power. In some cases, this was merely because of practical considerations, but in other cases, the treatment of the dead reflected a genuine shift in the attitudes of society at large. While the treatment of the dead could still be a solemn affair for the socially secure, for those who were ungrievable, death very often meant neglect, indignity, or even simply disposal.

Whether one was properly commemorated or not was (unsurprisingly) largely a matter of class and status. Many individuals of better circumstances or higher social standing were still afforded their usual distinction and were grieved by their communities.[49] For a death to be properly commemorated, it was important to prepare the body according to proper rites and within the proper time frame. If one had the money to pay funerary costs, this could be done easily and with grace. For those who could not, commemoration might be reduced to an anonymous ringing of a church bell or the call of a *muezzin* from the mosque. Given the sacred nature of death and the duties of the living to guide loved ones into the afterlife, religious institutions sometimes made an effort to intervene on behalf of the dead regardless of their social status (though as the volume of deaths increased, this ability diminished). In 1917, Edward Nickoley described priests who would remain in cemeteries to deliver final rites to the stream of bodies that trickled in.[50]

To fail to commemorate death would be both improper and dishonorable. To properly prepare and bury the body is to hide the harsh realities of decay from loved ones and to smooth their process of grief. As the anthropologist Robert Hertz writes, "The brute fact of physical death is not enough to consummate death in people's minds: the image of the recently deceased is still part of the system of things of this world and looses itself from them only gradually by a series of internal partings."[51] These partings, internal or otherwise, were complicated by the intense poverty of the famine. Though historical analysis of famine death tends to focus on the dead themselves, the responsibility for the body was ultimately a concern for the living. Indeed, for many who lost a loved one in the famine, death was both a source of trauma and an acute logistic problem. Lacking the means to appropriately prepare bodies or to adequately bury them, many families interred their kin hastily and poorly. In 1917, Nickoley wrote that the deepening of the famine meant a "multiplication of the gloomy mounds of earth by the road sides and in the fields. For people have long since passed the point of common decency where they feel the need of burying their dead in cemeteries and with a certain amount of form and ceremony."[52] Dodge similarly described overcrowded cemeteries filled with hastily covered corpses left vulnerable to the predations of scavenging animals.[53] There were reports of bodies dumped down wells or buried in shallow graves by the side of the road.[54] In small mountain villages, families who succumbed to starvation or epidemic disease were occasionally entombed in their own homes—the bricks that sheltered them in life becoming a cover for their corpses in death.[55] Secure writers like Nickoley and Dodge clearly viewed such acts of disposal as neglectful, and they may have had a point, because none of those examples were remotely appropriate forms of commemoration. Observers might question if the dead were even mourned. However, given the circumstances, the fact that such methods at least provided a modicum of concealment to permit the body to rot in peace made them better than simply leaving the body to decompose in the open.

The context of the famine demands that such abnormal practices be interpreted sympathetically and that accounts of them be viewed critically. For those who were weakened by starvation and unable to pay for a burial, dealing with a loved one's body was yet another traumatic obligation. Despite rumors of degenerated morals and hardened souls, there were hints of compassion buried in the hard choices that death forced on those who knew it was near. Stories circulated of mothers mournfully interring their dead children and of parents delivering children to orphanages in the hope that their loved ones might live after their own impending demise.[56] Some choices were merely a cost-benefit decision. In one instance, Doolittle observed a mother removing the clothing from her dead child before burial, explaining that her children who still survived would benefit more from the rags than the one already gone.[57] But we can also find stories of self-sacrifice for the sake of others. Dodge wrote of missionaries who encountered a man patiently digging graves for his family members. When the visitors passed through the village on their journey home, they found him lying dead alongside his buried loved ones. There was no one left to return the favor.[58]

As this last example suggests, respectful commemoration was possible when families made the effort to perform rites, regardless of how much they suffered. However, for many of the poorest in society, disposing of bodies was the province of local authorities who were far less concerned about respecting the dead than they were about efficiency. Collection had to be quick lest the presence of death have any further psychological or health effects on communities. By all accounts, municipal corpse removal was overtly depersonalized. Both the frequency and methods of disposal transformed the death of an individual from a tragedy into an administrative task. As epidemics struck and famine worsened, the mounting death tolls became a matter of terrible inconvenience for mayors and councils who were reeling from the fiscal austerity imposed by the war. When Ottoman surveyors Muhammad Bahjat and Muhammad Rafiq Tamimi passed through the southern coastal town of Tyre in 1916, the mayor complained bitterly about the increase in pauper's burials due to a typhus outbreak. Between the famine, migration, and the epidemic, the town had depleted its annual funerary fund in a few short months. For him, death had become a budgetary annoyance.[59] Anecdotal accounts suggest that this problem was widespread. Doolittle wrote that 217 bodies were collected from the streets of Jounieh between January and February of 1918 alone and that the town of Batroun buried 30 bodies per day in the war's final year. The latter is an obvious exaggeration, since thirty daily burials over ten months would have exceeded the town's prewar population of roughly six thousand, but the figurative implications of such an estimate are obvious.[60]

Predictably, the growing aversion to poverty and migration among the secure population influenced how dead impoverished bodies were handled and how the living were treated as death approached. Bahjat and Tamimi wrote that in Tyre the sick were rounded up and sent into recovery houses without a word or news of their outcomes. The surveyors remarked that "God only knows" how many died or what happened to their bodies.[61] Once they had died, even less respect was given to the impoverished body. For the sake of expediency, solutions to dispose of the dead tended to be uncreative and disrespectful as authorities prioritized speed over ceremony. While it is true that the presence of corpses decaying in the streets could spread disease or attract wild animals, the bodies were also bad optics for an administration that was fighting a public relations war for its very existence. In her account of the war, American Mission Press secretary Margaret Mc-Gilvary notes that in the central mountain town of 'Aley, the bodies were collected in the morning and dropped from the hillsides to keep the jackals and hyenas from eating the dead on the streets.[62] Larger cities faced greater problems due to the sheer number of deaths, but they seemed to have had better resources for dealing with the volume. Carts wound through the streets of Beirut several times a day collecting corpses, which would either be discarded in hastily dug pits in the sands south of the city or simply cast into the sea.[63] Tripoli's municipality initially dropped corpses into the Abu 'Ali River, but as this rather short-sighted practice created a visible nuisance and a public health risk when the bodies inevitably ran aground before reaching the sea, the city began warehousing the dead in an empty building until enough accumulated that they could be transported for burial (again) in "the sand" every few days.[64] Though the looseness of sand would have allowed for the rapid digging necessary for mass interment, it would have provided little protection from scavenging animals. The indignity of public corpse disposal was made achingly clear in a postwar interview with Mary Kfouri Ma'louf. As a child who suffered deeply during the war, she recalled watching carts collecting bodies "just like you were hauling boxes of cabbages, dirty clothes, or dirt."[65] There was similarly little guarantee of dignity when the body arrived at the cemetery, where the porters were said to have stripped the bodies of their clothing to divide among themselves,[66] a rather hazardous act in times of typhus, when infected lice and their eggs readily spread through used clothing.

The surfeit of corpses and the problem of their disposal eventually created a ghoulish death economy. For those willing to undertake the risk, graveyards offered a potentially lucrative (albeit grisly) harvest as thieves took to rifling graves in search of gold teeth.[67] However, even the formal famine economy offered legitimate opportunities for individuals like the professional porters who had lost their jobs to the Entente blockade. As death tolls mounted, they found a booming trade transporting corpses to cemeteries. In 1917, Nickoley described a "procession" of coffins that flowed from the center of Beirut to the cemeteries to the south and the southeast of the city. Eventually, the police began treating the congestion of coffins as they might handle normal traffic jams. In a sardonic passage that hints at the sort of macabre humor that grew out of the horrors of life in the famine, Nickoley writes that at one point the police "jogged" some of the porters for moving too slowly, leading one to retort that his pace was slow because the single coffin actually contained three bodies.[68] Whether that was merely a joke or not, this breach of protocol would have been indicative of an increasingly casual attitude toward the dignity of the dead. Doolittle describes a similar event with far less levity. A porter who was assigned to transport the body of a boy to the cemetery for burial arrived late and found the gates locked. Rather than return the child's body to his family or seek out the gatekeeper, the porter simply heaved the corpse over the gate, reasoning that someone would arrive to bury it in the morning.[69] This was the scene that leads Doolittle to conclude that death had finally lost all meaning.

At a time of rampant epidemics, the fear of disease was so great that it occasionally interfered with proper care for the dead. In his memoir, Mushin al-Amin describes the difficulties that even he as a shaykh and a religious authority encountered while preparing the dead for burial during a wartime cholera outbreak in his village. Fearing contamination, his neighbors refused to allow the body of a woman who died of the disease to be washed near their homes. Even after the body had been prepared, Amin was forced to press reluctant passersby into service to bear her coffin to the cemetery because nobody would volunteer.[70] In another instance, Amin was forced to assign the task of washing corpses to two villagers simply to ensure that the bodies would be prepared with dignity. Doolittle recorded a similar story in Tripoli, wherein a woman lay for hours in public view after dropping dead in the streets from an acute attack of cholera. Distraught members of the community implored a nearby guard to do something about the body. Although corpse disposal was evidently not part of his job description, he eventually relented, and, after demanding a few coins to buy lime, he dusted the corpse and then returned to his post. Wisely, he refused to remove the highly infectious body himself, much to the chagrin of the observers.[71]

As such examples show, to die poor or sick was to risk dishonor and decay. When a corpse was neglected and left to decompose in public, perception of the body conceptually shifted from tragic to horrid. As a body bloats, then recedes, its deterioration physically effaces the recognizable features of the person who once inhabited it. The corruption of the body and the erosion of its identity was both figuratively and practically a corruption of the self. To decay publicly and without care stripped the deceased of dignity and eventually anonymized them in the eyes of those who viewed them. Deprived of characteristics that defined the person in life, the body would have little left to offer but horror for the living and food for scavengers. In a best-case scenario, the body might be interred anonymously in a pauper's grave. But for many, to die poor was to be piled in a pit, to be dumped into the sea, to be cast aside the road to rot, to be scavenged by animals, or, unthinkably (and very rarely), to be eaten by another desperate human being.[72] There is powerful symbolism in this. As the anthropologist Timothy Taylor has observed, "Only those whom nobody cared about [are] left to the animals and the hungry."[73]

Finding Meaning in Mortality

For a fairly straightforward biological process, death is a surprisingly complex topic in famine. In eyewitness accounts, it was alternatively characterized as either a sort of ambient horror or as a very personal experience that severed the dead from friends and loved ones—depending on the meaning it was meant to invoke. Sometimes writers mentioned death to emphasize the suffering of the period. In other instances, they mentioned it to induce sympathy in the reader. Occasionally they used it to offer unsubtle symbolism or to highlight an impossible moral quandary. It was a particularly potent literary device since the severity of death made it a sort of superlative that could elevate the carnage of the crisis, highlight the humanity or inhumanity of a situation, or even simply set the tone for a scene by its mere mention.

As a literary device, a reference to death could be descriptive or figurative or a mix of the two. Writers often deployed allusion and metaphor to convey the gravity of the situation or to give meaning that would resonate with their readers. For instance, Doolittle dedicated an entire chapter of his unpublished manuscript to death. Provocatively titled "The Path of the Reaper," the chapter frames the famine in a point-by-point comparison with the biblical famine of Egypt.[74] Such allusions and even the basic terminology used may have provided additional meaning for the writer and reader, but the hyperbolic imagery of such passages often sensationalized the situation or reduced the dead and dying to euphemisms.[75] In these descriptions, the pity with which these individuals were regarded was mitigated by the implications of inhumanity that the words conveyed. When a person was made abject, their death may have been unfortunate, but it was also viewed as a natural consequence of the suffering and wretchedness that was deemed synonymous with poverty during the famine.

Some writers even portrayed death as an almost benevolent intervention when compared to the agony of long-term semistarvation. The American professor Edward Nickoley's diary rationalizes death in this way a number of times. In his February 1917 entry, he wrote:

> One method of destroying life is more spectacular and more sensational than another, it seems more horrifying to send several hundred persons to the bottom of the sea than to subject a community to starvation. It seems so, <u>until you have seen actual starvation.</u> Were I to take my chance between being speedily dispatched by a torpedo or being starved—give me the torpedo every time and give it quickly.[76]

In another particularly dour entry, Nickoley portrayed death as a "mercy" for the unsavable sufferers who were too far gone to recover.[77] For Nickoley, whose worldview had been shaped by years of ambient misery, the relative weight of suffering was an abstract matter. Certainly, nobody would *want* to die, but from his perspective, the horrors of life as a famine victim made death seem a better alternative than persisting so squalidly. His view of merciful death even extended to children suffering in the mountains during the terrible February winters. He wrote, "Their emaciated bodies, their swollen feet and faces are blue with cold. They must die, there is no saving them, for even what they now receive can merely serve to prolong slightly the miserable existence which they are leading."[78] It is curious that Nickoley would express this attitude even as he describes individuals going to desperate measures merely to maintain their lives in such a state. For a person who readily admitted to suffering from compassion fatigue during the crisis, Nickoley may have believed that death was a cosmic mercy because of his inability to process others' suffering, not because this reflected what his vulnerable subjects actually believed themselves.

In his diary entry on July 14, 1917, Nickoley offered an example that cuts to the heart of this point. While resting at home one evening, he heard the agonized moans of a starving boy drifting over the college wall near the Nelson family's house. As the boy's loud suffering dragged on, Nickoley became emotionally conflicted. He felt compelled to assist the child but was held back by an intangible fear of doing so. After pondering the matter for some time, his innate cynicism won out. Finally convinced that nothing could be done, he fell asleep. He woke the next morning to the sight of a cart loading a corpse where the boy had been.[79] Nickoley did not act, and as a consequence, the collectors of the dead were forced to.

The way that Nickoley depicted this scene is as interesting as his choice to record it for his family in the first place. In one sense, his writing conveys the clear ambivalence and guilt that he seems to have felt that night. He subtly tries to evade this by implicating the Nelsons for ignoring the boy's final moans, which they would have heard even more clearly than he. However, Nickoley also binds himself to the boy through his story in a way that never happens in any of his other anecdotes. Those other tales may have also revealed the compassion fatigue and psychosocial numbing that he admitted to feeling, but those anonymous cases were always someone else's problems. As callous as Nickoley would like the reader to believe he had become, his narrative carries a sense of responsibility for the boy's life that defies his attempt to rationalize the child's (inevitable?) death as he listened to the anguished cries in the dark. True, the boy was merely one among the thousands of starving individuals that populated the world outside the safety of the campus walls—but the inadvertent, one-sided relationship that was established through Nickoley's empathetic witnessing of the boy's suffering linked the two of them, even though the boy did not know who Nickoley was, or even that he was listening. If this temporary shared existence briefly joined them in life, for Nickoley, his unwillingness to help the child permanently linked the two in death. In many of Nickoley's earlier passages, death is merely an abstract concept—something that happens to other people. *This* body's expression of loneliness, pain, and fear before it died made its death very human. The fact that the boy's suffering had forced Nickoley to personally make a choice about his continued existence made his death more meaningful to Nickoley than any of the other corpses that the cart carried to the sands that morning. Not that it did the boy any good at that point.

The End

Conceptually, death exerts a powerful sway over the ways that we have understood (and continue to understand) life in the famine era. This is in part due to politics. In the immediate aftermath of the war, asserting that hundreds of thousands had died in the famine was a way of condemning an ostensibly oppressive Ottoman state and validating the sense of pain and loss that people within Mount Lebanon felt.[80] This, in turn, supported the controversial Maronite Catholic call for a French protectorate over the confessionally mixed region after the war. Conversely, citing smaller numbers somewhat invalidated those claims of persecution and suffering in the famine—as such, they were used by those who sought to defend the memory of Ottoman rule or to contest the need for a French protectorate. Beyond death's role in the postwar political discourse, it is doubtful that disputes over specific totals offer any value to either the historical analysis of the era or to our understanding of the crisis as we ponder it over a century later. What we do know is that many, many people died, and they often did so horrifically.

With little solid evidence for any of the estimates, choosing to cite a specific number is an implicit comment on the crisis and its severity. Death tolls tend to skew toward the higher, often unfeasible end of the scale because a "killing famine" that piles the dead in the hundreds of thousands feels far worse than one that "merely" kills eighty thousand. It is not surprising that more extreme figures gained currency as interest in the famine briefly spiked around the war's centennial and again as Lebanon slipped into economic collapse after 2020. In our new digital era, the stakes of such claims are not political gains but rather clicks and views that reflect how ghastly the subject can be made to appear in a headline. Though it may draw people to learn more about the era, in the end, the "clickbaiting" of history risks creating a misleading popular understanding of the period as a whole in its effort to attract the sympathetic or just the morbidly curious.

And it is unclear if the rhetorical use of death tolls has the ability to generate the sympathy the era deserves. As Nickoley's story shows, the death of one person can convey depth and pathos. The death of a hundred thousand is little more than a number. At best, it is a dark landscape onto which authors can impose meaning. Vast figures may be shorthand for suffering, but to what end? Death figures are embedded with semiotic and symbolic value that extends beyond the lives (or bodies) that numbers represent, and ultimately, the meaning that is attached to that mortality is more important than whatever arbitrary number an observer chooses to represent it. Citing unbelievable death tolls and describing starvation, disease, and mortality in gruesome detail was an easy way for a writer at the time to convey the terrible nature of the famine to an innocent readership. Though these descriptions sought to depict the undepictable, paradoxically, the use of such extreme descriptions was dehumanizing as well. By reducing suffering to a statistic to convey its scale, writers inadvertently converted each individual life into a tiny fraction of a percentage—a drop in the vast ocean of anonymous mortality.

While death understandably remains the morbid standard by which famines are measured, to overemphasize death skews our understanding of famine to the extreme, worst cases at their final, irreparable end. By focusing on the margins of the crisis, writers during the famine inadvertently confirmed themes of degradation and dishonor that they had consistently written into the disaster's narrative from their vantage as mostly secure observers at the famine's fringes. As a result, the microtragedies of daily life and its many struggles to survive were reduced to the sum of their outcomes:

people either lived or died. But we know that not all of those who lived through the war in Lebanon or coastal Syria starved, and that suffering was more of a spectrum than a binary. Even those who were dragged into poverty by the famine did not simply acquiesce to their fate, lie down, and perish. And even if many of the desperate attempts at self-preservation ultimately failed, the defining theme of the era was not death—it was survival.

3

Staying Alive

> When we had a bit of barley or wheat, mixed with dirt and other things, the women sorted it and prepared cakes which they placed in a chest locked with a key. They gave out one morsel per day to each child.
>
> —MUHSIN AL-AMIN

WHEN WE IMAGINE A PERSON coping in famine, the first things that come to mind are usually tragic or horrifying. On the lighter end of the coping spectrum, we might picture reducing rations, selling possessions, or migration. At the darker end, we picture prostitution, criminality, or even that most taboo of acts, cannibalism. Because we tend to fixate on the most aberrant behaviors of the most desperate individuals, such survival strategies have earned an undeservedly bad reputation. As awful as many of the preceding examples may be, they were often the final choices at the end of a long line of adaptive strategies. True, some of those behaviors were acts of futility. But most were simply examples of people adapting to new challenges as they attempted to maintain as much normalcy and comfort in their lives as the situation would allow. Though coping strategies were often improvised, few adaptations were wholly novel. Most reflected social memory or drew on a cultural resilience that was "baked into" a society forced to deal with the adversity of life in normal times.[1] Whether learned or remembered, such coping was a fundamental part of life in the famine. From the start of the war, individuals strategically adapted to high prices, scarcity, and their dwindling assets by creatively changing their behavioral patterns, their eating habits, and even how they obtained their money. Amid crisis, to cope was to live—or at least to live better.

One of the best descriptions of famine survival strategies during World War I comes from the memoir of Muhsin al-Amin, a Shi'i imam and shaykh from a small community east of Tyre in the Jabal 'Amil region. Al-Amin's initial, very literal, move began at the start of the war. Suspecting that Damascus would be a safer haven than his home village of Chakra amid the threat of conscription and the possibility of invasion, al-Amin hastily sold his food reserves and other belongings and prepared to move inland. Though he only received a fraction of the value of his items in the quick sale, al-Amin reasoned that the food would have spoiled before his return and that any cash was better than nothing as his family rebuilt their lives elsewhere. Unfortunately, a short stay in Damascus forced him to rethink his plan, and he soon returned home, where the consequences of his earlier choices would come to haunt him. Reminiscing on his return, he recalled, "We knew joys and sorrows there, then the situation reached a point that we had nothing left to eat."[2]

With his initial strategy in shambles and his situation more precarious than ever, al-Amin was forced to adapt on the spot. Back in Chakra, he mustered what little resources he had left to purchase an array of animals, then "threw himself" into agriculture. This was a fortuitous choice. What he produced from his animals and his farming helped to keep his family fed until the end of the war.[3] Amin's land and livestock were important assets during the war, but even this modest estate did not simply produce food at the snap of his fingers. Animals had to be maintained and milked. Annual crop cycles meant that certain types of food only came at certain times of the year, and not everything that he grew was sufficient, or even equally useful. Fresh vegetables and legumes may have been valuable supplements to his family's diet, but they were also relatively poor in calories compared to those usual staples like wheat and bread, which were the foundation of his prewar diet. To supplement his own yield with grain and seeds, al-Amin had to walk miles through agricultural land to the town of Nabatieh to purchase them in a market riddled with corruption and predatory speculation.[4]

His adaptations did not end there. After acquiring food (or what passed for it at the time), al-Amin and his family had to get creative with their meals to make strange ingredients edible. Like many in the famine, al-Amin purchased cheaper seeds and grains as replacements for expensive wheat and barley, even though the resulting meals were often a bit less nutritious and much less appetizing. As times grew harder, desperation inspired innovation. When his supplies of barley and millet ran low, he softened fenugreek seeds and boiled them with wild herbs, salt, and oil to produce a slimy, bitter sludge of nominal nutritional value. It was repugnant, but at least it kept his family alive. As bad as that seemed, other experiments were even worse. At one point he tried to replace wheat flour with ground acorns and vetch, but he abandoned the method after his son judged the result to be inedible.[5] The boy's hesitancy was probably a good thing. Acorns are filled with tannic acid, and vetch is toxic when eaten in large quantities, resulting in suppressed appetite, lathyrism, and in some cases even a favism-like condition.[6] Though Amin's status and possessions gave him a greater margin of error than many who were less fortunate, his efforts also showed that famine survival required flexibility. Even thoughtful plans were sometimes scrapped by the constantly evolving challenges of the wartime environment. Amin had it hard: he faced locusts, conscription, hunger, disease, and poverty—but in the end, he survived.

Amin's story, and indeed the topic of adaptation itself, is an important aspect of the famine picture that is often elided by famine narratives that revel in the wretched poverty and abject suffering of the starving poor. Of course, suffering was integral to the story of the famine, but so were the ways that people countered the ongoing threats as they strove to survive during the crisis. Some of these coping mechanisms were strategic ways to limit future vulnerability by preparing for what could be predicted, like anticipating the arrival of a harvest or the coming of winter. Conversely, some strategies—like flight—were reactive adaptations to unexpected developments or to the anticipation of ominous future conditions. Certain strategies were common, like eating less, eating differently, the sale of property, migration, and even crime. But just as no two households were identical, there was no one normative survival checklist. Strategies varied by need, location, a person's capital and assets, and their ability to procure food. Ultimately, each person responded to their own circumstances and adapted as they saw fit.

Some strategies may have seemed desperate or illogical to observers, but the choices people made were ultimately the result of a rational cost-benefit assessment that weighed the risk of maintaining an earlier strategy with the perceived benefits of changing it. A successful strategy demanded a careful balance between the perceived needs of the present and the anticipated needs of the future, as opaque as the latter may have been.[7] As al-Amin's wartime story suggests, not all of the strategies employed during the famine were successful, and we might even consider him lucky for surviving his numerous miscalculations. However, failure should not necessarily imply a shortcoming in the strategy or a deficiency in the strategist. Even well-planned adaptations were no guarantee of survival in an ever-evolving crisis. Disease, misestimation, misfortune, and misdeeds could dramatically transform one's risk profile over a very short period of time. Even when change brought suffering, it also demanded resiliency. Balancing the needs of the present with the terrifying variable of unforeseeable need in the future required ongoing recalculation and an understanding of which strategies worked and which did not. Over time, many adaptations became normalized, and the baseline of what "normal" meant began to shift to meet new realities.

Through such strategies, many were able to survive or at least to mitigate the suffering that they and their loved ones faced. Many, in spite of their adaptations, did not make it. Regardless of the success of the strategies, coping adaptations were deliberate, calculated choices that were rooted in a person's own assessment of their vulnerabilities and their assets. With logic, and perhaps a little bit of luck, coping could help to prolong life at a time when survival was not guaranteed and aid was rarely forthcoming. For those who suffered, and even for those who were merely pinched by rising prices and growing uncertainty, coping was a means of self-salvation, not just a sign of desperation.

Bad Bread and Less of It

One of the first victims of a famine is a normal diet. As in almost every famine, the problem was not necessarily the lack of food, but the fact that high prices and low incomes made all but the cheapest and least nutritious food inaccessible to a large portion of society. As prices increased and the currency collapsed, people began shifting their consumption habits to embrace different foods or to reduce the quantity of normal foods that they purchased. Although the early years of the famine were hardly comparable to the terrible situation that developed from 1916 to 1918, the fear of not having food or not being able to acquire it in the future soon became a reality for many among the poorest classes as early as 1914. This vulnerability was especially acute for those who were most affected by the initial shocks of the war—unskilled agricultural workers and urban wage laborers, migrants, and the families who had lost their breadwinner to emigration, conscription, or death. Driven by untenable circumstances, many went to great lengths to sustain their lives and the lives of their loved ones.[8] Many were able to eke out a living by adapting their diets to their incomes, but for some of the poorest families, the price fluctuations were almost meaningless. One woman in the village of Khiam told George Doolittle, "I have five persons in my house, with no income whatsoever. So what difference does it make to me whether a bushel of barley is one dollar or a dollar and forty cents!"[9]

Even when discussing dietary adaptations among the poorest members of society, we should not be tempted to overemphasize the most bizarre and horrifying examples. Famine writers frequently used the consumption of disgusting or taboo food as a symbol of social degradation in famine, particularly when it was consumed by the skeletal poor in the final stages of starvation.[10] This is not to deny that individuals relied on famine foods and sometimes went to extraordinary lengths to survive the crisis. For those without the resources to purchase good food, the aim was sometimes simply to fill their stomachs with anything that could provide the illusion of satiety or even just dull the pain of starvation.[11] Stories about this were heartrending. In their quest for life, destitute men, women, and children combed the trash heaps for potato and citrus peels, cactus pads, scraps of bone and gristle, melon rinds, rotten food, and other nominally edible, if mostly indigestible, materials.[12] Enterprising individuals rubbed the bitter outer peels from oranges to preserve the edible pith and removed every bit of meat and marrow that could be extracted from discarded bones, which themselves could be ground into a powder and boiled to capture their collagen.[13] Some preparations described in the sources made food more palatable but removed useful nutrients in the process. (For instance, boiling lemon juice destroys most of its vitamin C).[14] In addition to eating safe but strange foods, individuals also consumed more dangerous fare, like inedible grasses or materials that would have caused gastrointestinal distress.[15] Tragically, some of these strategies were actually counterproductive. Vomiting and diarrhea squandered precious calories, and writers described the devastating consequences that faced those who ate poorly processed famine foods, to say nothing of garbage and carrion from the fields and the roads.[16] Sometimes adaptive eating was little more than a symbolic attempt to fill starvation's yawning void.

However, as titillating as stories of desperate foraging and humans grazing may have been, not everyone rooted through trash heaps or picked grains of barley from animal dung to survive. For the most part, people tried to continue to acquire familiar foods in smaller quantities or simply found plausible replacements. The greatest obstacle to most diets was price. After 1915, speculation, production and transportation failures, unusual demand from the military, and the effects of hoarding all combined to price necessities like wheat, flour, and barley beyond the reach of even the middle class. Charting prices can help us to understand the challenges that people faced in the crisis, as commodities prices have long been used as a proxy to gauge the severity of subsistence crises.[17] However, in the Lebanese wartime famine, establishing price trends with any certainty is difficult because we have only fragmentary data, and what we do have shows that the cost of food varied by time, place, buyer, and method of purchase. For instance, paying in coin yielded cheaper prices than paying in the collapsing Ottoman paper currency. Likewise, flour in Beirut was cheaper than in the mountain, though apparently pricier than in interior regions of Syria. We do know that prices rose and fell by the season as in normal years, but the concerted effects of abnormal demand, the loss of global suppliers, and local stressors to the grain markets during the war all kept prices from correcting themselves to normal levels as typically happened in milder famines.

A few relatively complete, complementary price lists can indicate just what sorts of challenges people faced in the period. Prior to the war, a ratl (2.5 kilograms) of wheat or flour cost a few piasters. From the end of 1915, the costs of such basic commodities gradually trended upward, still largely following seasonal patterns, until they reached shocking peaks in the final year of the war. In September 1916, the Hamlin Sanatorium paid 17–19 piasters (in coin) per ratl for wheat. As expensive as that was, the report that lists this figure indicates that the sanatorium was actually getting a bargain compared to others in the area, who paid up to 25 piasters for the same amount.[18] At roughly the same time but farther north, the Yuhanna Maroun Monastery in the Batroun district paid a lower but still shocking 15 piasters per ratl.[19] By early 1918, wheat prices were reported to be 150 paper piasters per ratl, which had the nominal value of roughly 32 piasters in coin. For reference, this was roughly what the monks of Yuhanna Maroun Monastery paid for their wheat in the tremendously expensive months of March and April of 1918—30.6 and 33.6 piasters respectively.[20] But even these prices varied depending on where you were. The highest listed figure for a ratl of wheat was an incredible 300 paper piasters or 90 piasters in coin, as recorded by Wadih Bustani in Dayr al-Qamar on March 24, 1918.[21] Between hyperinflation and the long duration of the famine, many families eventually exhausted their cash reserves just trying to stay alive.

The price of wheat is especially relevant because it was the foundation of the regional diet—referred to in biblical terms as "the staff of life" by Lebanese sociologist Afif Tannous.[22] Apart from the periodic flour crises that afflicted the coast and mountain, wheat was mostly available during the famine if one had the means to acquire it. However, the quality diminished as the famine worsened. By the end of 1915, good white bread was little more than a memory for many across the region. As the price of wheat increased, merchants and officials began to cut the flour with higher volumes of bran, ground pulses, and even things like sand, wood, or worse. The result was a noxious "black bread" that so disgusted (and sickened) residents during the war that it was eventually remembered as a symbol of Ottoman mismanagement and cruelty.[23] Curiously, the scarcity of good bread also gave it a symbolic quality. In an interview, Hayat Mahmoud recalled that her aunt used to be proud of the fact that she was among those who ate white bread throughout the famine, indicating that being a "white bread-eater" became its own temporary social category in the depths of the crisis.[24] For those who could get it, such wartime luxuries offered an emotional crutch during a difficult time. Amid the misery and boredom of crisis, the act of eating white bead, drinking tea or coffee, eating sweets, or indulging in any of the other everyday extravagances that were eliminated by the war did not just serve to fill a person's belly—it preserved a bit of prewar normalcy and perhaps provided a morsel of joy at a time when it too was scarce.[25]

The increasing price of wheat was merely the most prominent example of a trend that touched nearly every consumable on the market. As staple prices rose, people were forced to adapt to their circumstances and eventually to reevaluate what a normal diet meant, both in quality and quantity. While this led to some unpleasant new realities, like the government-issued black bread, or creative and awful recipes like Amin's vetch bread, other adaptations were relatively well received, and some even stuck even after the war. A particularly interesting example concerns the propagation of the thin *saj*-style *marqouq* bread in the western Biqaʻ villages of Chtoura and Zahle. According to Liza Riyashi, this style of flatbread was largely absent prior to 1915 and was introduced when refugees fleeing poverty in the mountain brought the technique to the town. Toasting this thin dough atop the clay *tannour* oven rather than baking it in a larger oven reduced the amount of scarce and expensive fuel needed for baking while enabling families to produce a large number of the thin sheets of bread out of relatively little flour.[26]

High prices and scarcity demanded a creative shift in the diet patterns of even the relatively well off, who mainly restricted the quantity of more expensive foods in their diets or replaced them with more economical famine foods. Sometimes the change was nominal. In place of oranges,[27] George Doolittle noted that people switched to cheaper lemons.[28] Likewise, when wheat was too expensive, fodder grains and seeds like corn and millet replaced their expensive equivalents in daily diets. One family described grinding carob seeds and acorns into flour.[29] But there was often a tradeoff that came with these substitutions. While millet could be cooked like rice, mixed with *kibbeh* or boiled with milk, its fibrous shell meant it required far more fuel to soften than grains.[30] In the southern coastal town of Sidon, Doolittle observed that the dense, membranous seeds of the lupine plant (called *turmus*) were transformed by high prices from a quick snack into a "staple" that was sold by vendors on the street by the cupful.[31] Although less overtly dangerous than consuming rotten food, some of these replacement foods were potentially hazardous. In a minor famine prior to the war, Tripoli physician Ira Harris reported that children were particularly susceptible to famine diets, with some requiring hospitalization from the food itself.[32] Even something seemingly innocuous as corn was deemed harmful by contemporaries of the famine.[33] Fodder foods might have been filling, but what is safe for animal consumption may not be suited for human consumption, at least without additional preparation or technical knowledge. Curiously, traditional European famine foods like potatoes were grown in the region but were not commonly eaten at the time because they were considered more suitable for foreigners and animals.[34]

People in the lower and middle classes often added wild herbs and roots to their diets to supplement the food that they harvested and purchased. Typically, wild greens did not significantly contribute to the daily caloric intake of the residents of the region but rather provided relief from the limited diets of the winter months when they began to sprout in the countryside in February and March. Raw or prepared, herbs like *hindbeh* (curly chicory or dandelion greens), mallows, parsley, mint, nettle, and various *zaʿatars* (aromatic herbs similar to thyme or oregano) provided both satisfying flavors and important vitamins and minerals to otherwise deficient famine diets. In addition to their taste and nutritional value, herbs were also the backbone of folk remedies, offering treatments for ailments ranging from stomach problems to inflammation to malaria and stomach parasites.[35] Herbs would have been particularly valuable at a time when modern pharmaceuticals were in short supply, though the power of such herbs was often rooted in local lore and humoralist thinking rather than in empirical evidence (indeed, contemporary medical opinion tended to regard such folk medicines as scourges of the poorer populations, not cures).

Though herbs reduced hunger pangs and provided useful nutrients, wild plants alone were not the answer to starvation. The low caloric content of the herbs hardly compensated for the loss of carbohydrates from grain, and there were limits to the extent to which these plants could support an individual, let alone a population, in a crisis. For one, the plants were seasonal, so many were only available from February until around July.[36] Herbs were also a finite resource, and in extremely poor areas, the demand for wild greens could eventually exhaust an area's supply. Although the plants could be preserved to extend their shelf life—*zaʿatar*, which is used as a condiment, is dried, pulverized, and mixed with sumac, salt, and sesame seeds—the process usually stripped many of the delicate nutrients from the plants. Whatever their reasoning, contemporaries were skeptical of their nutritional value, often writing with pity about those who foraged for greens to survive.[37] George Doolittle described the inhabitants of the poor Christian town of ʿAlma in the southern region of Jabal ʿAmil as "devitalized" by a diet that was overly dependent upon herbs. He observed that once the poor had learned which plants were edible, one could "walk for hours and not find a bit of green vegetation suitable to eat, it had all been plucked up to satisfy the hunger pangs of the villagers."[38]

Survival strategies often required a keen sense of the calendar. It helped that people were already accustomed to adjusting their diets over the course of the year because of normal annual fluctuations in availability and price. Since grain tended to be most expensive in the winter and immediately before the harvest was released in the summer, many people staggered their diets to compensate. In his memoir, al-Amin comments that the *ful* (fava bean) harvest in midsummer was a relief for the population before the arrival of wheat, lentils, barley, and fruits in late summer.[39] Statistics and anecdotes indicate that prices typically dropped after the wheat crop that had been planted in the winter arrived in July. When seasonal crops hit the market, the drop in prices triggered purchases on a larger scale as people acquired and preserved food for use when it would be more expensive. Individuals would produce or purchase legumes, grains, fruits, vegetables, meat, and dairy products as they became available, then extend their shelf life by drying, salting, fermenting, or immersing them in oil, thereby arresting the process of decomposition.[40] Preserves from this annual preservation cycle (called the *mune*) were especially useful for the winter months when food was far more expensive or, in the worst cases, inaccessible in remote mountain villages. In the early years of the famine, leftover stores of preserved food may have allowed many to stave off hunger, or at least delay it for a while, but after 1915, the high cost of staple foods, restrictions on transportation in Lebanon, and the economic depression prevented many from acquiring the amounts necessary to sustain themselves through the severe winters of the famine years when suffering was greatest.

Ideally, expensive foods were produced by one's own hand on one's own land. Because of this, those best positioned to survive the famine in rural areas were those who owned land and animals, thus allowing for some self-sufficiency in times of high prices. Not coincidentally, these were the two factors that kept al-Amin and his family alive in the war. Unlike durable household goods and jewelry, which could be sold in times of need but ceased to provide any benefit once the cash was spent, ownership of arable agricultural land and animal husbandry were sustainable strategies. They not only could feed their owners with the food they produced, but those same products could be sold for cash to purchase items people could not grow themselves. One interviewee noted that her family was well off during the war because they owned agricultural land in the Gharb region where they kept goats and sheep that they milked for sale in Beirut.[41] While it was not a guarantee of survival, land and animal ownership offered a cushion that allowed many to stave off hunger or even achieve a measure of prosperity if the land or animals were sufficiently productive.

For most, however, self-grown food was no panacea. In the cramped, stony confines of towns and cities, growing food on a significant scale was impractical or impossible. In the towns of Mount Lebanon, agriculture within the villages and on their terraces provided little more than seasonal supplements to family diets or a means to augment annual preserves. As useful as the produce might have been, both the size of the plots (particularly in towns) and the seasonality of crops meant that most families could not rely on such small-scale agriculture for survival. In his memoir, Anis Furayha mentions that his family increased the cultivation of potatoes, onions, and beans in their garden to avoid the importation restrictions in the mountain but that this alone was not enough to sustain them once prices began to rise.[42] As a child of the famine, the future sociologist Afif Tannous was sent into Tripoli to sell his family's vegetables in order to buy the grain that his family needed to survive.[43] Ibrahim Khalil 'Awad, a mere child of nine at the time of the famine, wrote that his grandfather's fears of dearth and high prices prompted him to plant his various properties extensively with wheat and barley in addition to supplemental legumes and vegetables in an effort to avoid the high prices of the marketplace.[44] Although his grandfather prepared for famine strategically and thoughtfully, by 1916,

Ibrahim was forced to eat grasses and thin *saj* bread with yogurt and mint in order to meet his barest of needs.[45] In 1912, even the fertile market town of Zahle imported 4.05 million kilograms of wheat to meet local needs,[46] despite the 13.5 million kilograms of the grain produced in its immediate vicinity.[47] If Zahle could not feed itself, how could a small regional town or a family?

Land tenure arrangements also meant that simply having access to land was not necessarily a guarantee of survival. The often-complicated relationships between rural elites and the land's tenants almost uniformly favored the wealthy and powerful.[48] When the harvest came, farmers were usually forced to sell what they grew to pay taxes, obligations to elites, and past debts. Growing food did not always entitle one to it—many who lived in agricultural areas even encountered difficulties accessing food in the villages that produced it. Widespread poverty in rural villages gave them little economic gravity, so expensive cereals were drawn to the purchasing power of cities and market towns, where they were sold at prices far too high for many to afford. In his memoir, al-Amin recalls traveling nearly forty kilometers through farming communities to Nabatieh simply to pay thirty-two piasters per bushel for millet. Al-Amin's story reflects a trend that was evident not only in his home region of Jabal 'Amil[49] but also in the northern agrarian region of 'Akkar[50] and even in the interior town of Zahle, which was a magnet for grain, with its fifteen functioning mills.[51]

The biggest problem for most people in the famine was not so much the availability of food but rather finding money to pay for it. Those who had lost their jobs to the war or whose salaries failed to keep up with inflation had to adapt. For many, this meant selling movable items or even property for cash or food. Gold jewelry was useful both as an ornament and as insurance in hard times. If people needed money, they could sell their heirlooms for the value of the item or, if buyers were scarce, for the market value of the metal.[52] As the famine deepened and valuables were depleted, people resorted to selling basic household items and even land to meet their needs. Once simple items had been sold, people turned to selling the component parts of complex possessions like houses. In his account of the period, George Doolittle describes an "empty, roofless windowless, doorless house, with the solitary grave in the yard" as "emblematic" of the region.[53]

By stripping a house of shutters, tiles, windows, and doors, a family could immediately add relative value to the property while providing the cash necessary to keep its occupants alive.

The sale of possessions was not a long-term solution for those in need, but it provided a stopgap if staying alive was an immediate concern. Unfortunately, as time went on, this strategy grew less and less effective. When conditions worsened, people flooded the market with their valuables, causing the value of such items to collapse in an obvious buyer's market. An administrator in Beirut during the war, Muhammad 'Izzat Darwaza, wrote that middle-class families sold their furniture, their heirlooms, and their household items in piles when currency collapse had reduced their incomes to a fraction of the prewar value. He noted that the main beneficiaries were not the sellers but speculators and merchants from the wealthy cities of Damascus and Aleppo who came to Beirut to capitalize on its misery by buying valuable items at low prices, then transporting them back to the Syrian interior to sell at a profit.[54] According to Darwaza, even land lost value as homes that were worth one thousand gold liras began to sell for two thousand or three thousand in paper notes, a sum that he claimed was worth one hundred liras or less.[55] This began a vicious cycle: as prices fell, the rich purchased homes and either rented them to the former inhabitants at exorbitant rates or expelled the inhabitants into the streets in favor of wealthier tenants. The French scholar Andre Latron echoes this in his postwar analysis, citing stories of people who had bartered their land for indeterminate amounts of grain—the value of which was not even noted in the contract itself.[56]

From Suffering into Suffering

Migration in famine is often considered an act of desperation, and for those who fled the intense poverty in their home villages in the latter years of the war, this characterization often held true. However, migration was a rather complex coping strategy. Those who decided to move in the famine did so in response to a range of push and pull factors. Some left to take advantage of the perceived benefits of a new location, whereas others merely sought to escape potential hazards in their home villages. Migration might have been a last-ditch effort for some, but it was one of the first coping strategies for others. As with all aspects of life in the famine, class and circumstances frequently determined whether a strategy was successful or not. For many of the poorest, the slight benefits that a new location might provide often came at a great price.

Migration's negative associations are largely due to two challenges in particular that the vulnerable faced in their move. First, those who left were often already in poor condition and lacked the resources that they needed on their journey. Second, without access to their usual social support networks when arriving at their destinations, migrants were often ostracized as threats or intruders. In worst-case scenarios, they were pushed to the margins of society to live in poverty, poorly sheltered and often at great risk of disease. Such migrants were among the most vulnerable demographics of the famine, but for many, their odds would have been nearly as bad if they stayed. That their suffering was far more visible for observers made it easy for writers to associate their plight with the worst of the famine.

In fact, many of those who moved first were wealthy families who left rural areas for more populous communities like Beirut, Tripoli, Zahle, and Damascus. If a person had cash, migration was a protective factor, since urban environments provided additional insulation from potential suffering because their larger populations meant greater purchasing power. To have wealth in a city meant access to good housing, good food, and security. In contrast, those who moved from positions of poverty generally migrated once all avenues of support had been exhausted at home. As is common in such migrations, it was often men who, seeking work, made the initial move to the cities while their families remained at home.[57] In the rare cases where the men found a job that could support them, both the men and their families at home in the village were still vulnerable to the effects of starvation and disease. Moreover, the uncertainty of housing for migrants often meant that families found it difficult to contact their breadwinner, even to confirm that he was still alive.

In general, migration flowed from smaller to larger communities and from rural to urban zones. There was a logic to this. While no place was truly safe from the famine, urban areas came with some benefits, even if we take into account the wartime employment crisis, high mortality, terrible poverty, and epidemic diseases that were rampant in cities and towns during the famine. For migrants, the benefits boiled down to work and food. A larger population meant more competition for resources, but it also usually meant a larger and more diverse economy, a nucleus of reserve capital among the wealthy, and the availability of necessities due to a city's greater political and economic gravity.[58] This, in conjunction with the better rates of exchange for Ottoman paper notes in the larger cities, meant that important food items were usually both easier to acquire and cheaper for urban residents. There were some exceptions to this, notably during the Beirut flour crises, but those cases were outliers. As bad as things could be in the towns, circumstances were undoubtedly worse in poor rural mountain villages.

In theory, aid should have been easier to come by in urban areas as well. Even in crisis, major urban centers hosted a range of charitable foundations and offered a relatively functional bureaucracy that could look after hygiene, social welfare, and other basic needs. For those who could borrow, the wealthy elites of the cities had capital to provide credit—especially in Beirut. While this undoubtedly saved many lives, it was a mixed blessing, since the combination of a high demand for cash and the desperation of those needing credit meant that loans became increasingly usurious as the years passed, particularly since the odds of repayment during the war were almost nil after the value of collateral goods and property collapsed.[59] The political and economic importance of cities like Beirut also ensured that major problems were more likely to be addressed (if not always solved) by Ottoman officials, either through the patronage of local elites or occasionally by order of government officials. Such involvement was at times unfortunate, like when military governor Jamal Pasha himself teamed up with Beirut's merchants to solve the flour crisis (creating a nucleus of corruption in the process) or when he sought to slow currency speculation by deporting notable families at random to the interior.[60]

However, in practice, municipalities that had run deficits even before the war were ill-equipped to help the large numbers of locals who had fallen into poverty, let alone the migrants who flooded into the cities seeking work and aid. Both private and municipal patronage was often limited by the weakness of the wartime economy, which made it difficult to fund even the bureaucratic bare minimum.[61] While some towns had institutions in place to support the poor, the lack of funding, the high demand, and corruption limited their effectiveness during the crisis.[62] To balance tax shortfalls during the war, several local administrations were forced to adjust their budgetary priorities to meet basic municipal needs, usually to the detriment of those who needed help most. For local political leaders, migrants were an administrative nightmare, and they were treated as such. In the town of Sidon, the municipality slashed the budget for the poor from an already meager 15,500 piasters in 1915–1916, then justified the cut by classifying as charitable programs such political indulgences as public ceremonies and contributions to notables.[63] In his conversations with Ottoman surveyors, the mayor of Tyre openly depicted the refugees as drains on the municipality, and other larger cities were no different.[64] While Tripoli allotted funding to conduct charitable work, it also dealt with widespread poverty by incarcerating and expelling the homeless from the city.[65] Even Beirut swept refugees from the streets in advance of a visit by Jamal and Enver Pashas in an effort to sanitize the city's image in the eyes of Ottoman high officials.[66] Tragically, many who were caught up in the sweep would have been migrants coming in search of survival.

Despite the obvious suffering in the streets, large cities and towns like Beirut, Tripoli, Zahle, and even the smaller town of Tyre saw their populations increase during the years of the war as urban areas became convergence points for both refugees and wealthier migrants alike. Tripoli is an excellent example of this. Despite reports of terrible poverty and appalling mortality from famine and epidemic disease, wartime migration increased Tripoli's population from an estimated prewar level of around 30,000 in the combined region of the city and the coastal Mina quarter to around 32,000 in 1919. This suggests that the famine generated a nearly 7 percent increase in population even after subtracting the thousands of people who had perished.[67] Employment statistics from Ottoman surveyors Bahjat and Tamimi indicate that Tyre suffered similar effects. In their overview of the province of Beirut, they write that 2,700 out of the 6,000–7,500 people living in Tyre were unemployed. While this was clearly a result of the damage to the economy from the war, it was also in part due to the presence of large numbers of refugees in the town.[68] Similarly, the interior agrarian center of

Zahle became a target for migrants thanks to its agricultural labor market and its access to food.[69] Zahle would have seemed particularly hospitable when contrasted with the crumbling economies of the villages in the neighboring mountain district of Keserwan.

Unfortunately, the same effects that pushed people into larger towns devastated many small villages. Anis Furayha observed that even early in the crisis, those who did not own land left his family's village of Ras al-Matn for the coastal cities to seek work.[70] With the silk industry in stasis, there were few jobs to fill and many in need of employment, so many people left even before hunger began. Over time, with fewer people and less money in circulation, the small shops and markets that made up the backbone of the communities struggled, especially without the benefit of the mountain's twin economic pillars, sericulture and remittances. Adding to this misery, Ottoman restrictions on transporting grain cut access to wheat and drove up prices, forcing those with the means to take up smuggling to meet their needs. As small villages were drained by migration and death, the resulting economic and social disruption made acquiring basic necessities even more difficult for those who remained.[71] Not surprisingly, local histories of small mountain and coastal villages are filled with stories of villagers pouring into the cities seeking work, food, or both.[72]

As smaller villages hemorrhaged residents, destination towns filled with homeless refugees, who became conceptually synonymous with poverty and disease. Doolittle described the situation in Tripoli as "well nigh unbelievable,"[73] an assessment that is echoed in Bahjat and Tamimi's overview of the impoverished city in their report.[74] The poor and middle classes of both local and migrant groups suffered the worst of this situation. In Beirut, those locals who had been driven to sell their belongings or even their homes at increasingly lower prices faced hunger, eviction, and homelessness.[75] Tragically, the high cost of living mitigated what gains many of the migrants had hoped to make by coming to the city, prompting Darwaza to write that the poor "fled from hunger to hunger."[76]

Contemporaries of the famine often portrayed the refugees who flowed from the mountains into the streets of the cities and towns as desperate victims of the famine. While the choice to leave one's community in a time of crisis was indeed an extreme step, it was not an illogical one. As al-Amin's example demonstrates, migration should be more accurately regarded as a calculated risk that individuals and families took based on how they assessed their own vulnerabilities and the potential benefits they might find at their destinations. Those who were forced into migration as a last resort were certainly the most vulnerable in the famine, but the decision, no matter how difficult, was at least a rational one.

Support Networks and Survival

A survival strategy need not be overly complicated—sometimes it is as simple as asking for help. Although the state faltered and charitable giving decreased markedly during the famine, significant assistance provided in the famine era still flowed through the most fundamental support systems of all: family, community, and patronage networks. This is common in crisis. When social structures fail, societies tend to fall back on existing networks and forge new ones within their communities.[77] Like the informal sources of income that existed outside of official documentation, the support networks during the wartime period were part of the invisible socioeconomic threads that, even when frayed, still bound society together during the period.

Ibrahim Khalil 'Awad's memoir offers numerous examples of the complex nature of familial and communal support networks during the war. When Ibrahim's father migrated abroad in 1914 in search of greater economic opportunity, he left his family with a gold wedding ring and the promise of remittances to support them. These plans were dashed by the war and an Entente blockade that severed those ties, leaving his wife alone in an untenable situation. With three children to support and no income, she brought Ibrahim and his siblings to her father's home in the central Lebanese town of Bharsaf, where they lived with his grandfather, his aunt, and her family on his grandfather's land. Though just a boy, Ibrahim was expected to contribute to the household. During the war, he ran errands and worked his grandfather's fields in a nearby village, often spending days alone despite the fact that he was nine years old when the war began. Even though the family was supported by its own land, his grandfather's choice to add more mouths to an already extended household was a calculated risk. And indeed, by 1916, in spite of the food that the extended family unit had grown on its various properties across the valley, the family suffered through the wartime years.[78]

ʿAwad's story shows how the same kinship, community, and religious networks that were the pillars of prefamine society remained pivotal supports for many during the crisis. The most basic of these supports were local and derived strength from the kinship roots that were the foundations of the community in small Lebanese towns and neighborhoods. This is not an abstraction—the social order of village life was defined by blood, name, and family history.[79] On a practical level, this meant that immediate family and the extended kinship of the community were the first levels of support when people needed help, and often also the last.[80] This was especially important in times of crisis, during which Lebanese sociologist Afif Tannous averred that such ties were "binding." Tannous emphasized this point with a local proverb, which stated, "He who has no backing has no backbone."[81] For Ibrahim's mother, his grandfather was his backbone, so it was natural to seek out his support.

Since family and community were often coextensive, they did not merely provide safety to their members but often worked together to ensure it. ʿAwad's memoir also describes how his community initially looked after his family while his father was trapped abroad and unable to help. In the early months of the crisis, Ibrahim's mother sent him to the butcher to purchase meat using the only thing of value that she had left: her ring. The butcher refused to take it. Despite the fact that his decision meant that he was sacrificing precious income, he gave Ibrahim the meat anyway to ensure that his family would be fed. ʿAwad assures the reader that the honorable act did not go unpaid, stating that his father reimbursed the butcher for his kindness on his return.[82] Mahmud Khalil Saʿab writes of a similar act wherein kinship obligations overrode personal gain. Near the end of the war, a merchant from Dayr al-Qamar received a tip about cheap grain for sale in a nearby town and went to purchase it to bring back to sell in his shop. When he met a relative on the road, he shared his secret, knowing well that revealing it might limit his own profits from his own inventories. He even traveled with his relative to the town to ensure that he could acquire enough cheap grain to sustain his family. (Saʿab's story has a sad twist: while returning to the mountain with loads of what they thought was cheap grain, they learned that the Entente forces had arrived and that the price of grain in Beirut had collapsed. They had overpaid.)[83]

Help did not always come for free. Obligations could come in the form of a favor, or they could be financial. One rather ambiguous means of support was lending. Though it has a deservedly evil reputation in famine literature, lending could also constitute another layer of support within communities at a time when cash was scarce and prices were volatile. Some clearly took advantage of the need that drove people to accept loans. One missionary report tells of a man who mortgaged his land to a "friend" in Beirut for 53 gold liras at 55 percent compound interest. After the war, his small loan had turned into a 327-lira obligation.[84] However, in a period wherein survival depended on access to liquid funds, defaulted loans of food or cash could easily amount to a devastating loss because creditors could not easily redeem them during the disaster. George Doolittle wrote of one man who died with a safe full of unfulfilled IOUs.[85] Those loans that were not exploitative relied on both a sense of honor and the trust fostered by community ties. Though taking on debt assumes an unevenness in the social relationship between debtor and lender, village economics depended on such trust to function. 'Awad's story of the ring assumes as much, as does the scholar Nicola Ziadeh's description of his own experiences as a child in the war in Damascus. When his mother sent him to buy food, the local shopkeeper took his cash, and instead of giving back valuable coins in change, he started a tab in Ziadeh's father's name, then taught young Nicola how credit worked. This helped Ziadeh acquire the necessary items for his mother at home, though it also saved the merchant from having to give out his precious change in a time of currency volatility.[86]

Patronage systems represented the most visible part of this network, and they gained special significance during the war due to the negotiations between local elites, institutions, and the Ottoman officials tasked with the novel demands of wartime administration. Many patronage systems were extensions of religious and charitable institutions, the Red Cross and Red Crescent, or the state itself. While religious foundations had obligations to pay out when funds were available, support was only as forthcoming as the funding, and many still went hungry. Such patronage systems were inherently political, and many local actors used the crisis and the responses to it to work to their own advantage or to enhance their own reputations.[87]

Ottoman administrators were happy to use local patrons to enhance their governance. Within the particular patrimonial systems of both urban and rural areas, local elites could be harnessed as intermediaries or even mechanisms of state policy. This was most evident in the relationships of convenience that Ottoman high officials like Jamal Pasha and Beirut's governor 'Azmi Bey formed with local elites and institutions like Beirut mayor 'Umar Da'uq, merchant elites like Ahmad Mukhtar Beyhum, the Sursuq family, and the Syrian Protestant College. However, this exploitation went both ways. In exchange for their loyalty and assistance, elites could use their Ottoman connections to secure benefits like jobs, food, or favors, which they could then distribute to clients to benefit their communities while enhancing their own standing in the process. Such clientelism was a fundamental part of political life across the region in normal times, so it should not be surprising that much of the access to wartime aid was dependent on both benign and malign corruption.

Support networks offered layers of support that could be accessed at different levels and at different times in the famine. Each level of support came with different obligations and at times different costs—and all waned to varying degrees as the economic crisis strained the finances of individuals, charities, and the state alike. Some people, like 'Awad, survived because their networks held fast. Others who had been forced to migrate suffered because they lacked the "backbone" that kinship networks and social obligation (even in its reduced, famine form) provided. In new communities, the collaterals of blood, name, and reputation were not always available, especially when the loyalties of those in the destination community were first and foremost to their own. Like any survival strategy, seeking help was no guarantee of life. However, when available, support networks could be invaluable safety nets for those with nothing else to catch them.

Adaptation as Agency

Our dim view of survival strategies is more than an appraisal of their successes and failures; it is a reflection of how we understand the lives of those forced to adapt to survive. Unfortunately, sources that humanize famine strategies like Amin's diary are rare, leaving us dependent on third party observations that, while often sympathetic, still denied agency or respect to the poor in their efforts to survive. In such accounts, famine is broadly portrayed as something that just *happens* to the vulnerable: it is theirs to passively suffer, starve, and die from; if they are saved, it is by the mercy of fate or the benevolence of their social betters. However, as this chapter shows, those who were forced to adapt to survive deserve more credit. Even unsuccessful survival strategies were deliberately chosen, rational moves made by individuals trying to balance their uncertain futures against the immediate needs of the present. The poorest in society may have suffered, but they also actively confronted the challenges that they faced. They responded to developments and often sought to mitigate their risks by changing their diets, tapping support networks, or changing their environment altogether by moving away. Out of necessity, some individuals were driven to reinvent their own social norms and reconsider what options they could create. Even then, many merely struggled less while those around them perished. Not all survived, but no one lay down to die without a fight.

4

Trauma and Time

> New life began to pulsate within our bodies and within our souls, though the latter still bore scars that will remain to our dying day.
> —FREDERICK BLISS

WHEN THE GREAT WAR BEGAN, Frederick Bliss was a protected foreigner affiliated with some of the most prominent foreign institutions in the region, including the Palestine Exploration Fund, the American Red Cross, and the Syrian Protestant College. Though he was a vanishingly minor character in the historical narrative of a war that he endured in relative peace and security, we still know a surprisingly great deal about his wartime experience because of a retrospective that he wrote and then stashed away in the archive of the Syrian Protestant College after the war. Bliss's account is somewhat peculiar as a historical source. It is not especially valuable because of his skill as a storyteller or for the details it provides. In fact, his rambling and somewhat disorganized narrative is light on unique information and generally offers less insight into major events than other publications and diaries from the time. What makes Bliss's report fascinating is its perspective—most notably his raw insight into the difficulties of simply *being* amid an inescapable four-year disaster.

Scattered among meandering descriptions of politics and the aberrations of life under martial law are startling revelations about the emotional traumas of life in the famine and the awkwardness of living a life of privilege during a time of great privation. Not only does his text demonstrate an uncommon awareness of the human facets of the disaster around him, but it also reveals how much he agonized about the role he personally played in the crisis. Most remarkably, the physical draft of the document still attests to the difficulty that Bliss apparently felt in composing it. Now housed in the Jafet Library Archives and Special Collections at the American University of Beirut, the fragile onion-skin paper on which Bliss composed his draft is crisscrossed with edits and arrows where he nixed and relocated whole paragraphs in an effort to make sense of the jumbled cluster of ideas that were supposed to represent four terrible years of his life. Some corrections bear witness to the difficulty of admitting his own minor privations while writing on the abject deprivation of others—and in some passages, he despairs for even existing in security within their shattered worlds. One passage, stricken out as irrelevant or perhaps too honest, reads, "What if we seldom tasted coffee or sugar, what if the fat grew thin, what if we turned out clothes and patched our socks, what if we traveled by foot—did we not keep alive, and most of us keep well? No, it was not our own condition, but that of the people about us that was harrowing."[1] His writing is permeated with a sense of sadness and frustration but curiously also anxiety, and above all, guilt: guilt over the deaths of those he could not save, guilt for having to choose whom to save, and a tortured empathy for those whose lives had been warped by the power of the famine.[2] He even felt guilt for his own traumatization when he knew that he was one of the lucky ones. At one point, he wrote, "Our only real suffering during those long years was vicarious. To dwell on our own petty privations would be worse than irrelevant."[3]

Bliss shines brightest when describing his own feelings about the famine. Though his safety was not a concern outside of the risk of typhus or the tuberculosis that would eventually claim the life of his brother Howard, the famine was still a perpetual source of misery in his life. He frequently reflected upon the suffering and horrors of a world that had gradually transformed in front of him and the contrasts that he felt within it. Like most who wrote on the war, Bliss understood that he was lucky to be able to endure the famine without having to fear for his life or for the lives of those he loved. He even stated this outright. But safety and stability did not prevent him from suffering vicariously through the experiences of those around him. On this, he noted, "Although we Americans were exempt from actual personal suffering, we were by no means exempt from apprehension."

More so than most, Bliss saw himself as a participant observer within the crisis, even if only from its fringes. The famine was his disaster too, even if his suffering was simply by proximity. Indeed, his depiction of the famine's end is written as the lifting of a universal, shared burden that he projects onto all who survived the era—not merely those who starved. He wrote, "New life began to pulsate within our bodies and within our souls, though the latter still bore scars that will remain to our dying day."[4]

Such honest self-reflection is unfortunately rare in the famine literature. When mentioned, traumatic experiences are frequently treated superficially or as hollow generalities—stating the obvious to avoid having to explain the agonizing epiphenomena of four indescribably miserable years. Most references to emotional suffering in autobiographical works are merely attempts to harness pathos to convey the horrors of the famine.[5] The limitations of memoir are even more apparent when contrasted with the evocative emotional vulnerability found in some of the oral accounts and contemporary letters of the period. In one interview, Salwa Salibi recalled that her mother wept for a week after seeing people rooting through the garbage to find food.[6] In a 1916 letter, the Maronite priest and French intelligence agent Bulus 'Aqil earnestly describes the suffering he saw around him as something that "crushes ones insides and turns tears into blood."[7] In contrast, most retrospectives portray the rich landscape of lived experience as a meticulously posed, sepia-toned portrait.

The experiential aspect of trauma presents a daunting challenge for historians of famine. Though many of us at least attempt to engage with the issue of emotional suffering in crisis, it is difficult to do so with any substance. Writing about the social ravages of disaster is relatively easy. Writing about the particulars of trauma is a snipe hunt. Sources eagerly relay accounts of physical suffering or public poverty in exhilarating detail. In contrast, mental events are fleeting and are almost never recorded, and when they are, the writers are rarely inclined to be honest about them, leaving us to interpret the internal experience of famine indirectly or by proxy. Even then, both language and genre limit a writer's ability to express something as emotionally rich and confusing as feelings and memories about a direct experience of something so overwhelming. The passage of time only amplifies those problems.

To date, we have thousands of pages written about the famine but little real understanding of the deeper effects that it had on the people who actually lived it. It is hard to generalize from such incomplete data. A few sources may indicate parts of trends, but they cannot capture the broader experience of a whole society comprised of people who each experienced a slightly different famine. However, we cannot and should not ignore the issue of trauma simply because it is difficult to parse. Holocaust historian Dominick LaCapra has incisively wondered if it is even possible to write on the history of a traumatic episode without confronting the notion of trauma,[8] and the same question would seem highly relevant for any analysis of social life in the famine. Trauma, whether personal, anticipatory, or merely secondhand, was a fundamental part of life for everyone who experienced the wartime crisis. Without dabbling in the reductive alchemy of psychosocial history, I argue that it is essential to try to understand the emotional weight of the crisis if we wish to understand it as a lived experience and not just as events on a timeline.[9] Perhaps just as importantly, an analysis of trauma is necessary if we wish to understand both how the horrors of the crisis shaped historical actors over its duration and the social consequences of that transformation. As LaCapra has argued, "It is misguided to see trauma as a purely psychological or individual phenomenon. It has crucial connections to social and political conditions and can only be understood and engaged with respect to them."[10] Trauma is both infectious and transformative. It contributed to social attitudes that shaped social behaviors and even informed policies that had life or death implications. While we will never be able to see the world of the famine through the eyes of its beholders, it is worth empathetically trying to understand how the famine impacted them as human beings. That trauma was itself a profound, if hidden, facet of their lived reality, and any inquiry into life in the war would be incomplete without it.

Time in Crisis

To understand the nature of that trauma, we must also explore the concept of time in history—and especially in crisis. When we think of historical time, it is usually as a unit of measurement. We have dates that mark the start and end of a historical event more or less accurately. Between those dates, there is a quantifiable collection of months and days, each of which contain a set number of hours and minutes. A simple description of historical causality suggests that an event flows from a mutually agreed, historically determined start point until some ending resolves it. At that point, we can find causal connections between that event and others around it, or we can look ahead to a later period to give the event significance in the broad metahistorical narrative. Through this, we tie our event to an apparently universal historical timeline to show why it matters that it happened at all.[11]

Retrospectively, historical change and the passage of time can appear as objective, gradual, cumulative, and entirely passive processes that serve as the scenes in which historical actors play their roles. Such actors may alter their own historical circumstances, but they have no control over time. They ride like a river from their beginnings to their ends—or at least from the point they enter our historical awareness until the point they drop out of it. While this framework makes it easier to organize history, it also makes it easier to take time for granted as something to be lived. Historical actors are not passive riders, nor are they objective observers. They do not experience time retrospectively, even if their writings often homogenize time for us into a single, often omniscient timeline. They are subjective participants whose limited personal understandings of time are shaped by both their interactions with the world and the affective forces of their lived realities.

Time might be easy to quantify as an objective measurement, but as a subjective experience, it is far more complicated. Although we tend to measure time as a single continuum, the way that time is experienced and processed as we live it is actually quite relative. Time is a factor in economic or social cycles, like the annual planting and harvest dates that in turn affect food prices and labor demand. Time simultaneously can be a function of biological processes, marking the velocity of infection curves that spike and flatten over the course of an epidemic, or it can reflect the body's circadian rhythms, which rise and fall throughout the year in line with the angle of the sun on the horizon. It can be a predictable cycle like the changing seasons or the circuit of a clock. But it is also felt as we live through it. Anyone who has waited for urgent news or lain still in an MRI machine can confirm that the passage of the same amount of time may feel very different to the same person in different contexts, let alone for different people in vastly different circumstances.[12]

Such lived time can be perceived as both accretive and immediate, depending on how we look at it. Retrospectively, time can appear to be a cumulative force that alters the world around us. Our fresh experiences slowly supersede the old, which in turn fade into the past with only their consequences remaining. Our understanding of time ultimately allows us to reflect on the past, react to the present, and plan for the future. However, our consciousness is ultimately rooted in the immediacy of the present, which in turn shapes how we evaluate the world around us. Our interactions with new events can shape our perspectives and over time, even shape our identities. The passage of a few hours might change a person's emotional state from happy to wistful. The passage of a few months during a crisis might cause dramatic changes to their well-being or financial security, which in turn can lead to practical changes to their lifestyle. It can undoubtedly lead to new challenges that have to be endured. The passage of several years can (and did) reshape whole worldviews. Those in Lebanon who woke up to a world at war in 1914 (whether they were aware of it or not) were not the same people who with the very same eyes looked out on their ragged famine worlds as the armistice descended in late 1918.

If one looks at famine through a detached social scope, it is easy to forget that a traumatic event like a famine is still made up of that phenomenological "felt" time. And in the case of a long-term, horrifying ordeal like the famine of World War I, four years could have seemed almost endless. From the start of mobilization to the Ottoman withdrawal from Beirut—August 2, 1914, to October 1, 1918[13]—the inhabitants of the region spent 1,521 days of their lives in the thrall of the war.[14] Each of those 1,521 days had to be lived, often in depressing fashion. Over a dozen seasons passed. Harvests came and went—some bad, most worse. Exchange rates fluctuated; the price of food spiked and fell but generally climbed. The sun rose; the sun set. To survive this era meant surviving 36,504 hours of war, of fear, of sadness, of uncertainty and anxiety, of deferred hopes and fleeting joys, of crushing boredom and harrowing despair. Children who were born at the start of the war came to an age of comprehension in its darkest days. Some people who had lived almost their whole lives in a world of prosperity and progress died in a world of overwhelming tragedy. For those occupying this tiny stretch of the eastern Mediterranean, the war and the famine dominated the lived reality of the period from its chaotic beginning until its messy resolution.

As the days and months and years dragged on, the constant but variable trickle of horrors gradually altered the scenery that people saw in the famine worlds that they inhabited. The physical and social nature of the world itself changed as the crisis progressed, which in turn influenced what people experienced in their personal lives. These changes were most profound for those who lived in extreme poverty and starvation or for those who became ill, but the secure were not immune to them either. Observers watched with horror as the foundations of their worlds seemed to crumble before their eyes. Many of these changes were external—what people ate, how they lived, etc.—but many changes were subtler, hidden within the minds of the famine's participants. Such conceptual changes slowly altered how a person perceived the present and the way that they anticipated the future. Perceptions about institutions, organizations, elites, the poor, neighbors, family members, strangers, in-groups, out-groups, and everything in between transformed over time and under the influence of the crisis. This might be expected. But abstract ideas changed too. Perceptions of concepts like poverty, sickness, health, safety, and danger began to shift in response to the realities of the famine as well. Unintentionally, individuals even began to adapt their nonrational interpretations of ideas like justice, injustice, fear, aversion, pity, and sympathy into famine-warped synonyms that would have been unbelievable to them in the prewar era— and in some cases still horrified some of those who reflected on them long after the famine had ended.

Filling Time

It is easy to forget the mundane aspects of life in crisis because of the spectacular backdrop of a world war and a calamitous famine. But while Europe burned and starvation spread through the land, life for many on the home front simply dragged on in its usual sixty-minute, twenty-four-hour, 365-day cycles[15], which had to be filled in some way or another. Unfortunately, wartime existence was dominated by both the distant conflict, which residents of the region could do little to influence, and the immediate reality of the famine, which was equally resistant to individual efforts. The magnitude of both the war and the famine had a numbing effect that compounded the sense of helplessness that many observers reported in their writings.

Although the war began with a bang, the excitement quickly faded. For many, the formal patterns remained somewhat familiar. Days continued to revolve around sleep, food, domestic labor, and, often, work and school, even if the quality and quantity of some of those rituals had changed in the wartime context. However, with the blockade sealing off the sea; financial realities intruding on wealthy, middle, and lower classes alike; and government mandates hampering travel and leisure activities, the famine was surprisingly boring—even amid the horrific effects of widespread starvation and killer epidemics. Outside of one's daily routine, there was little to do and far too much to ponder.

Though safe from the war that burned around the fringes of the Ottoman Empire, life on the Syrian home front was increasingly dominated by the horrors of the famine and the sheer ennui of existence within it. Bliss describes the wartime period in his introduction as "those years of indefinite apprehension, when, in very exasperation at the deadly quiet, we fairly shrieked for something to go off with a bang, even if we ourselves should be annihilated in the crash. Anything, we cried, anything but this menacing monotony."[16] The term *monotony* found its way into missionary correspondence with striking regularity from 1916 onward. In a letter to the American Mission Press treasurer Charles Dana on April 25, 1916, W. S. Nelson of the mission's Tripoli Station wrote, "We reached home this morning after a most comfortable trip which had absolutely nothing in the way of incident to disturb the absolute monotony of existence."[17] George Doolittle actually used the same phrase, "monotony of existence," in his letter to Dana on August 1, 1917.[18] Press secretary Margaret McGilvary observed that over time, the initial excitement of the anticipated Allied invasion abated until it was reduced to a state of "dull apathy" as the crisis dragged on.[19]

Except perhaps for those suffering in the most extreme throes of starvation, the blandness of existence seemed to amplify the hopelessness of the social and political atmosphere to unbearable levels. While a student at the Syrian Protestant College, the future physician and historian William Nimeh wrote that due to the lack of things to do, "people became depressed and despondent, and it [sic] reacted at times in an unhealthy condition of mind."[20] Faced with the extraordinary suffering of those around them and the grating dullness of daily life, individuals in the more secure echelons of society often clung to those things that could provide them with emotional stability or a shred of normalcy at a time when their world had been thrown terribly asunder. For some, this involved maintaining rituals and practices that recalled vestiges of life prior to the war. This might mean splurging on odd, even ill-advised indulgences in order to tap into a comforting memory (even for just a few moments) or taking time to relax with friends over precious *nouveau-luxe* items like coffee or sugar. Sometimes it just meant symbolically replacing scarce items to approximate the feel of normal life—anything to momentarily distract from the grinding crisis around them.[21] Ramadan, Christmas, Easter, birthdays, baby and wedding showers, and various other celebrations continued to be celebrated by many, though the festivities themselves were hardly commensurate with what they had been before the war. Both nationalistic and religious ceremonies, though increasingly neglected as the famine dragged on, likewise provided a source of regularity and community at a time when each was needed. Such activities were not only important distractions from the suffering of the wartime period; they were also therapeutic means of alleviating the mental and emotional fatigue of the crisis.

The Entente blockade and restrictions on movement in the country contributed to a sense of caged isolation, particularly for foreigners. In his retrospective, Bliss writes, "Always before us, to the West, the smiling, treacherous blue sea, changed by the blockade from a way for us to get out to a means to keep us in."[22] Even temporary escape into the cool green reaches of Mount Lebanon was not as easy an option as it had been in the past for those living in Beirut. Though many affluent families along the coasts had made a tradition of summering in mountain resort towns like Brummana and Bhamdoun, the wartime environment threw up logistic and practical obstacles to this practice. It was not impossible to estivate in the mountain if one had the right connections—Arthur Dray's work on the famed soup kitchen in Brummana actually began as a chance encounter with starving individuals during his summer vacation—but long-term stays in Mount Lebanon required travelers to have permits to enter or to bring possessions and food across the border into the independent district. Margaret McGilvary mentions that such documents could take months to issue, unless of course one was willing to pay a substantial bribe to the official in charge to expedite the process.[23]

Even if they were granted permission to stay in the mountain, vacationers were still confounded by the difficulty of reaching it (in comfort). Because of the Ottoman requisitioning of pack animals and vehicles, most travel had to be made on foot or with the exorbitantly expensive assistance of local muleteers. Those who had money to spend could hire one of the few private carriages that remained in the cities. Syrian Protestant College professor Edward Nickoley availed himself of such a luxury on his journey into the mountain in 1917, and his record of the event suggests that even this novelty was much diminished from the prewar days. On July 23, 1917, he wrote (with characteristic sourness) that the three-hour carriage ride from Beirut to the nearby village of Shweir stretched to twelve hours due to the wasted state of the horses. For the privilege, Nickoley had to pay an astounding fifteen Ottoman liras (though accounting for currency collapse, it would have amounted to a more reasonable four liras at the currency's face value).[24]

Complaining about vacations while people starved on the streets might seem callous, but amid the stresses and the traumas of the famine, everyone coped in their own way. While observers often saw no problem with their own coping strategies, they at times regarded the efforts that other individuals or groups made to endure the crisis as irresponsible, disrespectful, or garish. This made the wealthy frequent targets of opprobrium because many of the leisure activities that they enjoyed during the war seemed to project indifference toward the suffering of those around them. Writers make numerous references to the opulence of the wealthy during economic crisis, in particular their insistence on hosting lavish parties while thousands starved on the streets. The contrast in living standards was often used as a metaphor for the social injustice of a crisis that killed the poorest members of society while enriching those at the top. Antun Yammine's disgust with the flagrant profiteering of the wealthy amid the suffering of the crisis inspired his class-critical Arabic language account of the war in 1919.[25] Turkish feminist reformer Halidé Edib's first depiction of wartime Beirut is a similarly scathing critique of the extravagant displays of wealth by the social elite of the city and the abject poverty of the beggars who lined its streets.[26] (Curiously, contemporaneous depictions of the famine are perhaps more class-conscious than they are sectarian, as the unequal social cost paid by different parts of society shaped wartime views of right and wrong.)[27]

However, the most despised elite behaviors were often as much about politics as they were about leisure. In a serial diary published years after the war, the shadowy figure falsely claiming to be "Aziz Bey," the self-proclaimed head of Beirut's General Security during the war (but who was likely another highly placed Ottoman official), defended both Ottomans and elites by showing that their social gatherings were primarily means of swapping patronage.[28] As much as we can doubt the authenticity of Aziz himself, his interpretation is not wrong. Venezuelan adventurer Rafael de Nogales wrote that "many of the well-to-do upper class . . . had enriched themselves and continued to grow richer every day through cooperation with and participation in the scandalous extortions of the Turkish bureaucracy" (of which the mercenary de Nogales was a part).[29] Undoubtedly, some of this went to the personal enrichment that de Nogales notes, but Anbara Salam al-Khalidi's memoir describes a scene wherein Jamal Pasha and other high Ottoman authorities were feted as a form of political theater that allowed Beirut's political class to bring their grievances to the regional authorities in a politically acceptable social venue. As the daughter of one of Sunni Beirut's brightest luminaries, Anbara herself was asked by the eminent Sunni leader Ahmad Mukhtar Beyhum to give a speech on behalf of the suffering multitudes of the nation. Though this was all part of the political game, Anbara nevertheless delivered her notes with some trepidation because she was addressing the very man who had investigated her father and hanged her fiancé in 1916.[30] Of course, Jamal had known the purpose of the gathering ahead of time and had even brought a relief plan to the meeting.[31] Even if we (very) generously assume that such parties were held with the best intentions, the ire that the associations sparked was unmistakable, particularly in the salacious rumors that such negotiations inspired (such as the allegation that the patriarchs of the Sursuq family had pimped out their wives to Jamal Pasha to secure control of the lucrative Beirut flour cartel).[32]

Filling time was difficult but necessary as individuals across society tried to endure the terrible wartime crisis. Each to their means, the upper, middle, and lower classes all coped as a way of gaining momentary respite from the trauma and stress of the crisis. This periodic frivolity helped to liven up wartime days that were lengthened by boredom, poverty, sickness, sadness, hunger, or some combination thereof. While retrospective sources might neglect this aspect of life in the famine except to judge the activities of others, the activities that filled the interminable hours of famine life were in many ways as defining as the tales of misery that fill the memoirs about the era. Contemporary descriptions of sporting events, movies, roller-skating, staring at the sea, or even joyously riding on the back of a wheat thresher reveal that life in the famine was not simply an unending string of miseries—it was as complicated as the emotions that people felt about it.[33]

Secondhand Suffering

This final observation about the complexity of life in the famine should not be read as a dismissal of the terrible traumas that the famine inflicted—because those traumas, as much as the activities that sought to minimize them, were fundamental to the famine experience. Understandably, when we discuss trauma in crisis our focus tends to rest on those who faced the brunt of it. Certainly, for the starving, famine suffering manifested in their constant search for food, their anxiety at the uncertainty of the future, and the physical and emotional pain that the famine caused. It was immediate, felt, and impossible to put into words. Sources frequently detailed the agony of hunger, the desperate struggles for inadequate food, and the misery of those who watched their children and loved ones wither away before their very eyes. However, many of those descriptions were not written by those who experienced suffering directly—they came from privileged observers of the famine who wrote about the world they saw and tried to understand.

For these observers, the suffering of the famine was traumatic as well, though in an entirely different way. Individuals who lived in a world transformed were faced with an unsettling sense of loss and were often horrified by the sights, sounds, and smells of their new famine world. The familiar streets of their cities were transformed into piteous menageries of suffering. In the eyes of their beholders, the bodies of the starving became caricatures of humanity that were fascinating, horrific, and shameful all at once. Need could change even erstwhile friends and neighbors into sources of guilt and sadness as relationships shifted from that of equals to that of a supplicant and a potential provider. Fears about the future forced some to turn inward to focus on their own uncertain circumstances, particularly with the crisis worsening without a clear endpoint.

For these secure observers, the effect of other people's suffering was itself a form of trauma. Like secondhand smoke, they absorbed the suffering of those around them merely by their proximity to the crisis, and like any carcinogen, it gradually changed them from the inside out. Unfortunately, such "secondhand suffering" was not openly discussed in many sources, as genre did not encourage emotional sharing in traditional Arabic memoir forms, and American writers in the war's aftermath were engaged in a sort of heroic mythmaking that left little room for ambivalence or weakness. Nevertheless, hints of trauma bled through the texts of many of the contemporaneous writings on life in the crisis. Even when trauma was expressed, technical issues often prevented writers from clearly conveying their feelings, since the simple vocabulary they had at their disposal appeared insufficient to depict the magnitude of what they experienced. It may have been possible to speak about the measurable effects of trauma like compassion fatigue, avoidance, and other concepts that help systematize our understanding of trauma and its pathologies in current psychological research, but of course, writers at the time would not have had access to the vocabulary to describe the psychology of trauma, let alone the ways that they internalized and interpreted their own trauma. They did, however, consistently note how impossible it was to really convey the *feeling* of being traumatized. And as Bliss's nervous edits suggest, even when writers tried, they were not always able to be honest about those feelings for fear of judgment.

Like Bliss, many American writers in particular admitted to being depressed, but their ability to express these emotions in a healthy manner was hindered by the haunting sense of guilt and unwarranted privilege that many who merely suffered "vicariously" had begun to feel when they contrasted their relatively petty emotional troubles with the immense and very existential suffering of those they saw dying in the streets. Amid the anguish and squalor of the famine, even their own depression could be depressing. In a 1917 diary entry, Edward Nickoley morosely noted, "There are all about us so many who are suffering so much more intensely that I am ashamed to let anyone know that I too have a regret and a sorrow, that I cherish a hope and a longing the realization and the fulfillment of which is indefinitely deferred."[34] Writers who expressed this sadness often seemed ambivalent, as if they did not know how to grieve the loss of the world they had known or whether they were even *allowed* to grieve its passing.[35] In a 1917 report, W. S. Nelson wrote, "Everywhere we missed old friends and strong men whose places had been vacated by disease or the unwonted hardship of military service. The somber dress of the widow and the dejected appearance of the orphan cast a gloom over all."[36]

The passage of time brought little relief, and perhaps even more anxiety, as the war and its famine seemed to stretch forever toward an unseen horizon. Bulus 'Aqil's reports on the situation in Lebanon to the French intelligence services on Arwad Island include the following terse passages: "Hearts are impatient, souls annoyed. Sadness has overcome us. Lost hope and expectation of ruin. So please inform us of what is happening. Is relief near?"[37] The anonymous mission report from Sidon Station in 1917 echoes these sentiments. The writer (undoubtedly George Doolittle, based on the handwriting), observed that the progressive destruction wrought by starvation, poverty, and disease had drained the population of hope. In Doolittle's eyes, the emotional demoralization had profound physical effects: "At first the people literally lifted up their voices and wept, but by 1916–1917, they still more literally lay down by the thousands and died."[38] In his retrospective, professor Jirjis Khuri al-Maqdisi specifically defined the years after 1916 by their despair, writing, "Where were the boys who were playing and shouting in the alleys of the towns and city? . . . Happiness ceased and was replaced by sorrowful sighs and unremitting sadness."[39] Others expressed a sense of confinement, frustration, and resentment at the situation that faced them. In her diary, the American hospital's superintendent of nursing, Mary Dale, poignantly wrote, "All news and conditions most depressing—even the beautiful, blue, utterly useless sea."[40]

The suffering of the famine taxed the empathetic capacity of those who experienced it to a terrible degree. The sheer volume of suffering made it impossible to avoid, as traumatic reminders of the crisis assailed the senses from literally every direction. In his retrospective, Bliss detailed the debilitating moans of the starving, "from which we could never escape, walk we never so fast or so far." Witnessing suffering among innocent children and families was especially devastating for some of the observers. Al-Maqdisi wrote, "The most severe sight for the soul was the sight of the children, sinuous from hunger, embracing their mothers who had fallen from weakness and emaciation, and (oh God!), from that gruesome situation!"[41] The humanitarian and professor Bayard Dodge concurred with this sentiment in his report on the soup kitchens in 'Abeih and Suq al-Gharb, writing that it was impossible to truly understand famine without witnessing the emotional agony of those who desperately strained to sustain their loved ones in the face of overwhelming odds.[42] Such trauma inevitably left scars on those it touched. As Judith Herman argues, trauma is "contagious," noting that "in the role of witness to disaster or atrocity, the [witness] at times is emotionally overwhelmed. She experiences, to a lesser degree, the same terror, rage, and despair as the patient."[43] When exposed to extreme suffering, even those who were not in physical danger were often still vicariously traumatized. In the case of the famine, the sympathetic responses that the suffering of others provoked was a terrible emotional burden, even if one only viewed it from afar—and as the famine worsened, that distance narrowed considerably.

The surge in poverty and the subsequent increase in begging increasingly dominated public interactions between the secure and the precarious. This not only forced elevated observers to confront suffering in their own lives, but it solidified the power disparity between the haves and have-nots. Contemporaries reported increasingly aggressive behaviors from the beggars, who began to specifically target the middle class because they were more accessible than the rich, even though they had less to give.[44] Margaret McGilvary wrote that "the foreigner was literally besieged with requests for help, which he could not grant . . . to give to one beggar in the street meant that twenty would spring up out of the ground to demand alms."[45] Bliss's retrospective echoes this observation, noting that it tended to inspire coldness. He wrote, "Cries of 'hungry, hungry, hungry' from which we could never escape, walk we never so fast or so far; cries pervading the city day and night, now faint, now loud, always despairing, cries from the stolid old man, from the frantic mother clutching the skeleton that was once her baby, from the bewildered little children."[46] Even if they were themselves safe, the effects of constant exposure to suffering traumatized such elevated observers. In McGilvary's words, the extent of the suffering made traveling about in Mount Lebanon "more than the heart can bear."[47] Each of these interactions insinuated the famine into otherwise secure lives—bringing horror, sadness, indignation, revulsion, and often guilt that those who lived above the crisis then had to confront.

Though their suffering was often only "vicarious," for the middle and upper classes, the emotional effects that this secondhand suffering produced were very real. However, the consequences of such traumatization were not always immediate—time was of the essence in the ways that social perceptions evolved during the crisis. Presented with the same scene of suffering, someone who had never witnessed such tragedy firsthand would respond differently than someone who had been repeatedly exposed to similar horrors and worse. Put in economic terms, the overwhelming supply of suffering diminished the value of the tragedy for those who were continuously exposed to it. This is not to be read figuratively. Al-Maqdisi observed that in the terrible year of 1918, "mercy diminished as the mouth of the famine gaped," swallowing even those who had been in comfortable circumstances before the war but who had fallen on hard times during the famine.[48] Although Bliss possessed a deep sympathy for the individual starving on the streets, his ongoing exposure to such suffering similarly made it difficult for him to bear continual reminders.[49] The ubiquity of starvation and the inability to assist a begging individual to any real extent drove many of the secure classes to avoid the poor or to at least try to exclude their suffering as much as possible from their own personal lives.

Some honest accounts even suggest that people began to accept the existence of suffering among the impoverished as a normalized aspect of their famine worlds. Rather than seeking to address the suffering, people became desensitized to the plight of the poor, and some sought to excise them from their daily experience altogether. In his retrospective, al-Maqdisi wrote:

> In 1915, the sight of a starving man falling would cause people to surround him and give him some water, some food, and some dirhams. By 1916 we would walk in the streets with men, women and children lying in the mud on both sides, whimpering for mercy or for a crust of bread. . . . Fewer reached a hand to relieve them because the burden was crushing and many were beyond saving. Most frequently, on passing, people turned their face and blocked their ears so they could not see or hear.[50]

In a diary entry in 1917, Edward Nickoley similarly observed that when the penetrating cries of the starving poor on the streets became too overwhelming for the Americans at the college, rather than assisting the starving person, they simply closed their windows to muffle the sound.[51] Such behaviors were common enough that they inspired harsh critiques from humanitarian writers during and after the war. In a postwar report on relief work, Bayard Dodge excoriated the wealthy for their dispassion, and during the harsh winter of 1916, when the suffering began to reach a truly calamitous level, al-Maqdisi dourly wrote that the well-off simply remained inside of their homes to avoid the suffering of the streets.[52]

The reports of the American Mission's Sidon Girls' School offer surprisingly vivid perspectives on this evolving view of poverty and on the growing aversion to it among the more secure members of society. The initial sympathy evident in reports from the early years of the war dissolves into distaste in the reports from the years 1916 to 1918.[53] Language in the latter reports reveals a community that had grown uncomfortable rubbing elbows with the impoverished, even when they were members of their own community. In her annual school report on the year 1916–1917, assistant principal Dora Eddy noted that the school had reduced its house calls because they had become "mere doleful recitals of the hard times and the high price of food."[54] In the school's subsequent 1917–1918 report, the principal Charlotte Brown unintentionally offered evidence of famine-inspired shifts in attitudes about class while discussing attendance at an annual student performance. She wrote, "We had prepared seats for a limited number but as the women and girls kept coming more chairs were brought, people were squeezed tighter and tighter and *what made it more embarrassing was the fact that some of the more honorable ladies came last after the most honorable seats had been taken*" (emphasis mine).[55] Such changes were also apparent in the Thursday meetings of the Sidon Girls' School women's club, which began to segregate itself in 1917 out of fear of typhus—and by extension, of the poor who were associated with it.[56] If such meetings were meant to preserve a shell of normalcy for the women in the group, the presence of their ragged "sisters" was yet another unwelcome reminder of just how abnormal their worlds had become.

Though such viewpoints seem callous, they were ultimately the sorts of coping mechanisms (and not necessarily conscious ones) that enabled people to endure the constant exposure to traumatic circumstances. Over time, as stress compounded stress, writers like Bliss, Nickoley, and al-Maqdisi all noted that they and those around them had hardened themselves to the suffering of others and looked after their own needs to the exclusion of those who suffered most. By far the best examples of such avoidance strategies were recorded in Edward Nickoley's wartime diary, which documents his life in the famine from February to September of 1917. Nickoley's writing is of special significance because of its detail and its unintentional honesty. At first glance, his observations appear detached from the intense suffering that his diary describes in detail. However, a great number of passages indicate that behind the wall that he had erected to shield himself from the grim reality of the crisis, he still felt intense distress at both the misery of others and at his own inability to empathize with their agony. While we cannot assume that he was a representative case, his details corroborate the observations that other contemporary writers had made about social attitudes that had begun to shift as the famine dragged on.

Nickoley's passages frequently express complicated and at times conflicting stances on suffering in the crisis and on the compassion that he had (or that he felt he should have had) toward it. This is particularly evident in his depictions of the wartime relief programs. Though he was a skeptic who derided the relief programs and their workers for their ostensibly selfish motivations and their overall ineffectiveness in raising society from the morass of the famine, his judgments varied by case and even evinced a sense of respect for those whose responses he deemed rational and useful.[57] He dismissed the primary relief efforts as mere "drops in the bucket" and criticized the generosity of the Syrian Protestant College's women's and children's hospital as absurd, or even cruel, because the people they cured were eventually released onto the streets to starve again. Nevertheless, he went on to praise certain individuals like the March family, who rented wasteland on the outskirts of the city for the sake of a few local families who used it to grow potatoes. In Nickoley's eyes, the tangible ability to support a few families in perpetuity overrode the broader benefits that came from those larger-scale relief efforts that would eventually fail their recipients.[58] Even within his practical critiques (which were not entirely wrong), Nickoley's observations provide an example of what Paul Slovic has termed "psychophysical numbing," a phenomenon in which we unintentionally minimize the relative good produced by humanitarian actions when the scale of a calamity is too great. Slovic has observed that "our affective responses and the resulting value we place on saving human lives may follow the same sort of 'psychophysical function' that characterizes our diminished sensitivity to a wide range of perceptual and cognitive entities—brightness, loudness, heaviness . . . as their underlying magnitudes increase."[59] Even lukewarm water can feel cold if one touches it after soaking one's hand in hot water, but the measure is relative, not objective. In a similar way, a situation as emotionally heavy as the famine could make even relatively effective aid appear inconsequential, especially when suffering persisted despite everyone's best efforts.

As cold as Nickoley's demeanor appears in his writing, a number of passages reveal the emotional burden that the crisis placed on him. In such entries, he candidly described his own process of disengagement from the suffering, referring to his response as "hardening." Even in his efforts to evade the stress of suffering, Nickoley struggled with the fact that he was actually conscious of the changes that had taken place in his attitudes and behaviors, and he was unhappy with the results. Because Nickoley was exceptionally self-aware, his diary provides a remarkable vantage from which to observe the personal struggles that otherwise good individuals faced when confronting their own situational badness. His entries reveal an intense internal conflict: he acknowledged that he *should* feel sympathy for his fellow human beings in suffering, but he could not. He wrote:

> The sights and the sounds haunt us, not only in our waking moments, but they pursue us in our dreams. And what can we do? Absolutely nothing. We feel as if we were up against a wall of stones, no, adamant. Our helplessness to give relief and our desire to avoid becoming morbid, tends to make us indifferent, to harden us and to make us cynical. It is a terrible sensation to realize that you are losing your power of sympathizing with a fellow man in suffering.[60]

However, we can suspect that even his own brutal honesty is perhaps too honest. Even as he projected his indifference, he subtly hinted at how deeply affected he could be by the suffering of others—but because he felt that the situation was hopeless, he chose not to act. It is interesting to note that

Nickoley—like Bliss and al-Maqdisi and Doolittle—slips into the first-person plural and the second person singular in this description, abstracting himself from his own feelings. Whether this is to suggest that others felt the same as he did (which is likely, since such sentiments were echoed rather commonly) or if he was simply ashamed of his own behavior, we cannot tell. What is evident is that this particular method of coping ultimately failed—it merely added a new form of emotional strain to an already troubled mind.

The Consequences of Trauma

The complexity of the social and emotional experience of the famine cannot be overemphasized, nor can the effects that such experiences had on individuals and society. Although individual behaviors varied from person to person and from context to context, the few writers that were willing to comment on their emotional struggles during the famine hint at the range of ways that people experienced the crisis and how they adapted to deal with it. They also indicate that the question of trauma in the famine was not simply a matter of individual suffering. Coping with crisis caused behaviors, attitudes, and worldviews to evolve over time. As people tried to come to terms with their own suffering, the ways that they dealt with it created a feedback loop that gradually and often cumulatively affected how they contextualized their experiences of the crisis. For every action there was an equal and opposite reaction—rather than simply absorbing the impact of their own suffering and struggling forward, those who lived in the famine reacted and adapted their responses to it. These changes were ultimately reflected outward through their social interactions, including in the ways that they tried to avoid further trauma.

In a sense, trauma shaped individuals' internal famine worlds like the famine itself shaped the external famine world. It also influenced how individuals interpreted what they saw around them. For the starving or vulnerable, this emotional adaptation was a matter of survival. However, even for those who were not in danger of starvation, the stressors and emotional hazards of the famine period led them to adapt and reshape their own behaviors in order to understand, rationalize, and, eventually, cope with the changes to their daily reality. Basic responses like compassion, sympathy, and even faith were twisted over time by the power of the famine, altering how people understood concepts like poverty, charity, suffering, and death. Many of the apparently aberrant behaviors and attitudes that appear in the sources were as much consequences of how people *interpreted* the famine as they were effects of the famine itself.

Although most of these changes were only visible on the social level, certain writers were very explicit about the effects that they observed in their own attitudes and behaviors. Because the authors of diaries, letters, and reports were often less aware of their writing's place in the historical record, they were more likely to honestly depict their perceptions or at least less likely to edit out their inadvertent admissions than in a piece that was deliberately intended to be a public record, like a memoir—or Bliss's retrospective. The diary of Edward Nickoley, which is frequently mentioned in this chapter, is perhaps the best example that we have of this genre. It provides a fascinating case study of the individual world of one person in the famine as he was living it. Not only does it detail the personal effects of the suffering and the stress that the famine added to his daily life, it also reveals the rationalizations and coping measures that he employed to counteract his own suffering. While such quantum-level microhistory is hard to generalize beyond the individual level, or at least beyond a personal cohort, the nuance that such an approach reveals adds texture to our understanding of the ground-level experience of the crisis.

Although merely existing may seem like a passive matter, the day-to-day traumas of the famine challenged contemporaries as they tried to physically survive and emotionally endure their own personal calamity. In this sense, experience should be considered to have deterministic power—to be an "active" thing—that altered how people understood the crisis and their role within it. Contact prompted change. The extent to which individuals were morally and emotionally impacted by such traumatic experiences depended on a variety of factors based on their own personal characteristics and their experiences from both the famine period and before. Even those who observed the famine from a position of safety were touched by what they saw as the moral collapse of society around them. For these individuals, the horrors of the crisis intruded upon the normalcy of daily life, introducing forms of secondary trauma that slowly altered their perceptions of the famine and others living within it. When viewed through the increasingly jaded and often disconnected eyes of the observers, the poor were seen as sympathetic, but they were often portrayed as passive victims of events that were beyond their control. As victims, they were not actors so much as objects who had actions happen to them. They were utterly at the mercy of an overwhelming famine. It gradually stripped them of their money, their flesh, their families, their humanity, and, for many, their lives.

This final point is a concern when we consider the broader secondary effects that trauma may have had in the period. Although Nickoley's personal conflict was the best documented among the famine writers, his was only one example of what other writers suggest was a relatively pervasive phenomenon. What happens if such effects occur on a grand scale? Though the traumatic experience of the famine was a largely personal emotional process, when projected as a broader societal pattern, such attitudes could have profound social and humanitarian implications. What this meant seems to have varied over time. Initially, the famine inspired pity, but in its later years, when desperation and starvation were severe, those who suffered the worst were depicted ungraciously. The famine changed society—that is a given. But it also changed peoples' perceptions of it and of each other.

5

A World in Decline

> They were clad in the clothes of hunger and fear and weakness.
> —JIRJIS KHURI AL-MAQDISI

THE FAMINE MUST HAVE BEEN terrible to behold. Even today it is still shocking to read about the appalling suffering that the famine wrought. With spiraling poverty came a rise in begging, homelessness, and starvation that filled the streets with humanity at its most desperate. As the crisis deteriorated in the latter years of the war, even those who were spared direct suffering by a buffer of privilege began to see a world falling apart at its increasingly visible seams. For some, the famine's physical effects became figurative—it was a corrupting force that ravaged souls as it emaciated the bodies that housed them. In an interview conducted decades after the war, Yusuf Rufayil stated that "everyone was forced by sheer self-preservation to look out for himself. A mother would sell her child for food. A brother would not give food to his brother. Once a man was taking a loaf of bread to his ailing father. Upon arriving home, he found a group of people gathered in front of the house. He kept saying to himself that he hoped his father was dead."[1] This abdication of familial obligation for the sake of one's own survival led Rufayil to conclude that "body diseases were accompanied by moral diseases. It was a period of *inhitat*."[2]

Rufayil's choice of words is interesting. Meaning "degradation" or "decline," *inhitat* is by its nature comparative, carrying the implication of a state of decay or a fall from a better past.[3] The idea that the famine had brought about a state of abjection within the population was a common social critique from those who sought deeper meaning in the changes that it wrought. Bayard Dodge succinctly encapsulated Rufayil's point in a postwar humanitarian report, observing that "the worst of famine is its effect upon the living, rather than its silence upon the dead." Like Rufayil's critique, Dodge's comment can be read both as a reflection of pity and regret for the behaviors of the starving and as a critique of the famine's moral effect on society at large.[4] Taking this one step further, Syrian Protestant College professor Edward Nickoley speculated that the moral degradation of the famine had left the people of the region generationally ruined.[5] In the eyes of such jaded social critics, the physical and spiritual degradation of the crisis had warped society, leaving behind a sorrowful land filled with skeletal structures and degraded people. This "darkest moment" in regional history haunted contemporary observers. One interlocutor even denounced it as "a tale of weakness and disgrace."[6]

Though it is tempting to view such firsthand narratives as simple reports of reality, they are more accurately viewed as subjective, often retrospective, perspectives. Ostensibly nonfiction, they had a clear literary nature in their narrative form and in the vocabulary and literary devices they employed to depict a world for their readers.[7] Many narratives were set within a Manichean world defined by its binaries—good and evil, rich and poor, sufferer and nonsufferer. This world was heavily populated by stock characters: villains, saviors, innocents, victims, wretches, and the like. Even relatively straightforward descriptions commonly relied on generalizations, allusion, metaphor, and famine commonplaces. We can forgive this to some extent because it was necessary for writers to selectively choose how to portray a complex event like the famine. It would be impossible to render the whole four-year period in precise detail, and even thoughtful accounts of the war were frequently somewhat chaotic in their organization.

However, the language that witnesses used to convey their observations frequently also offered subtle social commentary about both the famine and those within it. Frequently, these characterizations were intended to be sympathetic, but their execution often diminished the poor in the process, particularly when depicting starvation in its most wretched and piteous forms. Such themes of fallen humanity and victimhood were effective ways to generate pathos, but such imagery came with consequence: in rendering their characters abject, writers transformed the most vulnerable in society into little more than passive participants in their own fading lives and tragic deaths. There was an implicit class element to such descriptions. In contrast to the poor, who suffered terribly and often required the help of their social betters, those of the writers' own social class (or higher) were often the ones playing active roles in the narratives. These accounts reserved the traits of agency almost exclusively for the powerful, the nefarious, the secure, and the morally upright. They were the watchers, the saviors, and sometimes even the perpetrators. Such characterizations hinted at the bias of the writers amid the growing disconnect between the secure and the vulnerable as the famine worsened.

However, the portrayals were not simply a reflection of reality—they were a reflection of the constructs of poverty and suffering that had defined suffering and those who suffered in the declensionist famine discourse. This discourse relied heavily on secondhand knowledge and information networks because it conveyed not only factual information but implicit social judgments as well. Though it is clear that speculation about social decline during the famine reflected real suffering, the way that such suffering was portrayed often echoed common pejorative themes and evaluations that had developed about the crisis and those within it over the years. In doing so, the discourse of decline had the potential to be far more powerful than the sum of its words alone: it framed not only the world that people saw but also the world that they wanted their audiences to see.

Evidence of Decline

In one of his reports on the war, the young professor and wartime humanitarian Bayard Dodge depicted a society in an obvious state of collapse. In it, he observed:

> Laziness, pauperism and all kinds of dishonesty became prevalent. Petty thievery, highway robbery and assault grew common. The presence of soldiers and officers offered a never-ending temptation to thousands of starving and despairing girls. . . . Officers and soldiers carried on a regular business of corruption and oppression; priests grew selfish

and mercenary, and the poor sank into an extremity of moral weakness which can only be realized at a time of physical breakdown and religious despair.[8]

The apparent decay of the population from its prewar state of existence fascinated pious observers like Dodge, whose traumatic life as a wartime humanitarian began at the relatively tender age of twenty-six. Although such sentiments were common in American narratives, Lebanese observers like Yusuf Rufayil, Jirjis al-Maqdisi, Sulayman Dhahir, and others among their secure peers similarly bemoaned the social and moral decay that seemed to emanate from the famine throughout society.[9]

Some of this decline was attributed to real social breakdowns that took place during the crisis—as the sociologist of crisis Pitirim Sorokin astutely notes, "Calamity molds an entire culture in its own image."[10] One of the most persuasive examples of this was the rise in crime during the war. Though figures are scarce, anecdotal evidence suggests that basic property crime and disorder increased as poverty rose and enforcement lapsed.[11] In some cases, writers were understanding, regarding acts that would have been deemed inconceivable moral transgressions in years past as necessary evils when the situation worsened and social supports failed. Prostitution and theft were both reported to have increased significantly in the years of the famine, and even among the relatively affluent students at the Syrian Protestant College, petty thefts and the pilfering of necessities like clothing and blankets became commonplace.[12] George Doolittle observed that minor property crimes were generally condoned, "strangely, first of all by the losers" themselves.[13] Indeed, W. S. Nelson's report from the Presbyterian Mission in Tripoli exudes an almost apologetic forgiveness when noting that several starving boys who had been admitted to the local shelter "later proved their skill by helping themselves to certain items of moveable property belonging to the school." Though one might reasonably suspect Nelson of sarcasm, he generously added that "it was a satisfaction to know that they had been saved from death for a time."[14]

The surplus of abandoned buildings and the war-distracted authorities allowed both professional and situational criminals to increasingly get away with brigandage, theft, and murder, particularly as the war progressed and deserting soldiers proliferated.[15] Such opportunistic criminality was damning in the eyes of observers, who heaped scorn upon those who stole without starving, bandits who ravaged the innocent, corrupt officials who exacted bribes with impunity, and wealthy speculators who manipulated markets, hoarded supplies, and loaned money at exorbitant interest rates while their countrymen suffered. In his retrospective, Antun Yammine condemned the elites of the Lebanese system, who "sold their people and their religion" to join "the Turks" in delivering "tyrannical murderous blows upon our wretched mountain."[16] Nickoley similarly decried the venal predations of the "formerly struggling" merchants in his diary, singling out those who had shifted their business from trading to speculation and money lending.[17] American Mission Press secretary Margaret McGilvary echoed such sentiments, writing, "Among the influential classes in Syria . . . every man lived for himself, and every man's hand was against his brother. He who could snatched from those about him, and he who was robbed of everything laid himself down to die. . . . The rich ground down the poor, and those in power sacrificed the people to their selfish ambitions."[18] Amid the misery of the famine, such acts were clear violations of their obligations within the moral economy of the crisis.

The decidedly low-class crime of prostitution occupied a curious gray area in famine criminality. Although women who engaged in sex work were sometimes depicted sympathetically because their actions enabled their families to survive when vulnerable women had few legitimate options, many moralistic observers still levied judgment upon them for both their loss of honor and for their degradation of the men whose very demand for their bodies enabled them to work in the first place.[19] In his dairy, the young Palestinian soldier Ihsan Turjeman commented on the moral decline in Jerusalem with a mixture of scorn and pity, writing, "What miserable creatures, selling their bodies for pennies to satisfy the bestial needs of men. I am sure that most prostitutes would not practice their processions except for their financial need."[20] Turjeman's comments literally dehumanize the perpetrators on both ends, transforming them into "creatures" meeting the needs of "bestial" men. Such literary framing is common in wartime sources, as sexual transactions were often described figuratively, either out of a euphemistic sense of propriety or perhaps due to the writer's inability to separate the women's bodies from the ideal of feminine purity. In a passage about the moral collapse of the poor from "terror and hunger," Frederick Bliss bemoaned the fact that in addition to compelling men to lie for their own self-interest and to steal to survive, the famine led girls to sell their "virginal purity" for a loaf of bread.[21] The American hospital's superintendent of nursing, Mary Dale, similarly judged that a neighbor's friend had "sold herself" for a loaf of bread in November 1916.[22] As euphemisms go, "selling oneself" carried a harsh degree of permanence. Unlike a ring or a house, purity and honor were not things that could be purchased back when the situation improved.

Even beyond the cultural aversion to dishonorable behavior, the violation of sexual norms was a particularly damning form of corruption that was disproportionately associated with women. Part of this judgment may have been related to the public health issues that sex caused as syphilis ran rampant in major cities and spiked in smaller communities.[23] However, the stain was symbolic as well. The belief in the polluting effects of bodily fluids that a woman shares during sex made the act not simply a personal sin but extended the contamination to the male participant, and thereafter onto society as well.[24] For many among the honorable observers who viewed such trends from the safety of their social privilege, this particular act of desperation permanently reclassified the woman among the dishonorable, even if her ultimate goals were simply to survive or to keep her family fed.

Other hints of social decadence were evident in taboo breaking—particularly in the willingness to harm innocents for personal gain. As the very title of Najwa al-Qattan's article "When Mothers Ate Their Children" implies, among acts of desperation, those that involved family and children were perhaps the most repellant of all for writers at the time.[25] Witnesses recalled with alacrity tales of such social transgressions that involved the innocent or helpless. On his visit to the southern village of Khiam, George Doolittle wrote, "Parents lost their parental affections and fathers hid the food from the eyes of their starving children. One woman reported that she had sold her daughters to the Arabs [Bedouin], each for three bushels of corn, and seemed delighted to have got rid of them!"[26] In addition to his anecdote about the man rejoicing at the death of his father, Rufayil also relayed a story about a mother snatching food from the mouth of her hungry child.²⁷ The denial of food was such an important source of scorn that the missionary humanitarian Robert Byerly wrote in a report on relief work that the workers had begun feeding children on-site because of their distrust of parents. He noted that one father even refused to send his daughter to collect her portion of food if she could not bring it back to share.²⁸ In one of Nickoley's more morose entries on the rumors of the day, he cataloged a series of appalling behaviors reported from across the region as a simple summation of its decay: "A woman threw herself off the roof because she could not bear to see her children starving. Another woman is found beating, biting and otherwise mutilating her children, she has gone insane from the physical suffering and anxiety."²⁹ Such moral degeneration was unimaginable to those watching from above.

Breaking food taboos similarly prompted reactions of disgust and pity among contemporary observers. Nickoley's diary tells of a rumor about the villagers of Dbeih cutting up a dead donkey and distributing the meat through the town, leading to twenty deaths from "ptomaine" poisoning.³⁰ George Doolittle gives a similar account of a formerly well-to-do family who shared a baby goat that they found dead in their field—the food poisoning killed all but one boy, who was left alive but insane.³¹ The means by which individuals acquired their appalling fare was sometimes even more repellant for the observers than their actual consumption of it. Memoirs and interviews drew special attention to those who, in their desperation, scavenged undigested pieces of grain from animal dung.³² The filth of feces was clearly still a taboo that, like cannibalism, inspired both fascination and disgust. Nickoley described his own experience with the poor who haunted downtown Beirut in remarkable detail:

> We see children running after dogs to take bones away from them and then fight among themselves to determine who shall gnaw the bone. Children congregate at the meat stalls in the market and grab up greedily scraps of bone, gristle and skin that are thrown away and eagerly chew them. A woman with her finger nails picking bits of meat left in a hide and eating them as she peeled them loose, children chewing horns of animals to suck the meat taste out of the portion nearest to the head.³³

Descriptions of people killing pets for food or consuming grass and other herbs were notable, not only for the sheer desperation that this entailed but also for the savagery the act implied. We can see this in Nickoley's credulous report of a rumor that all the dogs of Mansourieh had been devoured by February 1917[34] and in Yammine's provocative description of starving Lebanese victims scouring the fields for greens among rotting bodies, an apocalyptic depiction penned to inspire both horror and pity in his audience.[35]

Perhaps more than anything, reports of necrophagy and outright cannibalism conveyed an unthinkable collapse of humanity within those who perpetrated such acts.[36] For contemporaries, tales of man-eating were a matter of morbid fascination. Writing from the town of Nabatieh, Sulayman Dhahir seemed particularly fixated on these events. In his account, he floridly described the various methods of butchery and the preparation of the "human flesh" that the police found when they raided a man's home in the coastal village of Damour. The text even provides detailed information on the cuts of meat that were discovered (for the record: liver and mince), as though the consumption of human flesh was somehow worse if artfully cooked into flavorful meals rather than simply torn raw from the bones like a dog.[37] In another case, Dhahir actually named victims, including a boy named Abd al-Hassan and a girl named Hafiza, whose heads were found in the home of their murderer.[38] Dhahir connected the most horrific events of the famine directly to both the personal deterioration of those who committed the acts and to the social dissolution that placed the victims at risk in the first place. He observed:

> These horrible events took place because of the famine. Hunger was what drove the Damouri and the woman to these acts and drove others to acts like them. . . . The children who had lost their mothers and fathers and support, whether from hunger or sickness or from conscription, were innumerable. Moving from village to village, as they could move, some like those children were attacked by criminals.[39]

Though Dhahir's examples are well documented, confirming tales of cannibalism in famine is difficult, and such claims have historically been prone to libels and exaggerations.[40] Most mentions of cannibalism in the sources are little more than vague rumors, but there are several cases that are corroborated with enough official detail that they can be considered valid.[41] The 1918 report of the Tripoli Mission Station includes detailed reference to the well-traveled story of two sisters who resorted to murder and cannibalism to support their younger siblings after their parents died. According to the story, the girls used their younger brother to lure children to their home, where they killed them, stripped them of their clothing, then cooked and fed the human flesh to their younger siblings. They discarded the bones in a well. In one report, the offense was made doubly horrifying because the sisters were said to have boiled the flesh to separate the fat for sale in the market—an act that corrupted others in society by making them inadvertent cannibals as well. (The story has a "happy" ending: A mother followed one of the brothers home when she noticed him wearing her son's shirt. When the police investigators found the skeletons in the well, they sent the girls to prison, where they died horridly of starvation.)[42]

If we are to be generous in our retrospective interpretations, the willingness to violate taboos to maintain one's life despite tremendous physical and emotional suffering shows not just the will to survive but the belief that the future is worth surviving for. However, for those observers consuming news of the crisis around them, such transgressions of social norms merely reinforced their own belief in the unspeakable collapse of society at large. Such a judgment had dire implications because it regarded human beings as objects that could be spoiled or tainted by physical degradation, desperation, or moral deviance. In his diary, Nickoley wrote that "the demoralization is so complete that it is sad to contemplate the condition of the people even after peace is established and after life once more resumes its normal course." He speculated that it would take generations to overcome the effects of the famine.[43] Jirjis al-Maqdisi seemed to concur with this sentiment, estimating that many in the famine were "beyond saving."[44]

Documenting Degeneration

If we are to take suffering and its consequences as proof of decline, we must account for Didier Fassin's observation that suffering is not "just a physiological or psychological fact; it is also a social construction."[45] As easy as it might be to take descriptions from famine observers as reflections of reality, their ideas about what was happening during the famine were not simply pieces of objective knowledge, and even the most precise observations posed a number of epistemological problems. Writers recorded what was seen (but often not with their own eyes) and what they knew (which they heard from others), and they usually had a keen sense of the audience that they needed to convince.

The most obvious bias came in those accounts that were written after the war to achieve a political or humanitarian end, but even relatively innocent texts were written for a reason. Some, like Frederick Bliss's postwar retrospective, seem to be attempts by the writers to unburden themselves or to rationalize the overwhelming, highly traumatic effects of the crisis that they carried with them after the war ended.[46] While such accounts are perhaps more trustworthy in some respects, they, like their politically motivated counterparts, are still held hostage to the perspectives of their writers and the language that they could use to depict their experiences. As writers compressed the ineffable fragments of their lived personal experience into simple representative depictions, they often relied upon imagery, metaphor, allusion, and other linguistic shorthand to convey the depth of suffering that so resisted normal language. As a result, their descriptions are often as imprecise and as leading as they are evocative.

This is also apparent in the sparse photographic documentation that we have of the era. In many images, the photographers sought to depict the most horrific or the most pitiful aspects of the famine to represent its essence to their audience in its rawest form. The choice of subjects and the framing of the images often suggest a scene in a tragic narrative—and perhaps because of this, the images are tremendously effective. Even today, it is difficult to view the most famous famine photos snapped by Ibrahim Naoum Kanaan without feeling intense feelings of sympathy, sadness, pity, and horror.[47] Many of Kanaan's photos feature starving individuals in states of great vulnerability. In one, a woman sits naked and bony, nursing a hungry child from a withered breast. Many are emotionally devastating, like that of a father sitting bewildered while his family starves around him or that of a child crying at the loss of their sibling. However, the photos are not neutral documents either. As a humanitarian, Kanaan shot those images with a purpose, and he chose his subjects well. Most scenes involve innocent subjects like women, children, or families. He deliberately feminized the victims of the famine in an attempt to "sanctify" their trauma for the sake of a sympathetic viewer.[48]

As Judith Butler argues, such framing is "actively interpreting, sometimes forcibly so," the subjects on our behalf.[49] For Kanaan, the intent was to document suffering in a way that could otherwise only be tangible for those who experienced the horrors of famine firsthand. However, in this sense, the framing is somewhat ironic. While the people in the photos are legitimately starving, many of the shots were clearly posed for effect.[50] The subjects of the images are undoubtedly sympathetic, but their behaviors are directed by the photographer to capture the dark scenes and cadaverous characters of the calamity in the most evocative way possible—an act that we might now consider "disaster porn."[51] (It is for this reason that I am not including photos in this text.) The characters who appeared in the images were not people who could have a good day. As shown, they were individuals who existed horrifically, and in some cases, died wretchedly. Thanks to the camera, they have remained immortalized in a timeless, framed existence as a constructed symbol of the horror, the sadness, and the pathos of that terrible era.

Without the aid of a camera lens, writers were forced to use words and concepts to at least try to frame the crisis for their audience. The horrors of the famine were often written as brief, colorful images depicting a lived context that confounded the normal array of adjectives and adverbs that the authors had at their disposal. Lacking the space or ability to clearly articulate what they had experienced, authors often depicted horrid scenes in surreal language. According to Nickoley, "the daily sights along the streets seem like a dream—like a horrible nightmare."[52] Perhaps because of this, many descriptions of suffering are excessively florid or simply admit that the famine was "indescribable" as a way of conveying its severity. In a passage intended for his wife and children, who had remained in Greece during the war, Nickoley described the sight of a starving person as "indefinable" and wholly unforgettable.[53]

He is right. But writers *did* describe the famine and often sought to define it, despite the complexity of what they witnessed. Even in sympathetic descriptions, the rich language that depicts such suffering carries with it value judgments, and often an implicit critique. Alongside sanctified representations of passive suffering, the poor are often reduced to odious caricatures such as "monkeys," "skeletons," "waifs," and worse.[54] In practice, such terms are less descriptive than they are conceptual contractions. The skeletal poor suffering from marasmus or from the bloated bellies and rough skin of the nutrient deficiency kwashiorkor inspired a mixture of pity and horror in the writers—and I do not use the term loosely. "Horror" is a common term in American texts in particular as writers sought to sum up the ghastly realities around them. Something horrific is unthinkable, warped, denatured, mildly fearful—the normal made appalling. In famine, horrors are often humans with their humanity annihilated.[55] Horrors are also reflexive in that they require a witness to comprehend, recognize, interpret, and feel them—to be revolted, unsettled, or "horrified" by them.[56] Even in sympathetic accounts, a horror is also a value judgment. As a form of revulsion, it is the opposite of sympathy. This distinction was problematic at a time when power disparities between the secure and the vulnerable not only differentiated people within society but left people "out of the patterning of society." Their "placeless" status identified them as marginal, even dangerous, for those who viewed them.[57]

This ineffable, degraded form of humanity that the sufferers possessed seemed to inspire the same sense of uncanniness as the monsters of zombie films. Nickoley likened the scenes of his daily life to living in a nightmare. The diary asks: "Did you ever see a starving person? I hope you never may. No matter how emaciated a person may be from disease he never looks exactly like the person suffering from pangs of hunger. It is indefinable but when you have once seen it you can never mistake it, nor ever forget it."[58] In a later entry, he reiterated his point: "No description can do justice to the situation. . . . No one who has never seen famine and starvation knows what it looks like in its physical embodiment. It is a ghastly subject."[59] But it is worth asking what exactly Nickoley saw as ghastly. Was it "starvation" in the abstract, or was "it" a sterilized way of referring to the starving people themselves?

Among more pious writers, religious allusion was a particularly powerful literary shorthand that was often used to link the horrors of the crisis with familiar and profound cultural reference points. This was most common among Christian writers, who frequently deferred to the Bible when casting about for profundity. Jirjis Khuri al-Maqdisi invoked scripture when he wrote, "Those who once ate sumptuous foods fell in the streets. They who were brought up in crimson embraced the dung."[60] This allusion was apparently compelling enough that the exact same biblical verse was lifted by Reverend George Doolittle in his own English-language description of poverty in Beirut.[61] Using another biblical reference, al-Maqdisi wrote, "Their image became the severest, blackest oppression. Their bones stuck through their skin. They became as rough as wood. Their skin blackened like a *tannour* from the heat of the fire of hunger."[62] It would not be lost on his readers that the original quote from the book of Lamentations is in reference to divine punishment and abandonment. While allusion to an altogether different crisis by its very nature makes this an inexact description, his use of scripture conveys meaning to his readers with the severity of the word of God.

Writers also used the concept of degradation (which was at the very core of the famine construct) to show a hierarchy of suffering among the famine's victims. In some cases, this was to distinguish those whose fall from grace made them especially tragic. Al-Maqdisi, who was one of the most sympathetic of those to write about the suffering of the famine, was particularly struck by the physical and behavioral transformation of respectable members of the middle class who had degraded into the desperate creatures he saw scrabbling along the wayside to survive. In his retrospective, al-Maqdisi specifically identified two different classes of beggar, both in undeniably pejorative terms. The first group was still healthy and mobile enough to "mill about" the doorways and stores to beg for handouts or to rummage through garbage heaps in search of edible waste, which in his estimation made them stink like "a skunk." The second "were the ones who cried out with all their strength from the severity of their suffering from malnutrition and hunger, bowing at the sides of the roads, appealing with words crumbling in pain."[63] Both al-Maqdisi and Nickoley deemed the saddest sight to be those individuals for whom the physiological effects of long-term semistarvation made them captives to their search for sustenance. Nickoley wrote, "Their eyes are constantly fixed on the ground, moving restlessly from side to side in the hope of seeing something that they can pick up and eat." He marveled at "how tenaciously the human being clings to life, to what desperate measures the individual will resort to keep the vital spark alive."[64] Nickoley's language is curious here. Even in his reference to the humanity of the sufferers, he filters his thoughts through detached vocabulary, using "human being," "individual," and "the" vital spark, rather than more personalized terms such as "person," "man," or "his."

As Najwa al-Qattan has argued, descriptions of taboo breaking, particularly regarding food, made for especially potent imagery.[65] And indeed, the disgusting fodder that individuals were driven to eat in their desperation captivated those observing the actions of the starving, since both the foods and the acts of obtaining them were often so appalling that they seemed to have been used in the sources for their shock value. Some of the nonsufferers were emotionally devastated by the spectacle, weeping as they watched their neighbors devouring garbage in the streets.[66] In her memoir, Anbara Salam al-Khalidi wrote that the ragged, distended children appeared more like apes than humans as they descended upon the discarded peels of the bananas that she had purchased downtown.[67] Such descriptions, like accounts of cannibalism or dead bodies with grass in their mouths, show how the physical state and the desperate behaviors of the suffering poor had further divided them from the secure.

This distinction is codified in the imagery and descriptions that render the starving poor as denatured human beings, or worse, as beasts. Even when framed compassionately, the dehumanizing language used to describe suffering erases the humanity of the individuals who are portrayed. Nickoley concluded his depiction of skeletal sufferers mechanically seeking out scraps of food by writing, "Their eyes have been turned from the higher and better things in life, with them it is simply the existence of a brute."[68] Antun Yammine's sympathetic account similarly reverts to bestial language to depict the Lebanese "racing the animals to eat various grasses."[69] Such sentiments are relayed in even greater detail in Sulayman Dhahir's account of the famine in Nabatieh, in which he wrote, "We saw with our own eyes the victims of starvation fallen on the roads, in the alleys, on the streets, their cries filling the air. We saw them degrade into scared animals and compete against each other for scraps."[70] In such extreme depictions, the language choices deny the humanity of the sufferers, rendering them in what the Italian social historian Piero Camporesi has described as "the last stage in a troubled metamorphosis: the long voyage in the destruction of what is human and the passing birth of the man/animal."[71] Such imagery allowed writers to convey a complex situation relatively efficiently, but the implications of the description are hardly flattering for those who struggled to survive a crisis beyond their control.

Such linguistic quibbling may seem trivial in light of the severe suffering on the ground. However, such accounts are examples of the discourse about poverty and the starving poor that developed during the crisis in response to widespread suffering and its social effects. To some extent we can read such accounts as proxies for how the writers understood their own world, or at least the world that they sought to convey to their readers. While such depictions ostensibly aimed to generate sympathy for the poor, the effects were often anything but sympathetic. Visceral descriptions of taboo breaking, bodily decay, filth, and stench were certainly evocative. But such portrayals implicitly demeaned those who suffered in the famine while also physically and figuratively distinguishing them from the secure. Such depictions of filth and degradation ultimately had a depatterning effect. If dirt is simply "matter out of place," what does this say about those defined by their filth?[72] As the famine unraveled the prefamine world and replaced it with a horrific facsimile, those who endured the crisis were forced to revise their understanding of society, often by editing old social constructs or crafting new ones through which they could better rationalize the horrors that they saw. In the social context of the famine, such distinction was further incentive to push the poorest to the margins of society.

The Hunger for (Mis)information

Reading the postwar narratives, one is struck with the omniscience that exudes from the writers' detailed anecdotes and their incisive proclamations about the famine, its causes, and its effects. The fact that many of the writers were themselves members of the intelligentsia, or at least the social elite, might explain the confidence of their diagnoses. Their words sound authoritative because many of them *were* authorities in some fashion or another. However, this confidence was also augmented by a real sense of knowledge that came from the writers' avid consumption of fact and rumor, which was one of the few pastimes openly encouraged by the stifled wartime social environment. This makes for engaging reading, but when we find the same richly depicted anecdotes in several sources, each conveying slightly different facts, we have to wonder how people in the famine came to know what was in many cases second- or thirdhand information. Perhaps just as important, we might ask if the method of transmission conveyed more than just information to its consumers.

Despite the widespread desire to keep up to date on news about the famine, staying informed during the war was (by design) not particularly easy, especially in the Ottoman Empire. Locked in an existential battle with enemies who possessed an unsettling familiarity with the regional administration's internal affairs,[73] Ottoman regional authorities went to great lengths to prevent espionage and boost morale, or at the very least to keep morale from falling even further than it already had. Administrators like Jamal Pasha and his intelligence services pursued this goal through stifling censorship and the strict regulation of topics that might offer strategic benefits to the Entente powers.[74] Journalists were muzzled, and presses were shuttered. Even sending the wrong piece of information to the wrong person could (and did) result in arrests and deportations. However, the strictness also backfired on the state. Rather than improving perceptions of an administration that seemed dedicated to enacting unpopular policies, wartime censorship reinforced criticism and amplified rumors in ways that unsettled the state's effort to stabilize the region.[75] By issuing unreliable propaganda and narrowing legitimate modes of professional journalistic discourse, the state inadvertently strengthened less reliable, informal modes of public discourse that it could not control.

The lack of authoritative information vexed those on the home front who were left straining to divine the progress of a distant war and to understand the festering social crisis on their doorstep. Trapped in their own myopic corners of the famine, contemporary observers obsessed over what pieces of information they could acquire. Thanks to censorship, people were increasingly reliant on person-to-person communication such as discussions among friends, whispers among neighbors, or casual conversations in the shops.[76] Though the rumor mill satisfied people's need for updates, the wartime discourse that this produced was somewhat disorderly. While some of the information that spread was at least superficially accurate, the fact that news was conveyed through what was essentially a convoluted, morbid game of "Telephone" meant that any fact came with a risk of editorialization, loss in transmission, fabrication, misrepresentation, or some combination thereof. The horrific nature of the crisis also made it easy to sensationalize an already gruesome spectacle by focusing on the most appalling events, thereby obscuring the difference between outliers and the mean.[77] Much of this was due to the fascination with the horrid developments of the famine, but it also may have been a natural effect of the crisis itself. As the historian of trauma Dominick LaCapra has suggested, such hyperbole "enacts stylistically the fact that one is affected by excess and trauma." And in the wartime famine, both were in ready supply.[78]

Because of the traumas of famine suffering and of the uncertainty and boredom of the famine atmosphere, many in the region were driven to "consume" the catastrophe around them in a form of "empathetic hedonism."[79] This is a common effect in times of crisis, though there is some question about why it happens. Explanations seem to have an intrinsically positive value for those who spread them, even if they are false.[80] Recent psychological research on conspiracy theories indicates that spreading information actually offers people a form of emotional stability, regardless of its truth value.[81] However, such obsessive information gathering was not necessarily therapeutic, despite the emotional void that it seemed to fill. Diary entries by Mary Dale and Edward Nickoley suggest that satisfying their thirst for information actually *increased* the growing sense of hopelessness that permeated their daily lives. Other explanations suggest that information gathering may have been a way for individuals and societies to rationalize a dangerous situation and help them navigate it more safely.[82] However, the wartime rumor mongering appeared to serve more purposes than mere self-defense or explanation seeking. People obsessed over information. Pitirim Sorokin argues from his own experience that the cognitive processes of individuals in famines become increasingly "monopolized" by a crisis that surrounds them, causing people to frame their existence around the crisis to the exclusion of unrelated topics.[83] Sorokin notes that this obsessiveness is not restricted to those suffering—everyone in society grows obsessed with the morbid developments around them.[84]

The informal methods of transmission and the consistent topic matter meant that many rumors favored familiar themes and extreme examples. Famine commonplaces like cannibalism, infanticide, grave robbing, and taboo breaking were sources of fascination, and even the most absurd fabrication could find enough credulous ears to circulate it through the claustrophobic famine environment if the report was compelling enough. Margaret McGilvary passed on a number of such tales in her wartime account *The Dawn of a New Era in Syria*, which had been written in part to generate sympathy and financial donations for the massive Near East Relief program after the war. Perhaps the most incredible among them was the story of locusts stripping children to the bone after they were left unattended in a field during the plague of 1915.[85] Since locusts are herbivores with jaws incapable of devouring human flesh (even if they wanted to), such a claim might be considered (at best) an unverified rumor. But it is telling that such an obvious falsehood was deemed compelling enough to report.

Though examples of extreme horrors surely existed, the focus on such terrible topics seemed to be more related to how people perceived the crisis or how they wanted to consume it than about the rumors themselves. Since titillating examples that were memetically "fitter" were repeated with a greater frequency and remembered better than mundane stories, they were more likely to be incorporated into the broader discourse.[86] Successful famine rumors (defined as ones that were repeated most) spread effectively because they were either exceptionally ghastly or appealed to a believable, coherent narrative that reinforced ideas that people already held about the world. They did not have to be true or even objectively plausible, but if they resonated enough with the storyteller, then they were deemed important enough to be inserted into the discourse and passed on. Nickoley suggests as much in his diary, noting that people readily digested and spread even gruesome claims because what they heard either confirmed their preexisting beliefs or adequately explained the terrible things that they saw around them.

Lest we imagine that the people of the period were merely naive parrots of unreliable information, a few writers confirmed that they were fully aware of the unreliability of their sources. In her 1916–1917 report, the head of the Tripoli Girl's School Harriet LaGrange wrote that "wild rumors filled the air, none authentic."[87] Likewise, while Nickoley often reported on the local news in his diary as a matter of curiosity, he sometimes openly doubted the veracity of what he had written, given the uncertainty of the wartime climate. In a particularly telling February 9, 1917, entry, he wrote: "These are the days when we can believe only one fourth of what we hear (and we are often in doubt as to which particular fourth) one half of what we see, and three-fourths of what we ourselves say."[88] In an entry on February 12, 1917, he listed the news of the day as rumors, rather than fact, writing that he had heard that the Ottomans intended to eradicate the Arab male population through conscription and that it, along with Turkish language instruction, was part of a grand plan to Turkify the region and eliminate its politically independent tendencies; that Jamal Pasha had intentionally refrained from aiding the mountain as it starved; that Mount Lebanon was to be annexed by Damascus and Tripoli, ending the independent status of the *mutasarrifate*; and that either 50 or 70 percent of the population of Mount Lebanon had starved to death.[89]

Though the conspiratorial tone of some of the reports and the hyperbole of others cast doubt on their veracity, Nickoley observed that many people had witnessed such terrible things in their own daily lives that even the most unbelievable of claims were almost plausible.[90] In some cases, facts were conveyed with a reference to a source (often a vague one) to counter skepticism. Though such hearsay would hardly stand up in a court of law, it at least lent an air of authority within the epistemological vacuum of the war. In one case, a writer emphasized that his information came on the authority of an anonymous, but well-placed, colleague in the administration when reporting that Jamal Pasha was considering killing all of the camels that had been requisitioned due to an insufficient fodder supply.[91]

We must consider what effects such information networks had on the famine discourse and on the people who took part in it. By consuming and sharing information, people plugged in to a shared famine epistemology. The discourse that this produced both reflected and shaped contemporary interpretations of the famine because of the type of information that tended to be shared and the values that were attached to it—it was indubitably a discourse of decline. The truth value of that information is important, but ultimately somewhat irrelevant for the influence that the discourse had at the time. Even if the knowledge conveyed was flawed, the discourse still provided a framework for ways that contemporaries perceived reality during the crisis.[92] Through these interpersonal oral information networks, individuals from across the region were able to empathetically share in the suffering around them. To some extent, the act of bearing witness to that suffering helped them rationalize their trauma.[93] While in practice this gossip tended to reinforce negative perceptions, it was apparent that many contemporaries engaged in the discourse out of a legitimate sympathy for those who suffered. This was evident in common topics of discussion, like the universal impacts of high prices, the greed of the upper classes, or the cruelty of Jamal Pasha's Ottoman state. Over time, all of these elements fit into a collectively understood famine narrative that allowed individuals from across society to imagine themselves to be a "community of sufferers" based on their shared experience of the crisis.[94]

Unfortunately, this shared identity was largely illusory. Even if everyone lived through the same famine context, each person ultimately filtered news that they heard about the disaster through their own individual identities and class-centered perspectives. In turn, these perspectives were also inherently colored by subjective personal experiences and preexisting and developed beliefs about the lives of others in society. These filters not only defined what information people deemed important; they also provided a framework of interpretation and a consistent set of imagery and vocabulary that was used when conveying it. Whether conscious or not, such generic representations ultimately embedded commonly understood value judgments into both the knowledge transmitted and the medium that carried it.

In the end, though the process of information acquisition and transmission succeeded in circulating facts about the crisis, much of that information was unverifiable, hyperbolic, and prone to social interpretation. Rather than conveying an accurate understanding of the famine situation, this process instead reinforced and created prevailing beliefs about the calamity and those within it. For observers who already believed the worst about the famine and the world it had made, the hyperbole of the discourse effectively made their belief a self-fulfilling prophecy.

A View from Above

Whether they intended to or not, all of those who participated in the famine discourse contributed to the construction of the historical narrative of the crisis. Though vivid, contemporaneous works about the famine are epistemologically suspicious. Even when not overtly political, they often present the writers' own interpretations of the crisis as authoritative reality.[95] However, the works themselves are anything but objective. Witnesses wrote from a perspective shaped by their own experience and for a specific audience.

The language used in writings about the famine is shockingly visceral. For historians, this can be useful, since the rich and often figurative descriptions in the famine narratives provide partial access to the writers' understanding of their worlds and how they suffered within it. However, such descriptions also impose the writers' perspectives upon the world that they purported to show to their readers.[96] Like the insinuations of decline that appear in so many accounts from the era, such figurative elements of famine literature are often tinted by a subtle didactic quality, or even overt moralism. Writers often tried to serve as mouthpieces for those who either could not speak or who lacked a platform. Yammine, Dhahir, and al-Maqdisi all fashioned their narratives to generate sympathy and to try to explain the causes and consequences of the disaster according to their own understandings and inclinations. For McGilvary, Yammine, and Dhahir in particular, it was important to ensure that the villains of the disaster were thoroughly outed.

However, even sympathetic portrayals of the famine took the general degradation of the starving poor as a given and used their suffering as a literary device or for emphasis. At times, such dehumanizing portrayals can be seen as relatively innocent examples of metaphor and allusion, but many writers also used the physical decay of long-suffering individuals and the decrepitude of stripped, neglected buildings as metaphors for the slow erosion of social norms and the collapse of morality. In such cases, the "disease of wretchedness" suffered by the poor and the nation alike was more than an observation;[97] it was a social judgment that saw suffering individuals as tainted to their very core. This was all the more problematic because this discourse broadly overlapped with new famine-specific reinterpretations of poverty, need, honor, and the like that were applied to the groups of people who inhabited the world of the crisis.

When the behaviors of starving individuals were weaponized against them in the social discourse to deny them empathy or even life-saving aid, the ostensible state of decline depicted in the sources was not necessarily figurative. For many writers, it represented an *actual* state of physical and moral deterioration that was readily apparent to them as privileged observers surveying the wreckage of society from the safety of their social perch. Retrospectively, it is true that the people of the famine suffered. But their state of decline was a matter of interpretation. The poor might disagree with that characterization, but in the famine discourse they were rarely granted a voice with which to object.

6

The Unwashed and Unwell

> On top of all of the other catastrophes that we have mentioned, the residents received the blows of disease.
> —JIRJIS KHURI AL-MAQDISI

EPIDEMICS ARE THREATS WHEREVER THEY emerge, but they are especially devastating in times of famine. During the wartime crisis in Lebanon, familiar diseases acquired fresh virulence, and newer pathogens spread with dreadful efficiency through a society racked by rising poverty, displacement, poor hygiene, inadequate shelter, and malnutrition. The combined effects of both crisis and disease were terrible and well documented. In his postwar retrospective, Jirjis Khuri al-Maqdisi wrote of "armies of microbes" that exploited the poverty of the famine to ravage the residents of the region. He noted that church officials and local shaykhs reported that disease and hunger had claimed a third of the residents of some villages—and all of the residents of other villages.[1] George Doolittle echoed these observations in his famine analysis and humanitarian surveys. In one village, the famine brought "the ravages of typhus, typhoid, dysentery, cholera, smallpox, severe malaria or torturing ophthalmia. Two-thirds of the population died. Frequently no one was left in a family to wait upon the sick."[2] In his account of the war, Antun Yammine reported a calamitous spread of dysentery, typhus, smallpox, and cholera through a vulnerable population, hyperbolically claiming that the 1916 typhus epidemic alone killed seventy thousand in a few short months.[3]

Although the numbers cited by such writers may have been exaggerated, their accounts are a clear indication of the trepidation that disease inspired in the region during the war and the damage that it caused. While infectious disease was no stranger to the region—and the coastal areas and the Biqaʿ Valley had particularly insalubrious reputations—the synergy between social disaster and human ecological shifts created new opportunities for infectious agents at a time of great vulnerability. These evolving threats in turn inspired new attitudes about the relationship between humans and their microbial adversaries. Until deadly infections begin burning through our populations, we, the apparent masters of our destiny, tend to forget that we have spent most of our recorded history at the mercy of unseen antagonists of indeterminate origin. When epidemics *do* strike, the "immanence of evil and the anxiety of indeterminacy" that they inspire inject uncertainty and fear into the lives of even the most protected members of society.[4] In the famine, it was this uncertainty that gave diseases power beyond their ability to infect and kill.

By far the best example of this was the dreaded disease of typhus. Spread by troop movements and migration and catalyzed by the social breakdowns of the famine, typhus first became epidemic in mid-1916 and again from late 1916 to mid-1917, killing roughly a fifth of those it infected and menacing the captive population with uncertainty and fear. Thanks to the deadliness of the disease and the terror it inspired, the wartime typhus construct left a deeper social impact than any other disease in the era.[5] Amid the horrific suffering of the famine, this unpredictable novel disease began to shift how people understood the relationships between human and pest, human and disease, and even human and human. Typhus's louse-based etiology and its association with starving migrants entwined the construct of the disease with that of the poor and the hungry. As social concepts like poverty, begging, suffering, and hygiene became coextensive with the concept of the disease itself, the neediest were pushed even further toward the margins because they were seen as sources of risk for the rest of society. Unlike the more ubiquitous vector-borne malaria or the deadlier dysentery, typhus had the unique ability to infect the very social status of the poor and the migrants. As the historian J. N. Hayes has cleverly observed, "the poor get not only the blame, but also the disease"[6]—in a time of typhus, their poverty was no longer just distasteful, it was potentially dangerous as well.

Health and the Famine

The habit of hyperbolizing in famine writing naturally crossed over into accounts of disease in the period as well, so amid all of the health crises that struck the region, the loudest and deadliest afflictions tend to be the ones that we remember most. The 1916 bubonic plague "outbreak" in the central coastal village of Antelias provides a fine example of this. Despite the fact that only two (albeit fatal) cases were recorded, the plague's very presence in the region during the war has left it indelibly linked to the famine in both popular and professional histories (for reference, the plague made another brief appearance after the war, but this is generally forgotten).[7] Though chilling tales of sensational diseases like plague and cholera may have shocked and titillated the readers of famine literature as much as they terrified the residents of the region by their very presence, the limited spread of such diseases meant that their social impacts were significantly less than those of the ubiquitous malaria or enteric diseases like dysentery and typhoid.[8] If we pull back from the great killers, we can see that many of the health challenges in the period came from everyday risks that had been amplified by the social effects of the wartime crisis and by a regional medical system suffering from oversubscription, overworked staff, and medicine shortages due to the Entente blockade.[9] Although most of the mundane afflictions that threatened the region were not particularly exotic, they could still be debilitating or even deadly at a time of famine.

Most health risks in the war were either perpetual problems that carried over from the prewar period, or they were secondary effects of social crisis. Some diseases, like tuberculosis, skin afflictions like scabies, blinding diseases like trachoma, and enteric diseases like typhoid or intestinal worms, increased during the war due to rising poverty and poor living conditions.[10] Other diseases seem to have been boosted by the famine, but without leading to significant mortality. For instance, health statistics from Mount Lebanon indicate that viral diseases like diphtheria and measles were prevalent but apparently not major killers during the war. Smallpox was an interesting exception—it did not spread widely in the region due to the prewar Ottoman vaccination campaign,[11] but its periodic outbreaks were still sources of dread because of its grisly symptoms and grim reputation. Of the 191 cases tallied in Mount Lebanon in 1917, the explosively contagious virus killed over a fourth of those it infected, for a case fatality rate (CFR) of 26.7 percent.[12] Despite the vaccination campaign, smallpox still flared in poor and rural areas where residents distrusted the state's applications of biopower and often avoided modern medical interventions that conflicted with folk wisdom and local practices.[13] The movement of people also brought or encouraged disease. Along with epidemic typhus, migration and troop movements also brought a bizarre new form of cutaneous diphtheria, which produced foul-smelling gangrenous ulcers on the limbs of the infected.[14] Syphilis thrived during the war amid the rise in prostitution encouraged by poverty and the presence of troops with disposable income.[15] Residents also continued to face mundane chronic illness, and cancer, rheumatism, and cardiac disease were common afflictions of older residents before and during the famine. Health statistics from Mount Lebanon (flawed though they were) suggest that heart disease remained the *greatest* recorded killer of individuals over the age of forty in the district during the terrible famine year of 1917—starvation and epidemics inclusive.[16] Some of these diseases would not have been fatal by themselves. However, when problems like starvation or secondary infections intervened, any of them could become far more serious, or even deadly.

Perhaps the most understated wartime menace was malaria, which reached epidemic proportions during the war in a number of susceptible areas across the Mediterranean and in Ottoman Iraq.[17] Even in normal times, malaria was described as the "most characteristic and important" of all diseases in neighboring Palestine,[18] and contemporary health reports indicate that the war only worsened its impacts.[19] While it was rarely described in the hushed tones of typhus or cholera, malaria undoubtedly had the most dramatic effect of any illness on the overall health of the region's population.[20] In his 1917 mission report, George Doolittle (perhaps hyperbolically) claimed that *every* inhabitant of the tiny village of Alma in the southern region of Jabal 'Amil was afflicted by malaria.[21] Hikmet Ozdemir's suggestion that 75 percent of Ottomans were afflicted by the parasite during the war is probably also an exaggeration,[22] but his error likely stems from assuming that 75 percent had active cases. Given the prevalence of malaria in the Mediterranean basin, it is entirely believable that well over three-quarters of the Ottoman population suffered from malaria at some point in their lives, with the worst effects falling on the young and the poor. One study conducted by E. W. G. Masterman on Palestinian schoolchildren at the peak of the malarial season determined that 27–30 percent of students in Jerusalem tested positive for the parasite, which echoed a similar study that found the parasite in 26.7 percent of those sampled from the population at large.[23] It was certainly a problem in prewar Beirut. In the list of recorded afflictions that the French doctor Benoit Boyer provides in his 1897 study of health and hygiene in the city, he notes 2,937 malaria cases out of a population of roughly 120,000 (a morbidity rate of 24.47 out of 1,000), making it by far the most prevalent disease charted in the study. For reference, the second most common ailment was the gruesome blinding disease granular conjunctivitis (also called trachoma), which afflicted 1,376 individuals.[24] Moreover, Boyer's estimate only accounts for individuals with active malaria—patients can be asymptomatic for long periods, only to have it flare up again later.

Like plague and typhus, malaria is not transferred from person to person, but via an arthropod vector—in this case, the *Anopheles* mosquito. Because both the mosquito and the parasite respond to factors like moisture and temperature, malarial outbreaks follow specific geographical and seasonal patterns.[25] This means that malaria concentrates in areas that have water sources that allow mosquitoes to breed and a population of infected individuals or infected mosquitoes.[26] (A person moving from a malarial zone to a clean one could actually infect a whole area if he exposed otherwise clean mosquitoes to the parasites in his blood). In Mount Lebanon and the province of Beirut, the malarial season began in the fall around October, when temperatures suited mosquito movement and parasite reproduction.[27] Malaria season lasted until roughly December, when colder temperatures and precipitation sent the mosquitoes into a state of relative dormancy, sheltering in structures like barns, cisterns, or houses for the winter.[28] The coastal or plains regions in proximity to still water and poorly housed refugees were at greatest risk. For instance, Tyre was a natural malarial hot spot, as it sat in a flood zone near rivers and the sea.[29] Ottoman sources identified coastal cities like Sidon, Tripoli, and Beirut as particularly susceptible, and in Mount Lebanon, the larger population centers near the coast (like Bourj Hammoud, Antelias, and Bourj al-Barajneh) and Damour, Zahle, Jounieh, and the towns of Byblos (Jbeil) and Batroun tended to suffer the worst from the disease. However, malaria clusters were recorded even in the elevated reaches of Mount Lebanon.

Malaria was usually not in itself fatal, but its risks were elevated by the effects of the famine. Infections of the rarer malignant *Plasmodium falciparum* strain were far more violent, potentially leaving sufferers with profound neurological effects, kidney failure, cardiovascular problems, and jaundice as the parasite ravaged their livers. However, even with milder strains, common symptoms like fever, vomiting, and diarrhea would have dehydrated those afflicted while worsening their state of malnutrition. Affected individuals displayed an ashen or yellowed complexion, a distended abdomen from their enlarged spleen (the "ague cake"), edema,[30] and an absent state of listlessness.[31] Symptoms like distended bellies may have been mistaken for the protein deficiency disease kwashiorkor, which is common in famine.[32] The secondary effects of the illness could also be devastating, as high fevers and anemia made infected individuals lethargic, hampering their ability to work, find food, or care for others.[33] Without care, a starving malarial person would be at much higher risk of death. It was especially deadly in infants and young children, whose lack of prior exposure made their initial infections far worse.[34]

It is impossible to know how much malaria contributed to mortality during the period because its symptoms were not as dramatic or horrifying as those of diseases like typhus or smallpox. Moreover, since so many had it, malaria may have been overlooked in part due to the more obvious effects of starvation or a comorbidity with another, more visible infection. However, to put things in perspective, Dr. Masterman (who was not prone to exaggeration) estimated that the disease was directly and indirectly responsible for more deaths among children and young adults in Palestine than any other disease, an assessment that undoubtedly extended to the neighboring province of Beirut, the coastal regions of Mount Lebanon, and the malarious rivers and swamps of the interior Biqaʿ Valley.[35]

In general, the conditions created by the war and the famine worsened the epidemiological situation across the region. The famine is largely to blame for this. This was not necessarily because starvation makes infections worse, but because famine ferments a complex mix of biological and social problems that encourages the spread of disease while leaving people more socially and biologically vulnerable to it. Once the vulnerable are infected, disease is often harder to fight off. In sum, famine is as much a social catalyst for disease as it is a biological one.

Famine's biological influence is somewhat misunderstood. Of course, famine *can* make a person more susceptible to disease. On a cellular level, malnutrition lowers the production of defensive antibodies and enzymes that help the body fend off infections, and it can also hamper cell-mediated immunity and phagocytosis—meaning a starved body has more trouble identifying and evicting invading pathogens than a fed one.[36] Malnutrition can also heighten the severity of infections: symptoms that might be manageable under normal circumstances might be fatal for a starving person. For instance, anemia from intestinal parasites could be debilitating during the famine because it caused sluggishness even as the afflicted worked to sustain themselves and their freeloading worms.[37] Likewise, diseases that caused diarrhea and vomiting worsened the malnutrition and dehydration of famished individuals. Not only did the fever and constant bowel evacuations squander the (literally) precious resources that the victim had managed to consume, but the symptoms made it harder for the infected person to replace and retain those nutrients. The implications of this were clear in the 1917 data from Mount Lebanon in which the deadliest diseases on a per-case basis were not the dreaded typhus or smallpox but rather the diarrheal diseases of cholera and dysentery, which had shocking case fatality rates of 57.5 percent and 33 percent, respectively.[38]

However, malnutrition does not always make a person more susceptible to disease. Malnutrition can hamper the development of certain diseases whose infectious parasites and microbes rely on the same nutrients as their host. Some diseases multiply faster in a well-fed host, so a starving or anemic host would leave the pathogen starved as well. The human body's innate immune system has actually evolved to capitalize on this fact—when our immune system's early warning alerts are triggered, our bodies begin to sequester zinc and iron to try to slow down any opportunistic microbes.[39] The relationship between malnutrition and illness thus varies on a disease-by-disease basis. While hunger may not necessarily make a person more susceptible to malaria or tuberculosis, which are more dependent on exposure to malaria's mosquito vector or to a "consumptive" person's bodily fluids, those diseases can be deadlier when the synergistic effects of starvation are added.[40] This is especially the case for malaria.[41] On the other hand, the impact of hunger is negligible for diseases like typhus, plague, smallpox, and typhoid, which are all deadly enough that a large percentage of individuals die from infection whether they are well fed or not. In most cases in the famine, access to effective nursing care factored far more into the survival of an infected person than did nutrition alone.[42] Even when suffering from a relatively moderate disease, an abandoned patient could not expect a good outcome.

This is not to suggest that widespread starvation did not contribute to high mortality but, rather, that the connection is more complicated. Theories tying hunger to disease mortality ignore the link between disease and poverty and the secondary economic, social, and environmental vulnerabilities that famine creates. Poverty alone placed individuals at far greater risk of infection with far fewer means to support themselves.[43] Disease ecology was also important during the famine, as poverty, the mass movement of refugees, and the introduction of epidemic pathogens created social and ecological circumstances that made certain susceptible localities veritable Petri dishes for their vulnerable residents. The squalid living conditions of the poorest residents left them exposed to diseases of filth, and, in an oblique way, wartime poverty also increased the prevalence of social diseases like syphilis as unemployed women increasingly relied on sex work to survive.[44] Syphilis was more widespread than one might expect. A map published in 1918 identifies syphilis hotspots in ten Lebanese municipalities, including such relatively unexpected locations like the small coastal village of Damour and in interior mountain towns like Zgharta, Bsharri, and 'Aley.[45]

The fluidity of disease ecology in a time of mass population movement also altered the relationship between humans and their pathogens. Social changes due to the crisis created new biological niches that allowed an endemic problem like malaria to transform into a killer and encouraged a deadly pathogen like typhus to become epidemic.[46] These changes were chiefly brought about by the worsening social conditions across the region as the famine progressed. Many of the poor were badly housed and subsisted on insufficient or insalubrious food and unsafe water. Inadequate housing in low-lying locations led to a wartime spike in malarial infections,[47] and poor living conditions increased the risk of contact-spread diseases like typhus, scabies, and trachoma; pulmonary afflictions like tuberculosis and pneumonia; and enteric diseases like typhoid, dysentery, and the dreaded cholera. For many of those who were thrust by circumstance into conditions of poverty, wartime diseases both loud and silent could mean suffering or even an untimely death, especially when medication and medical care were both in short supply.

Old Disease, New Threat

The wartime typhus epidemic is an interesting case study of the complex relationship between the human and microbial worlds. Though malaria was far more prevalent and likely contributed (both directly and indirectly) to a larger number of deaths than typhus, it never captured the social imagination in the same way as the more virulent louse-borne disease. Thanks to the famine, typhus was transformed from a dangerous but rare disease into a terrifying social phenomenon by 1916. As epidemics burned, the fear of the disease became affixed to other social afflictions within the wartime crisis, much to the detriment of those who became associated with its threat. The terror that typhus inspired and the ways that people responded because of that fear made the epidemic disease more than simply a biological scourge during the war: it was a social one as well.

Though fear often led reporters to exaggerate typhus's effects, the louse-borne pathogen was perhaps the one example of a loud disease whose bite nearly equaled its bark during the war. This was true for more than just the eastern Mediterranean region. Generally speaking, World War I represented a sort of reversion to the terrible mean for the once-fearsome affliction's relationship with western Eurasia. Throughout the latter part of the nineteenth century, medical advances, changes to social and hygienic practices, and the shifting focus of warfare from Europe to the imperial periphery caused typhus to shed its unsavory reputation as the "inevitable and expected companion of war," eventually settling into what the epidemiologist, entomologist, and "biographer" of the pathogen Hans Zinsser delightfully called the "quiet, bourgeois existence of a relatively domesticated disease."[48] This all changed when the Great War stoked the smaller epidemics sparked by the Ottoman-Balkan wars of 1912–13 into an epidemic conflagration that allegedly killed one hundred thousand in Serbia alone in six months. The tragedy of typhus's reemergence in its epidemic form was that, much like the famine, it was an entirely unnecessary consequence of the war. The vast armies mobilizing for the Great War and the deteriorating conditions on home fronts and battlefronts alike caused the epidemic disease to take root across Russia, Eastern Europe, and the Ottoman Empire with alarming speed and appalling virulence.[49] Cramped military quarters and the unwashed clothing of refugees provided excellent breeding grounds for lice, who thereafter found a reliable mode of transportation from the battlefronts to home fronts on the backs of both soldiers and the civilian victims of conflict, famine, and genocide. Across Ottoman Syria, fuel demands from the army and the rail systems made sanitizing clothing and bedding a costly luxury outside of government-sponsored boiling centers, so lice flourished amid the neglect.[50] By 1915, the unfortunate trinity of army movement, poverty, and displacement caused typhus to circulate among vulnerable populations. As conditions deteriorated, the disease abandoned Zinsser's state of domesticity to become feral for the first time in Lebanon's regional memory.

While many of the diseases that plagued the region during the war remained relatively unheralded, the novelty, deadliness, and rapid spread of epidemic typhus ensured that outbreaks of the disease and its various mythologies were well documented by observers and historians alike. According to contemporaries, the pathogen was brought by soldiers returning from the Balkans after the Ottoman army withdrew in 1913, resulting in small regional outbreaks that reached deadly levels during the war. This earned it the wartime nickname "military fever" (*al-huma al-ʿaskariyya*), along with its phonetic Arabic spelling *tayfus* and the more descriptive term "spotted fever" (*al-huma al-namashiyya*), due to the speckling of papules that appeared on those it infected. Though typhus was reputed to have arrived only during the war,[51] it had in fact been present long before, though in its muted form it was overshadowed by the spectacular new affliction of cholera and familiar terrors like tuberculosis and bubonic plague. Indeed, prewar accounts attest to the fact that it had been spreading in Syria during the nineteenth and twentieth centuries, and likely well before.⁵² Benoit Boyer recorded nineteen confirmed cases of typhus in Beirut during his public health survey of late nineteenth-century Beirut and also unintentionally provided the best argument for the pathogen's prewar circulation when he personally died of the disease in Beirut in 1897.⁵³ Though it never reached epidemic proportions, typhus appears to have periodically sparked and fizzled roughly once every ten years, including in Palestine in 1913 and 1914.⁵⁴

During the war, patterns of typhus outbreaks traced the impacts of the famine. Areas with high population density, migration, and poverty had the most—and deadliest—cases. This made major cities like Beirut and Tripoli as well as large towns like Zahle, Dayr al-Qamar, Tyre, and Jounieh major sites of infection. The connection between suffering and both infections and mortality can be clearly seen in the wartime analysis of Mount Lebanon's typhus outbreaks. In the populous and famine devastated Keserwan district, typhus accounted for 73.2 percent of the total infections in 1917. Similar impacts held in the central district of the Matn, which had by far the greatest number of typhus cases reported in Mount Lebanon and the greatest proportion of typhus relative to other disease at 80 percent of the 1,132 infections recorded. This is not surprising, given its large population along the coastal plain near Beirut and the nearly twenty thousand Armenian refugees who were encamped in appalling conditions in the mosquito-ridden riverside village of Bourj Hammoud. We can draw similar conclusions for the interior district of Zahle, which hosted many migrants from Keserwan in its large eponymous town. There, typhus comprised 70.5 percent of the reported instances of disease for the year 1917.⁵⁵ In contrast, the southern mountain district of Jazzine had a mere 90 typhus cases in a population of 24,593, representing a relatively meager 57 percent of the 158 total recorded cases of infectious disease. Since the small villages in the remote regions were more likely to push refugees into nearby towns like Nabatieh, Tyre, and Sidon than to draw them in, the town of Jazzine faced fewer of the risks associated with crowding and displacement than market towns like Zahle or the coastal towns of Batroun, Byblos, and Jounieh.⁵⁶ The geographical isolation of the district of Jazzine may also have provided physical barriers to migrant travel compared to the more accessible areas of central and southern Mount Lebanon,[57] and the lighter populations and weaker economies of smaller towns would have been less attractive for migrants seeking work. The size of these smaller towns also helped, since sporadic outbreaks were likely to fizzle quickly due to the smaller and more diffused population of susceptible human hosts. This does not necessarily mean that smaller communities were better off during the famine. Though less susceptible to epidemics, small towns were often hardest hit by the economic turmoil and still faced the chance of epidemic outbreaks or endemic diseases as well.[58]

Statistics suggest that during the war, typhus killed at least one in every five people it infected after inflicting splitting headaches, high fevers, mental fog, and its characteristic spotted rash. However, this was simply the mean—morbidity and mortality varied widely across space and time. The deadliness of the disease seems to have been closely linked to the social and individual circumstances of those infected and even to the point in the epidemic at which an individual had fallen ill. We do know that the 1916 epidemic was the most dangerous phase of the outbreak. Infections spread widely amid growing social malaise, and mortality rates were estimated by one contemporary doctor at an apocalyptic (and probably exaggerated) 30–40 percent.[59] One statistical report indicates a CFR of over 30 percent, but the sample size is too low to draw solid conclusions.[60] However, time also seems to have played a role in the deadliness of the outbreaks. Official statistics from Mount Lebanon from the second wave of the epidemic, which ran from late 1916 until mid-1917, suggest the outbreak burned hottest from March until the end of June, producing thousands of infections and many deaths. However, deaths plateaued and dropped in the early summer of 1917. Though many new cases were recorded in May and June, fatalities dropped substantially from May onward, and infection numbers followed suit at the end of June.[61] For whatever reason, infections later in the epidemic seem to have been less severe, or at least more survivable. The author of the mission report from Zahle Station in 1918 confirmed that July 1917 marked the end of typhus's reign of terror, astutely surmising that the strain had become less virulent and that so many had already been infected that there were few susceptible individuals left to help the disease spread.[62]

It is difficult to fully grasp the effects that typhus had in the war because of the uneven reporting about the disease in contemporary sources. Riveted by both the deadliness and the terrifying randomness of the affliction, many writers sensationalized typhus in their accounts and inflated both case numbers and death tolls.[63] Their exuberance was encouraged by an information stream comprised mainly of common knowledge and rumor, neither of which was especially accurate. Though typhus was terrifyingly dangerous, the fear of the disease obscured exactly how deadly and widespread it had actually been during the famine. Antun Yammine's account of the typhus epidemic in the war offers a prime example of this. In his description, Yammine claims that 70,000 individuals died of the disease in the city of Beirut and Mount Lebanon during the spring 1916 epidemic alone.[64] Though this tally is instructive as a reflection of the alarm that typhus inspired in the population, especially in its initial wave, his estimate is statistically unlikely. Using Mount Lebanon's already alarmingly high 1917 case fatality rate of 19.3 percent as a baseline,[65] a death toll of this magnitude would mathematically require a *minimum* of 362,294 individuals to have been infected in a two-month period alone, which would amount to slightly more than the entire estimated population that was present in Mount Lebanon during the war.[66] Even assuming that the epidemic in 1916 had been deadlier than in 1917 because it struck a virgin-soil population without much prior exposure,[67] a death toll of 70,000 would still require an extraordinary 233,333 people to have fallen ill over the course of a few months. Outside of Yammine's claim, there is no indication in any of the sources that a disaster of this magnitude took place, nor does it seem epidemiologically feasible that it could have.

The best statistics that we have on typhus and its role in the war come from Mount Lebanon public health director Husni Bey Muhieddine's report on the health situation in the district during the war. According to the report, government clinics recorded 2,539 cases of the disease in the shortened Ottoman administrative year of 1333 (which confusingly only stretched from March to December 1917 because the Ottoman state switched from the Julian to the Gregorian calendar midway through the year). In that period, typhus infected 3.5 out of every 1,000 men and 2.5 out of every 1,000 women in the mountain.[68] Such numbers contrast sharply with anecdotal accounts, which pointed not only to a greater prevalence but a higher mortality rate as well. Certainly, the state's statistics are not without their own problems.

The official figures undoubtedly underestimate the incidence of the disease, since it would be impossible to identify each case, let alone the cause of death of each individual in the mountain thanks to widespread displacement and poverty.[69] Moreover, the distrust of state officials and the difficulty of traveling while sick meant that many infected individuals would have never made it to a clinic. Many would have avoided professional care in general since widespread skepticism about modern medical practices in poor and rural areas would have deterred the ill from seeking professional medical attention, if the splitting headaches, high fever, and mental fogginess of a full-blown typhus infection would have even permitted the arduous journey to seek help at all.[70] The statistics may cut off the margins as well—relatively minor infections that did not require medical attention would never have come to the attention of the authorities, whereas those with the worst cases may have died alone in a miserable fever-induced delirium. Finally, death statistics in particular can be skewed by confounding factors like starvation and comorbidities from simultaneous infections. In short, as with nearly all demographic data on the region at this time, the numbers are clearly wrong, but we are not sure exactly how wrong they might be and should thus be cautious when applying them to contemporaneous claims.

However, corroborating estimates indicate that a lower death toll was likely accurate. Ottoman surveyors Muhammad Bahjat and Muhammad Rafiq Tamimi's comments on the effects of the disease in Tyre in 1916 offered a relatively clear take on the deadlier initial epidemic. As a relatively poor, migrant-laden town, Tyre had all of the risk factors in place for a major outbreak when typhus arrived in July 1916—and when it hit, it was deadly, killing a third of those it infected. All told, within a population of five thousand to six thousand people, 5–6 percent fell ill, and 2 percent died. Still, despite the virulence of the pathogen, the fact that the outbreak only produced one hundred deaths in one of the largest urban centers in the province suggests that seventy thousand deaths in the 1916 outbreak would have been highly unlikely.[71] (It should be noted that Bahjat and Tamimi were merely reporting figures from their sources and could themselves be somewhat unreliable. In their overview of Nablus, they reported that seventy people had died of cholera and five hundred of typhus over the course of a few days[72]—Nablus had an official population of 3,787.)[73]

Death records from the large central mountain town of Dayr al-Qamar also support a lower figure. As a major population center, the town drew migrants from nearby communities during the famine, making it susceptible to outbreaks. However, annual burial records indicate that the epidemics of 1916 and 1917 may have been deadly, but not deadly enough to distinguish typhus mortality from other famine mortality. Between 1913 and 1915, the Church of Our Lady of the Hill buried an average of 27 parishioners per year (including 35 in the early famine year of 1915). These numbers rose to 171 in 1916, to 177 in 1917, and to 196 in 1918.[74] Though the excess mortality of the epidemic years of 1916 and 1917 was extraordinary compared to the usual levels, the deadliest year was the one in which the effect of typhus was negligible but poverty and high prices peaked. The church's totals are corroborated by official government statistics, which showed 160 typhus patients in Dayr al-Qamar in 1917, leading to 57 deaths for a high case fatality rate of 35 percent. But Dayr al-Qamar was also an outlier. Per-case mortality was high in the town compared to the surrounding district of the Chouf, which in 1917 saw 88 deaths out of 354 infected individuals—resulting in a high, but lower CFR of 25 percent.[75] The statistics show that typhus was certainly terrifying, but the epidemic was not the scourge that Yammine portrayed.

Although we can reasonably question some of the myths about the typhus outbreaks during the war, we should not take that to mean that typhus was insignificant. Case fatality rates were incredibly high compared to other less prevalent diseases, and unlike many other afflictions that simmered endemically during the war, typhus produced alarming epidemic surges that touched even those in society whose status should have left them relatively well protected. For those who lived through the famine, the widespread fear of typhus was neither exaggerated nor unfounded.

The Consequences of Constructs

Perhaps the very existence of the myths surrounding typhus indicates the potential power of typhus as both an infection and a social concept. Although the biological pathogen (or the symptoms it causes) is the part of a disease that actually makes us sick, our understanding of a disease includes a range of ideas that constitutes that disease's construct. A construct might include ideas about symptoms, risks, how it is spread, what it looks like, and who is susceptible. During outbreaks, such conceptualizations are important because they help us to quickly assess how we might avoid a disease and whether we should fear it. Constructs define how we understand diseases, even if we are not aware of them. For instance, our mental image of the common cold is very different from what we imagine the Ebola virus to be. Not all of those ideas may be accurate, but a construct is a commonly shared idea, not a textbook definition. Even similar pathogens can have wildly different constructs—just think of how our conception of "the flu" differs from "the Spanish flu." Ultimately, the ways that we construct ideas of disease vary depending on their severity, their novelty, and the apparent risk that they represent (especially for the socially secure).[76]

As a relatively unfamiliar epidemic that spread in waves and killed one in every five of those it infected, typhus as a construct was a potent source of terror during the war for people across society.[77] Some of this was rooted in the virulence of the disease itself, but adding to that a cocktail of rumor, randomness, and fear transformed a dangerous but somewhat obscure disease into a horrific plague in the eyes of contemporaries. There is a logic to a disease construct. Creating such conceptual definitions of a disease allows people to understand and rationalize its relative threat and to manage their own risk by avoiding situations—or people—that they believe might endanger them.[78] During the famine, this aspect of the construct extended typhus's reach beyond the medical realm to the social realm as well.

One reason for typhus's social influence is due to the pathogen's primary vector, the human body louse—or at least the social attitudes toward it. Like typhus itself, the wartime epidemic transformed the body louse from a relatively benign pest into a deadly threat. From our vantage in the present, it is difficult to conceive of lice as anything but repugnant vermin. Yet at the time, because the region had only felt periodic brushes with typhus (and as lice were not yet associated with a deadly plague), the creatures had actually spent thousands of years living somewhat harmoniously on the clothing and flesh of the region's residents. Ubiquitous and mostly harmless (if itchy), the presence of lice was considered normal and even oddly reassuring in certain cases. In an article for the *Palestine Exploration Quarterly*, Dr. E. W. G. Masterman writes that the flight of lice from a body was considered a sign of imminent death among his Palestinian patients (possibly since the lice could sense an irregular body temperature), which Masterman claimed gave rise to the colloquial exhortation "May God not remove them [the lice] from me."[79] The sentiments were certainly mutual from the louse's perspective, as it could contract fatal diseases from a sick host (including typhus, which was universally fatal to the louse).[80] And, if it separated from its human, the delicate louse would have to find suitable alternate housing quickly or risk a wretched death of starvation, exposure, or predation.

Unfortunately for all parties, this prewar state of parasitic comity was shattered as declining living conditions of the wartime period improved the lot of the louse at the expense of its human hosts. This was not necessarily because of starvation but because a louse-ridden population forced into crowded, filthy spaces provided ample fuel for deadly epidemics once they began. The abundance of lice during the famine made the disease terrifyingly unpredictable in a time of poor sanitation and widespread poverty. The epidemic was undoubtedly aided by the theft of clothing from the dead and the sale of used items in the marketplace, but typhus had an unsettling randomness about it that gave secure individuals pause. Something as minor as brushing against someone in public or a chance encounter with an infested piece of clothing might pass on the single louse that sent a person to their grave. In a postwar interview, Dr. Joseph Hitti even claimed to recall the *exact bite* that gave him his case of the disease.[81]

The association of typhus with its louse vector transformed lice from bodily passengers or minor irritants into harbingers of doom. Perhaps more poignantly, the association of the disease with those fleeing the famine helped transform those who were most associated with the parasites from objects of sympathy into dangerous nuisances. As appalling as that may be, there was some validity to this association. Although anyone could be infected, a person's risk of contracting or dying from the disease was closely associated with their level of exposure to its hosts and its vectors (or their prior exposure to them, since some immunity was conferred if one recovered). This was evident in the high mortality among doctors and relief workers in the period, especially in the military, where typhus was responsible for 222 of the 300 deaths among Ottoman medical officers in the war.[82] In 1916 alone, typhus killed Dr. Ira Harris of the Kennedy Memorial Hospital in Tripoli,[83] Dr. Kaiserman of Beirut, and Drs. Alam al-Din and Iskander Zeine of Zahle while also infecting several medical students (including the aforementioned Joseph Hitti). The following year it killed Muhammad Effende Abu ʿIzzedine, who had helped to organize relief work in Mount Lebanon.[84] The elevated risk to medical professionals can be explained by the greater exposure that health and relief workers had to infected individuals and their body lice. George Doolittle wrote that even the resplendent ʿUmar Daʿuq, who headed the Beirut municipality during the war, was forced to carefully remove lice that had collected on his clothing after his stints in the municipal relief shelters. Daʿuq was well aware of the risk that lice presented because the disease had killed his brother.[85]

Though the wealthy were less likely to contract the disease, the sense that typhus posed a universal risk made it a particular concern for the wealthy and middle classes who otherwise escaped the worst of the famine. A number of sources were keen to note when the wealthy sickened and died, even though they did so at a rate far lower than their poorer countrymen. In 1917, American missionary Harriet LaGrange (who also caught the disease during the war) pointedly recorded that typhus had killed some of the most influential Muslims in Tripoli,[86] while George Doolittle reported a similar situation in the southern city of Sidon. Doolittle's account includes a short anecdote of a "well-to-do" woman who was reduced to poverty by typhus and a subsequent bout of malaria. She died (in Doolittle's baroque terms) "a gaunt skeleton, far beyond hope of recovery. Oh the pathos of her outstretched hands and pleading voice!"[87]

In Beirut, the fear extended among the relatively elite ranks of the students and faculty of the Syrian Protestant College. Though the school may have had the protection of the Ottoman high administration in the war, this did little to dissuade lice and their infectious microbes from intruding. In his May 23, 1917, diary entry, Edward Nickoley notes that the ongoing outbreak of the disease had spread to three members of the faculty community and a large number of students.[88] Fear of the randomness of typhus's etiology encouraged obsessiveness and conspiracy theories. Nickoley repeats rumors of lice riding on flies like tiny arthropodal Huns in search of fresh human hosts.[89] This sense of helplessness drove some to action. Young Philomela Van Zandt gamely volunteered in a Beirut typhus ward, explaining to Nickoley that "the question seems to be whether I am to get these beasts or whether they are to get me."[90] However, apart from the resident foreign medical staff, Van Zandt's initiative was rare among the financially secure segments of the population, who wisely preferred to avoid infectious situations if they could.

The suffering of the famine gradually augmented the already growing aversion to the poor among the wealthier classes. This was a complex process that had a variety of causes. As previous chapters noted, the rise in begging and compassion fatigue led many to avoid interacting with the poor whenever possible.[91] However, the wretchedness and filth that stigmatized the starving poor also marked them as potential carriers of deadly disease. Practices that might accurately be described as "social distancing" became common in 1916 as the secure sought to use their status as protection from their impoverished neighbors. In the town of Sidon, the Presbyterian missionaries deployed countermeasures to prevent the spread of the disease during outbreaks, including posting a guard at the Gerard Institute to ward off the poor for fear that they would drop deadly lice while pleading for aid.[92] Similar policies were enacted in the women's sewing circle at the Sidon Seminary, which had been a social fixture of the local community before and during the war. In the seminary's 1917–18 annual report, the school's principal, Charlotte Brown, expressed the following sentiments:

> We found that it was neither agreeable nor sanitary for the well-to-do to have their unwashed sisters of the very poor sitting too near them in those days of typhus fever, and with soap beyond the reach of many, we quietly let the clean people go upstairs to one meeting and had a second gathering on the ground floor for the unmended, unwashed and underfed, some of whom were practically beggars.[93]

Brown's phrasing hints at the dark consequences to the reassessment of poverty in the famine. At a time when dire circumstances already threatened the lives of the poor, such social attitudes had social consequences: the poor were not only unsympathetic in the famine; they were now regarded as threats.

The intersection of the social constructs of typhus and the famine-era constructs of starvation and poverty not only dehumanized the poor and the potentially ill but ultimately devalued their lives and deaths during a time of intense suffering and mortality. Edward Nickoley in particular makes this apparent in his diary entries. In one poignant passage, Nickoley morosely speculates about the conditions in the mountains, noting that many would inevitably die in the typhus outbreak that had flared alarmingly during the winter of that year. Not that this was necessarily a bad thing in his view. He wrote, "In a way it is a mercy and a relief to those who are so far gone and there are no means of rescue in sight. The quick action of the fever would seem preferable to the lingering torture of famine with a no less sure result."[94] In a famine with no apparent endpoint, death from an incurable illness seemed an acceptable solution to the gruesome suffering of the starving poor.

As a deadly, unpredictable, and somewhat novel epidemic, the fact and fantasy of the typhus construct captivated local discourse, influencing social behaviors in ways that extended beyond its power as a simple infection. In this sense, typhus was a singular phenomenon among the many deadly risks that individuals faced during the war. Malaria, the other great vector-borne illness of the time, was undoubtedly far more prevalent, but malaria was simply associated with the mosquitoes that spread it—it did not have a "type." Because typhus was associated with the filth of the poor and the lice that they carried, the typhus construct during the famine made it more than just a medical affliction; it was a social affliction that further stigmatized the people who might carry it. The famine-era typhus construct encompassed not just the disease itself, its symptoms, and its six-legged mode of transmission but also the circumstances that favored its proliferation and the way that a potentially infectious person might look and behave. This all influenced the measures that a secure person could take to avoid risking contact with a stray louse. In a period of overwhelming poverty and of compassion fatigue among nonsuffering individuals, typhus became yet another justification for the separation of society into new, famine-specific social castes. In the end, this aversion to poverty and its effects represented an additional barrier to survival for those who needed assistance the most.

7

The Sheep and the Goats

> Personally I can only believe that this struggle between American philanthropy and Turkish lust for destruction was only another phase of the world-conflict of civilization against barbarism, of right against might.
>
> —MARGARET MCGILVARY

IN 1920, THE PRESBYTERIAN BOARD of Foreign Missions published a marketing pamphlet entitled *A Story of Our Syria Mission*, written by the former secretary of Beirut's American Mission Press, Margaret McGilvary (who had by then added the last name "Zimmerman" by marriage). Praising American humanitarians during the war, she boldly declared that a "small army" of foreign relief workers had saved the entire Syrian people from "annihilation" during the crisis.[1] The hyperbole of McGilvary's statement is palpable, but as the document aimed to mobilize cash and bodies for the vast postwar Near East Relief program,[2] accuracy was less important than effect. Such tales of heroism and sacrifice certainly played well for an American postwar audience that was already pouring vast sums of money into the shattered region.[3]

With the worst of the famine in the past and much of the work focused on the Armenian Christians orphaned in the genocide, postwar aid work basked in the glow of a receptive public that was well fed by images of misery and the heartening tales of the humanitarians they funded.[4] At the time, publicists and journalists alike took the opportunity to cast the relief workers as benevolent white knights dedicated to raising the helpless, wretchedly suffering Syrians from their misery. Apart from a few negative reports in the press and some minor internally documented incidents of corruption and debauchery,[5] the luster of the missionary aid work provided pious Americans with a warm sense of Christlike accomplishment as they donated to relieve the biblical suffering that the war had brought to the Holy Land.

Initially, McGilvary's characterization of the dauntless self-sacrifice of the wartime humanitarians may not have been far off. Though retrospectives written about the famine ominously characterize the early months of the war with foreshadowing and grim portents, reports that were written in 1914 and 1915 reveal a mission community that was mostly naive to the horrors that would come and eager to help when it could. Even as the blockade, food shortages, and locusts brought mounting hardships in the first year of the conflict, the American missionaries and volunteers from the Syrian Protestant College remained optimistic in their correspondence. For them, the growing social malaise was tragic, but it also presented a unique opportunity to aid their neighbors from their position of privilege. As "modern missionaries," they could show the light of Christ through their deeds rather than by proselytization.[6] Their zeal was not necessarily selfish. Many of the Americans living in the region had either been born there or had lived there long enough to have developed a strong personal connection to their adopted homes and neighbors.

For those first few months, many of the foreign humanitarians were fresh faced, eager to help, and not a little proud of their initial achievements. In one especially radiant report written at the end of the first year of the crisis, George Doolittle declared, "Over against this appalling picture of suffering and want, of heartless cruelty, of bribery and corruption, of a nation's crucifixion on the cross of military absolutism, stands out in pure–white light the resplendent altruism of the American people."[7] William Jessup's 1915 report on the Beirut Station echoes this sentiment, noting that the Good Samaritans of the Beirut Mission community were "harrowed by the sorrows and anxious for the welfare of the people of Syria, with whom they deeply sympathize . . . we have a very real affection for them and their welfare."[8] In this relatively halcyon phase of the crisis, the missionaries reveled in the opportunity to lead by example, and perhaps even to augment their flock in the process.

However, optimism faded as the situation deteriorated. The work grew grim, and the humanitarians could not simply hide from the stressors of their daily lives because it was their job to expose themselves to suffering so that they might ameliorate it. And the suffering was terrible. Despite their hopeful initial reports, those who actually delivered famine aid during the war eventually found themselves in a situation that was quite different from the glamorous exercises in piety that were depicted in postwar literature. Although the humanitarians' lives were largely free from hunger and poverty, the futility of their efforts began to take a toll on their mental well-being. As the years passed, the ongoing work left many jaded and emotionally scarred. Those who worked in their own communities found themselves turning away those who had been friends or associates before the crisis. In the uneven humanitarian hierarchy of giver and receiver, those friends had become particularly vexing supplicants asking for help that the workers often could not deliver.[9] After years of trauma, vicarious suffering, and guilt, many of the aid workers admitted to developing a distant, coldly objective stance on aid and on those who needed it.

Though this chapter is ostensibly about relief work in the famine, it is not concerned with providing an overview of all relief work in the region, or even in assessing its effectiveness. To avoid redundancy in a topic that has been brilliantly covered from a variety of angles,[10] this chapter focuses on two groups of humanitarian workers in particular: the members of the Red Cross and the humanitarians from the American Mission. The often brutally honest contemporary letters and reports that the workers from the latter group in particular wrote during the war offer uniquely personal insight into the traumas of the job. This chapter tries to use those documents on humanitarian practice as a framework to better understand the effects of the crisis on those tasked with solving it and, moreover, to understand how the shifting constructs of poverty influenced aid work over the course of the famine, particularly with regard to ideas of worthiness.

The American humanitarian experience raises particularly interesting questions about the hierarchies between savior and saved, which McGilvary inadvertently highlights in her postwar pamphlet. Whether she was correct in claiming full credit for saving the whole region (she was not) may be less important than whether she was correct in how she characterized the power that humanitarians exercised over life and death during the famine. As providers of care in a deadly calamity, the workers were not merely handing out aid; they were specifically choosing who would live. To accomplish that, they defined those traits that made a person worthy of salvation . . . or not.[11] Triage is always an ethical problem because it requires people to make value judgments that have direct consequences for the health or even survival of both the ones chosen and the ones rejected. In a hospital emergency ward, this might mean weighing the relative urgency of a person's affliction to ensure that someone with a stab wound in the neck is treated before a person with a severely broken leg. One might save the former, but the latter may not walk again due to the delay. However, in the world of the famine, relative need was often also determined by values other than simple urgency or severity. The applicants had to prove *why* they should receive help—implicitly—over others. This was particularly apparent in the American humanitarians' unified relief policy from 1917, in which the need to ration aid intersected with both preexisting beliefs about worthiness and new famine-based constructs of poverty and suffering. For the American humanitarians, triage was not merely a practical necessity but a moral one as well. And in an era when poverty and suffering had become increasingly pejorative, the moralization of worthiness had consequences.

American Wartime Humanitarianism

McGilvary was very wrong about one thing: the Americans were not the only ones helping during the war. Most examples of crisis support during the famine were undoubtedly invisible examples of normal kinship, community, or patronage relationships in which family helped family or others in their circle. In times of crisis, the first level of aid was always local and familial until circumstances made such support impossible. It is no surprise that some of the larger aid projects that developed during the crisis were smaller local programs that expanded with private or government assistance (or both), as in the case of Beirut mayor ʻUmar Daʻuq's relief projects and the soup kitchen started by the Cortas family in Brummana. (Ironically, it was

McGilvary herself who transformed the memory of the Brummana kitchen from a local project into a missionary success story in her book.)[12] Religious organizations, private and religious charities, and social organizations took the lead in offering aid from the start, though like the aid that flowed from person to person, the declining circumstances within the famine caused a substantial drop in donations as the famine worsened. Since this infrastructure was already in place, local and regional leaders, including the reviled Jamal Pasha, often allocated additional funding to help them address their communities' needs. (An odd and very notable exception was the influential Sunni Maqasid foundation in Beirut, which was largely sidelined for political reasons during the war). Even the much-derided Ottoman administration had been offering assistance through existing charities as early as 1915. During the war, the state preferred to delegate relief because it lacked both the resources and the mechanisms to offer direct aid while it managed the ongoing war. However, in lieu of direct assistance, the state dispensed various forms of patronage through normal clientele networks and contributed to emergency assistance through the shelters, distribution centers, and work programs implemented by regional leaders, like Jamal Pasha and 'Azmi Bey, and local administrators.[13] Eventually, the state's preference for sparse indirect assistance became politically problematic, leading administrators like Jamal Pasha and 'Azmi Bey to finally expanded the state-driven programs in 1917. At that point in the famine, the programs were mostly cosmetic.[14]

Though it was not unique, the American aid work was an outlier among foreign outfits for several reasons. Apart from the Johanniter Hospital and other German humanitarian groups during the war,[15] most of the foreign-based organizations were tarred as agents of the Entente and shut down. Foreigners carrying the passports of belligerent nations were nearly all deported or relocated and, like the Jesuit Université Saint-Joseph in Beirut or the orphanage at 'Antoura, their facilities were confiscated for state use. Though they faced some harassment by the authorities, the American humanitarians benefited from the fact that the United States maintained a stance of tentative neutrality in the war until April 1917. Even after it entered the war, it refrained from opening hostilities with the Ottoman Empire thanks to the efforts of committed lobbyists of American institutions (who knew the consequences for their investments if the United States broke its neutrality). Bolstered by the American diplomatic stance, key figures like American consul Stanley Hollis and Syrian Protestant College president Howard Bliss cultivated strategic (and even warm) relationships with the Ottoman regional authorities, which ultimately allowed resident American institutions to endure the war in good standing. The Beirut Chapter of the American Red Cross even provided assistance to Ottoman troops on the Suez front in 1915 to demonstrate its good-faith service to anyone who needed it. For this, the state rewarded the Red Cross with permission to engage in relief work, sometimes even with its help. Some conflicts with Ottoman administrators were inevitable, of course. Humanitarian aid is inherently political, and some nationalistic Ottoman officials, like Beirut governor 'Azmi Bey, saw it as a zero-sum affair. However, by adjusting and adapting, the programs continued to function in some form from early 1915 throughout the war—and in some instances for years afterward as part of Near East Relief programs.[16] After the war, American aid was augmented by and at times competed with the more selective beneficence offered by the occupying French forces and their local allies, who sought to burnish their reputations in advance of their colonial allocation in the eventual peace deal.[17]

The legacy of American relief work in Lebanon and the province of Beirut during the war is somewhat more complicated than the congratulatory genre of postwar humanitarian-aid literature might suggest. Before American humanitarian groups began collaborating at the end of the war, aid was funneled through two main sources: the Beirut Chapter of the American Red Cross, headed by Consul Hollis and members of the Syrian Protestant College, and the Presbyterian American Mission. There was some natural overlap between the groups, which collaborated in a "joint relief committee" as early as December of 1916, but they each ran distinct projects during the war that only sometimes intersected.[18] It should be noted that though both factions were technically linked to religious institutions, the "humanitarian reason" driving the aid work at the time was not necessarily conversion (though some saw it as a potential bonus) but rather a concern over the correctness of action in a time of distress.[19] As such, the aid was mostly distributed without regard to sect, though Maronite leaders sometimes regarded the Americans warily due to their prior evangelical activity among their flock.

The Red Cross's affiliation with the American Consulate gave it some official diplomatic cover during the war, and it benefited from the personal relationship between college president Howard Bliss and Ottoman officials like Jamal Pasha. From January 1915 until aid operations were banned in the province upon the arrival of new governor ʿAzmi Bey in July, the Red Cross and the college's YMCA club conducted extensive work in Beirut, offering both direct aid distribution and a job program that employed men to repair terraces and destroy locust eggs after the swarm of April 1915.[20] After ʿAzmi's ban, the college community continued to offer subtle support through private distribution centers across the city and other aid that was cleverly sheltered to evade restrictions.[21] Such aid included a free pharmacy that was administered partly by the college's students[22] and the wasteland that the March family rented to the south of Ras Beirut to allow a few needy families to grow potatoes to support themselves.[23] The college as an entity had little latitude to directly assist the poor because it was provisioned at military rates by the Ottoman state. However, it did use its influence and institutions to benefit the community, including offering charitable admissions to its women's and children's hospital.[24]

The governor's ban more directly affected the Beirut Chapter of the Red Cross because it was solely a foreign aid organization. After its operations in Beirut ceased in 1915, it was invited to move its work to Mount Lebanon under the patronage of district governor ʿAli Munif Bey on the condition that it work with its Ottoman counterpart, the Ottoman Red Crescent. Ostensibly, this was to better coordinate aid, but it also ensured that the Americans did not outshine the state's own efforts.[25] This alliance with the Red Crescent was mutually beneficial, as it further augmented the Americans' political clout by linking them to the influential individuals connected to the Ottoman state, including the treasurer of Mount Lebanon, a Turkish professor from the college, and a respected judge from the mountain's Druze community, Muhammad Effendi Abu ʿIzzedine.[26] The American Mission was represented by George Doolittle, who was placed in charge of the relief bureau in the Lebanese government headquarters in Baʿabda.[27]

While some of the joint operations were marred by blatant corruption, including ʿAli Munif Bey's disastrous wheat distribution scheme,[28] the reputation of the Red Cross was apparently not tainted by its involvement. On the contrary, its soup kitchens and shelters in the central mountain towns of Hadath, ʿAley, ʿAbeih, ʿAinab, Suq al-Gharb, and especially Brummana were deemed resounding successes. At those sites, Syrian Protestant College professors Bayard Dodge and Arthur Dray helped to administer the relief work alongside local volunteers, students, and other members of the college community like Dr. Dikran Utidjian. Though I am loath to McGilvarize their roles, the importance of those two figures for the success of the projects cannot be understated. In addition to his college ties and apparently bottomless energy, Dodge's name also linked the projects to his father, the multimillionaire vice president of the Phelps Dodge Corporation, Cleveland Dodge, and thereby to Presbyterian capital in the United States. The dynamic Dray's influence was perhaps even more potent during the war. Not only was he fortuitously married to an Austrian noblewoman, but he secured the personal patronage of Jamal Pasha himself by providing emergency dental surgery for a mysterious Ottoman notable who had been wounded in an attempt on Jamal's life. This (worst-kept) secret procedure earned Jamal's official blessing for the shelters that Dray sponsored in Brummana, ʿAley, and Shweir, while also allowing Dray to cadge five months' supply of food at military rates to launch the operations.[29]

In contrast with the successful appeasement strategy used by the Red Cross and the college, the American Mission's attitude toward the Ottoman state was far more antagonistic. While many college staff members quietly objected to Howard Bliss's courting of the highly unpopular Jamal Pasha, they muted their criticisms far more than the workers of the American Mission, who wore their contempt for Ottoman authorities like a badge of honor. Although the mission stations ran soup kitchens and engaged in charitable work like the Red Cross, the crown jewel of the mission aid program was a controversial remittance smuggling operation that it conducted in defiance of Ottoman restrictions on foreign money transfers. Developed after Syrian Americans approached the American Mission's headquarters about crisis relief in 1916, the smuggling system eventually evolved into an ingenious manipulation of the Ottoman bureaucracy, harnessing global financial exchanges, international corporations, and local capital markets to funnel cash to the American Mission Press in Beirut, from whence it was distributed to recipients via mission employees and local networks.[30]

This provided an absolutely vital source of support for many people in the country who were otherwise cut off from normal sources of funding from abroad.

To circumvent restrictions on bank transfers into the Ottoman Empire, the missionaries capitalized on the piety of the Presbyterian oil tycoon John Rockefeller and the cephalopodic reach of his Standard Oil Company in the region. Checks from Syrian family members would be deposited with instructions for their disbursement with the mission headquarters in New York. The cash would then be transferred to Standard Oil's accounts and changed to lira through the New York Corn Bank at a market rate that varied from $4.60 to $2.78 to the lira (not counting conversion fees).[31] Standard Oil's Istanbul branch would be instructed to deposit lump sums in the name of the American Mission Press or its treasurer Charles Dana at various Ottoman institutions, including the Ottoman Post Office, the Tobacco Regié, the Ottoman Bank, and the Agricultural Bank, among others.[32] Dana would then stroll into one of these institutions and draw substantial sums on the press account, then leave with nobody the wiser. Based on the instructions sent separately from New York, that cash would then be secretly conveyed across the country by mission affiliates using ledgers that recorded both sums and intended recipients.[33] As the system evolved, the press was also able to offer interest-free loans using money that it took out locally in its own name, staking both its reputation and the deposits made in New York as collateral. By the end of the war, it had offered 403 loans totaling $89,372.66—or almost $1.75 million in 2022 dollars.[34] This was somewhat risky, as the press could have literally been holding the bag on vast amounts of debt had the loans not been repaid at the end of the war, but such support prevented many people from having to take usurious loans out from local lenders.[35]

Comprised of missionaries affiliated with a foreign power of dubious neutrality, the American Mission took a substantial risk with its illegal operations. Ottoman officials were justifiably fearful of Entente espionage and skeptical of American foreigners. Several members of the American Mission community (including prominent Lebanese Protestant, Asʿad Khairallah) became targets of the state in the war. The Tripoli Station's William Nelson was arrested for espionage in 1917 and deported for merely writing an offhanded remark about sensitive matters in a letter that was confiscated by a gendarme on the road to Beirut. Charles Dana and his niece (the one and only Margaret McGilvary) were also jailed and expelled for simply being the intended recipients.[36] Though the missionaries' fear was warranted, their concern for secrecy also produced a giddy embrace of cloak-and-dagger measures that they perhaps ill-advisedly relayed in reports generated for the Presbyterian Mission Board in America. For instance, rather than openly requesting the transfer of cash from the press, the satellite missions would note that they needed innocuous products like *dibs kharrub* (carob molasses), code for paper money, and Lyle's Golden Syrup, code for coin.[37] Similarly, when following the progress of an ill-fated aid ship between New York and Beirut, rather than mentioning the USS *Caesar* by name, they instead referred to the ship as "Calpurnia's husband," hoping that the censor was neither well-versed in Roman history nor perturbed by that awkward title. When the *Caesar* failed to arrive, the American Mission sent the following cryptic telegram: "Calpurnia's husband unable to make delivery. Can you duplicate amount your cable twenty ($100,000), enabling make purchases locally pending reaping (Stop). Reply, using only this cable number (37)." Dana was arrested for this missive, but he was released after (allegedly) convincing the authorities that Calpurnia was merely a woman who had been separated from her apparently fantastically wealthy husband.[38]

As clever as they believed they were, signs indicated that the local Ottoman authorities were well aware of the relief operations and sometimes even supported them. Although several individuals were arrested at various times for conducting illicit aid—including the redoubtable Mary Dale, the American hospital's superintendent of nursing and sister of college president Howard Bliss—some of the authorities knowingly cast a blind eye toward American programs. In January 1918 the press reported that the Ottoman authorities were "friendly" to their distribution scheme when people flocked around its headquarters to receive remittances,[39] and some officials even took part in the aid or conspired with the missionaries. Prominent local leaders and *mukhtars* (local political heads) were instrumental in disbursing remittances to remote areas. At one point, officials in charge of inspecting the American Mission properties in Sidon subtly informed the Americans in advance of their visit and even suggested that some items be hidden and excluded from official inventories in case a second inspection was conducted by other, less deliberately neglectful agents.[40] The Sidon Station even received 720 kilograms of wheat from the governor at a fifth of the market rate, which allowed it to continue its operations in 1917.[41]

The remittance operation was a qualified success. Between February and November of 1918 alone, it helped to bring $298,298.90 from New York to family members back in the region—the equivalent of $5,837,709.47 in 2022.[42] Though vast sums flowed through the system, many of the payments never found their intended targets. In May of 1916, a letter from Paul Erdman showed that $11,390.95 of the Zahle Station's remittances had been collected, $27,601 had gone uncollected, and $13,807 was still pending—meaning that at that time, 78 percent of the remittances were not (yet) issued.[43] It was sometimes quite difficult to find people in the chaotic wartime environment; in many cases the intended recipients had died or migrated. It is probable that most failures were innocent mistakes or glitches in a complicated process. The lists themselves caused havoc because the identifying Arabic language details of the recipients were recorded by the untrained ears and hands of American secretaries in New York. Their transliterations of local names and places had to be successfully decoded before payments could be dispatched to intended recipients. George Doolittle recalled that when the American Mission Press requested an inquiry into a payment for a "Nochela Tonnuse Ossite in Nebite," the American Mission scoured maps until it found a Nebite near Sidon. But the actual recipient turned out to be Nachle Tannous Assad in Nabye, Matn—halfway across the mountain from Nebite.[44]

Because of such honest failures and some unwise actions on the part of the press itself, the mission and its workers were accused of corruption and embezzlement several times. Sometimes this was not entirely their fault, like when local brokers skimmed remittances they were supposed to deliver[45] or when recipients objected to the loss of value that inevitably took place when converting or transmitting the cash. Still, even the missionaries themselves were not immune to the confusion that the highly fluid economic situation often produced. W. S. Nelson in Tripoli wrote in 1916 that because he was unaware that the Ottoman currency had fallen to 124 piasters to the lira from its original value of 108 piasters, he had paid out two-thirds of the station's remittances at the original value, only to have to pay out the remaining third at the weaker rate. Those who received the reduced payments were understandably upset.[46] Paul Erdman from the Lebanon Station in Zahle wrote several letters to Dana outlining the difficulties posed by the internal Ottoman exchange rate in early 1916. In March he complained that converting paper to coin in order to provide remittances in smaller denominations cost him 25 percent of its value, and in April 1916 when the authorities arbitrarily fixed the value of the flagging paper currency at 100 piasters per lira, he scrambled to get 80 percent of its value in the town.[47] The American Mission itself took on significant risk with this voluntary activity, as well as significant debt. By 1917, missionary correspondence indicated that some of the individual stations were broke. George Doolittle's Sidon Station carried a four thousand-lira debt by November 1917.[48]

American aid from both the Red Cross and the American Mission began to taper around April of 1917 after the United States entered the war, but this trend was reversed by late 1917 as administrative decisions in America brought more certainty to the funding situation. The American Mission was promised $200,000 in October 1917 and managed to spend $97,127.29 before fully joining forces with the Red Cross in the American Relief Committee later in the year. Once the two united, the promise of $150,000 by the Presbyterian Mission Board in America allowed the joint committee to effectively plan work for the most terrible year of the famine.[49] Between February and November of 1918, the committee spent a total of $530,000 in the region—the equivalent of $10,372,000 in 2022 dollars.[50]

Despite the volume of aid and its undoubted value to its recipients, the memory of the American humanitarian work in Lebanon is decidedly mixed. The neutrality and impartial support delivered by the Syrian Protestant College boosted its reputation and even defined part of the college's identity when it became the American University of Beirut in 1920. Its main gate is still engraved with the quote from John 10:10 "That they may have life, and have it more fully"—a motto intended to be read both figuratively and literally. Despite their efforts and the benefit that they provided, the American Mission's operations generated skepticism. Charles Dana was perhaps the most common target of opprobrium by missionaries and Lebanese alike until his deportation to Istanbul alongside McGilvary in 1917. At one point, W. S. Nelson sent a series of hectoring letters to Dana about aid work in 1916, one of which ended by commenting, "Your silences are getting to be almost overwhelming, tho [*sic*] you will not take offence if I say they are hardly golden."[51] Doolittle similarly chided him for his reluctance to pay fair wages or offer assistance to struggling mission employees, pointedly stating, "This is a job for the Good Samaritan, not for the bank accountant or the lawyer."[52] This sentiment was echoed by nurse Affeffi Saba in a 1916 letter about the condition of the poorly paid laborers who had been contracted to construct a road for the Hamlin Sanatorium as a charitable project.[53] Dana's alleged use of the press's cash holdings to acquire land at discounted rates was also problematic and poorly timed given the community's sensitivity to such criticism following the (ungrounded) controversies surrounding Asʿad Khairallah, who was accused of land speculation in 1917.[54] Though Khairallah was vindicated, Dana's legacy seems to have stuck. When I asked the renowned historian of Lebanon (and Protestant) Kamal Salibi about Dana, he mainly recalled his reputation as a crook, an embezzler, and a land speculator. While this may merely be seen as further anecdotal evidence for the maxim that no good deed goes unpunished, there was apparently enough discontent among the missionary community that an anonymous writer (who I presume to be Margaret McGilvary, based on the style) submitted a brief but vehement report denying accusations to the Presbyterian Mission Board,[55] and George Doolittle felt compelled to defend the relief workers in his own postwar account.[56]

Both the hyperbole and the controversy about the American aid work is somewhat unfortunate because it was effective within its own limits. Famine specialist Alex de Waal has made the point that even the best humanitarian programs fail to meet their targets,[57] and the aid was undoubtedly a substantial help those who received it. In the absence of effective state intervention, humanitarian programs offered a lifeline for many who had no place left to turn. Even in places where numbers were small (in 1917 correspondence, it was noted that 350 people were receiving aid in ʿAbeih, 50 in Shimlan, and 300 in Suq al-Gharb and its vicinity),[58] those people might have died without the help. Postwar tallies of the various American programs suggest that thousands, perhaps even tens of thousands, were assisted through direct aid programs, shelters, workshops, and soup kitchens, and that over 30,000 more benefited from the loans and the $500,000 to $2,000,000 in remittances smuggled through the American Mission Press from Syrians and Lebanese abroad.[59]

It is clear that McGilvary overstates her point in her pamphlet. American aid no more saved the whole Syrian nation than Turkish perfidy doomed it. But it is also clear that without the American projects, circumstances would have been far worse for thousands of people across the region.

A Famine of Faith

I refer to the Americans as "humanitarians," but aid work was often just an additional duty added to their normal day jobs. Even during the famine, the lives of the temporary aid workers continued to revolve around teaching, administrative work, and their duties as religious leaders. Nevertheless, for the missionaries in particular, the lines between humanitarian duties and pastoral ones were often somewhat blurred. While this did not cause them to discriminate to whom they delivered aid (at least by faith), it did lead to frustrations that they detailed in their reports and correspondence with the Presbyterian Mission Board in America. Such accounts provide unique, and often unintentionally honest, insights into perceptions of the famine and its human consequences throughout the war.

The famine's initial effects were regarded as a boon by several missionaries. In his 1915 report for the Sidon Station, George Scherer celebrates a rise in conversions, writing, "Undoubtedly the troubles which the people have been experiencing have driven them to God."[60] This did not last long, however. After the first year, church attendance lagged, attentions drifted, and the famine increasingly diverted the efforts of the missionaries and their flocks. Later reports dismissed falling participation as an effect of the war, because sickness, poverty, government interference, or even the need to guard crops from theft kept people at home.[61] As the famine deepened, the missionaries sensed a growing disillusionment with faith and even with God in general. In his 1916 report from the American Mission's Tripoli Station, Arthur Fowler acknowledges the terrible social ills that the city faced but expresses irritation that widespread "despair" had not pushed the suffering into the arms of God as a means of "deliverance." He complains that people seemed more concerned about how to obtain remittance money from America than about "how to get eternal riches from Heaven."[62] Fowler ends his overview of the spiritual situation in Tripoli with two revealing statements. The first is little more than a formality typical of such reports, but it is framed with a dehumanizing sort of pity: "Let us pray to Him with an intensity and a faith that we have not yet known that He will show us how to present the Gospel to these poor dying creatures that they shall turn to Him in repentance." The next hints at his own frustrations at what he saw as a failure to capitalize on the situation: "One feels that it would be comparatively easy for us to stand the oppression and the burden of physical misery, were we but surrounded by souls turning to God and asking the way of salvation."[63]

Like many of his peers, Fowler capitulated in the end. In a subsequent report written in late 1916, he admits that he "could hardly blame" the parishioners for their inactivity but that he also felt as though the failures of the community had rendered his report "unsatisfactory."[64] Reports indicate that a number of the missionaries similarly grew to accept the trend as a natural consequence of the crisis. The writer of the 1918 report of the American Mission's abandoned Lebanon Station in Zahle (penned after the start of the Entente occupation) explained: "Quite generally, the bodily needs so engrossed the attention of all that the soul needs were very generally left aside. Where whole villages were left and people migrated in the hope of getting a meager living, it is perhaps no wonder if many, not to say most, dropped out of mind every interest but that of food."[65] Another report on the situation in Tripoli in 1917 concurs: "It was not found easy to instill any great amount of spiritual instruction, since, on their arrival, [the needy] were too hungry to give close attention; and when they had received their pittance they were eager to go on their way in search of something more for the [sic] emaciated bodies."[66]

As conditions declined and the famine worsened, missionaries began dismissing proselytization altogether in their reports. The Sidon Station report from 1918 notes that "many people turned away from God saying, 'God has turned his face from us God has left us.'"[67] Similar observations are made in the 1917 Lebanon Station 1917 report, which judges that the religious life in Zahle's mission school "left a great deal to be desired."[68]

The anonymous author of the 1917 report of the Lebanon Station (in what appears to be Paul Erdman's handwriting) openly repudiated typical evangelism as useless when compared to the value of aid work. He wrote: "At this time when so much of conventional Christianity proves ineffective and life is [gauged] by material standards and by deeds, even more than commonly . . . a demonstration of Christian work is perhaps as valuable if not more valuable than the spoken word. Certainly the latter seems to carry all too little weight in these troublous times."[69] The surprisingly frank (and anonymous) report of Tripoli Station in 1918 suggests that even the missionaries themselves were not altogether convinced of their own words or of the forthcoming mercy of God. It reads: "If even the thought of doubt entered our heart, we may be sure that it was very strong in the hearts of the poor dirty hungry creatures who were listening as if to a fairy tale."[70]

These comments on growing faithlessness came at the same time that people across society began lodging social judgments about the poor and their desperate attempts to survive the crisis. For the missionaries, the two issues overlapped: they sought to understand the impoverished, suffering people around them—and how to attach value to their behaviors. The missionary correspondence places value on those who struggled in vain and died nobly in pious misery, unlike those who experienced the famine from within, for whom adaptation and sacrifice are often depicted as indications of moral strength. In the Beirut Station report of 1917 and 1918, missionaries laud the tragic deeds of a man named Aneese Fayadh, who sold scraps of scripture to passersby to feed himself and his two companions until he finally succumbed to hunger and exposure.[71] Such stories are presented as examples of upright morality to give value to the deaths of individuals who had, in the missionaries' minds, persevered and stayed true to their spiritual duties at a time when so many others transgressed in order to prolong their lives. Indeed, those who compromised their moral character to ignobly eke out a living presented a problem for the missionaries. Since their duties during the famine had shifted to include emergency relief, the famine's insidious impact on behaviors and values created a conflict between their professional obligation to save the souls of the poor and their newfound obligation to save their lives.

The Problem of Triage

One of the most difficult and ethically problematic duties for any of the relief work programs during the famine was determining how and whom to help, particularly as the famine worsened and funding grew unpredictable. While some charities gave freely until their coffers were empty,[72] the American aid organizations strategically rationed aid to avoid having to withdraw support because of a funding shortfall. And the aid was not cheap. At the famine's peak prices in the summer of 1918, Bayard Dodge estimated that it cost $7–$9 a week to sustain a single person—the equivalent of $135–$174 in 2022.[73] The cost of running Arthur Dray's immense relief network in Brummana for thirty months was $180,000,[74] whereas the cost of Dodge's more modest series of shelters and his collaborative agriculture project with Druze landlords in the Chouf district totaled $27,000.[75] In 2022, Dodge's programs would have cost over half a million dollars, while Dray's would have exceeded $3.6 million. For the time, such outlays are remarkable, especially since the soup kitchens were considered a more sustainable way to deliver aid thanks to high prices and transportation difficulties.

With funding tight and demand high, both American organizations implemented a strict triage system. For each person helped by the American Mission or the Red Cross, dozens, if not hundreds, of others had to be turned away to ensure that the relief was sustainable over the course of the war. While their policies ensured the survival of their programs, the selection process required rigid criteria to ensure that those who received the scarce support were the ones who *should* receive it. In the depths of the famine, this triage process ultimately assessed not just who would receive aid; it defined who was worthy of living.

Initially, the missionaries were relatively permissive. In 1915, the Tripoli Station's Arthur Fowler wrote, "Being only finite, we probably erred more than once, sometimes on the side of mercy in helping the very needy whom we considered comparatively worthless and sometimes on the side of justice in helping the unfortunate but worthy ones who perhaps did not need our aid quite so much."[76] As time passed, the need to ration funds, the high demand for aid, and the effects of conducting triage over the years of the famine demanded clear guidelines to determine whom would be helped. In this system, candidates were rated based not only their neediness but also on their worthiness to determine who qualified as "deserving objects of humanitarianism."[77] As a result, the "worthless" who may have been helped in 1915 would not receive aid in 1917—if they survived that long.

Just who might be worthy of salvation was explicitly outlined by the joint American Relief Committee in late 1917. The adopted plan provided a comprehensive set of guidelines and a system of investigation that evaluated the applicants to ensure that aid was distributed to those whom they deemed to be the right people. The policy was:

1. To select those most "deserving" of aid. Reasons to be excluded included having an "evil disease" (undoubtedly meaning syphilis, which was rampant), being a confirmed beggar, or rejecting "suitable work." While typhus and malaria sufferers could be helped, "helpless cripples" and those who were a burden to caretakers were labeled unworthy.[78]

2. To aid only those who would survive the war. This may have eliminated those suffering from acute starvation and possibly the elderly.

3. To "personally" ensure the worthiness of applicants to prevent local leaders from adding unworthy names (either corruptly or out of compassion). While a vetting system had been in place since 1915, the stakes were far higher by the end of 1917.

4. To prioritize children and to distribute food on-site to maintain control over who received aid.

5. To give food instead of money (however, there was a pilot program that distributed cash assistance at the end of the war).

6. To provide scarce medicine and a special diet to those suffering from malaria.

7. To offer clothing that had been produced in shelter workhouses to those who needed it.[79]

The criteria for receiving aid accounted for merit and need, but the technicalities ultimately privileged certain classes of recipients over others. Instead of seeking to preserve the helpless, the policy deliberately excluded those whose physical or perceived moral characteristics rendered them unworthy. This meant that the policy excluded the chronically poor, who would have been more likely to commit disqualifying acts of desperation to survive until 1917. Byerly makes this explicit in his report, noting that as the economic crisis worsened and members of the middle classes began to sink into poverty, the American Mission started making exceptions to aid those from the "best classes" whom they deemed "more deserving of help."[80] Ultimately, the aid policy looked as much to the future as it did to the present: as Byerly writes in his 1918 report on Sidon Station, the policy aimed to ensure that after the war they would not "find that the worthless had survived the worthy."[81]

The humanitarian attitude toward the impoverished (and toward society at large) was especially evident in two aspects of their relief strategy. The first was their distrust of the needy. The preference for food aid over cash was an implicit critique of the judgment of the poor, who might be tempted to spend on items that would provide emotional comfort beyond their bare subsistence. Other mission reports confirm this attitude. Byerly's justification for the investigation board provides another example, as it was explicitly designed as a check against "deceitful" (or sympathetic) local leaders who might add those deemed less worthy or the elderly to their lists. (Note: the issue is complicated, but current thinking among certain humanitarian experts has been less critical of direct aid to local actors, as they are most aware of their own problems.)[82] This was particularly evident in the preference for on-site distributions to children, which writers note was a way to keep parents from taking the food or sharing it among the family. Paradoxically, this policy clashed with the aim to save whole families because it risked a scenario wherein children survived while their parents starved to death in front of them.

The second, and far more serious, aspect was the assignment of relative values to individuals in the crisis—in biblical terms, separating the sheep from the goats. Judith Butler has argued that our willingness to protect a particular "body" depends on how we define whether a life is worth living, preserving, or even being mourned when it passes.[83] Although such classifications were often rooted in general beliefs and ideologies that predated the war, many of the conceptual frameworks that the Americans used to determine the value of the poor were products of the very horrors that their work sought to address. As previous chapters have shown, shifting attitudes about the impoverished increasingly devalued their bodies and redefined them as a dependent, often dangerous out-group in famine society. Though Fowler's use of the terms *worthless* and *creatures* in his correspondence may appear to be innocent slips of the pen, they are indicative of the revaluation of humanity that was common in that time of perceived moral and social collapse.

At a time when writers openly depicted society in collapse, the terminology that the humanitarians used in their correspondence was significant. As humanitarian expert Tammam Aloudat has written, the language of relief first "defines the field of action, humanitarianism, and draws its parameters, principles, and tactics; second, it justifies and moralises the act itself and asserts the legitimacy of its existence and consequences; and third, it sustains the power, worldview, and future of those who control the narrative."[84] In a situation like the famine wherein triage relied on not only technical but moral factors as well, such definitions were clear value judgments. Using vague terms like *evil* to describe illness moralized aid, using its refusal as a cudgel to punish someone who was already suffering. Likewise, placing "helpless cripples" or those who were a "burden" to others into the excluded list made physical defects into fatal flaws. The missionaries readily acknowledged the life-and-death implications of these decisions, using verbs like *save* to describe their relief work rather than neutral terms like *assist*.

The relief workers considered such policies to be consistent, and even necessary, with the underlying aim of their mission, given the terrible task that faced them. Still, the fact that many who voiced concerns about the decline of society were the same people tasked with managing the crisis suggests that such attitudes inevitably biased the selection process in favor of members of more sympathetic social groups. This made the selection criteria more than a justification for aid; it was a judgment about the very quality of the beneficiaries' humanity. Such attitudes were also evident in the creation of workshops in conjunction with the shelters. Workshops were partly a pragmatic cost-saving measure, but they also reflected prevailing Protestant attitudes about making the poor work for their keep. Contemporary reports proudly proclaim that the workshops sought to inculcate a sense of duty and diligence in the women and children in their care—whether they wished for it or not.[85] As the policy states, a refusal to perform "suitable" work was a criterion for denying aid. Such practices indicate that American humanitarian aid ultimately sought not only to save but also to "remoralize" the poor by using the conditional distribution of relief to encourage productive behaviors, thereby eradicating mendicancy in the country.[86] By stipulating that those who would be saved must meet a moral standard that could only reasonably be achieved by those of a certain social status, the burden of weighing need and worthiness was somewhat lessened. But this came at a cost. The needy, because of their very desperation, would be less likely to remain worthy, leaving the aid to those who, while worthy, ultimately needed it less. As a result, those who were regarded as social deadwood would be left to die in order to save the younger, educated, and more vital members of society, who would presumably form the nucleus of a bright postfamine future. Though we might be horrified by the social engineering inherent in the 1917 policy, for the humanitarians, such conditions were entirely logical outgrowths of the attitudes toward poverty and the moral collapse of society that had circulated since the crisis began to worsen.

The logic of the decision-making process should not diminish the inevitable human factor of triage, which was especially poignant given the terrible traumas that the relief work inflicted on the humanitarians. It is not uncommon for the "raw emotions" of humanitarian administrators to trickle into the logic of their planning processes.[87] This would have been especially likely in the famine, during which such frontline care workers held the lives of hundreds, even thousands, of people in their hands. Like present-day humanitarians, their work would have placed them at an elevated risk of psychological distress and burnout.[88] However, unlike humanitarians of today, the relief workers during the war were amateurs thrust into a crisis for which they had no training or ethical preparation. The situations they endured were harrowing, and with no institutional or professional support to relieve them, they were forced to weather the traumas of their work alone.

The Burden of Relief

The words of the workers themselves indicate just how raw those emotions could be. If we compare George Doolittle's description of relief work in his unpublished 1920 retrospective "Pathos and Humor in the Wartime Years in Syria" to his earlier reports, it becomes readily apparent that the optimism he exuded in 1915 became yet another victim of the famine by 1918. In contrast to McGilvary's effusive praise of the humanitarian efforts, Doolittle wrote that the "service" that aid workers provided was in the end a thankless, Sisyphean task that extracted a deep emotional toll. He noted that over time they found themselves under "a tremendous sympathetic strain, growing more and more intense as the years dragged on, because they were waging a losing fight against famine, nakedness, disease and death,—against injustice, oppression, brutality and robbery,—'against the rulers of the darkness of this world!'"[89] An anonymous report from the Beirut Station in 1919 similarly shows a dramatic shift away from the warmth of William Jessup's empathetic 1915 missive. Complaining that relief work consumed most of the missionaries' time, the writer dourly wrote, "The sight of many dying on the streets from starvation and disease and the constant cries of 'juaan—juaan' (hungry, hungry) have given us such nervous and physical wear and tear that no one has been up to normal strength and capacity."[90] Such comments not only show the complex humanity that tends to disappear in more congratulatory retrospective accounts; they also indicate a darker side of humanitarianism and its impacts on those who directed famine relief.

The traumas that workers faced were incredible. In a February 1917 diary entry, Edward Nickoley observed that in the soup kitchens, "there is more evidence of distress and suffering . . . than there is on any battle field, I am sure."[91] He was probably right. Workers confronted the visual horrors of the late stages of starvation and, perhaps more poignantly, had to witness the intense emotional pain of those who had already lost everything. In a postwar report, Bayard Dodge empathetically defined the essence of famine by what horrified him the most—the futile struggle of parents trying to save their families. He wrote, "Unless you have heard the wailing of little children in your ears for days at a time and seen weeping mothers clasping their dying babies in their arms; unless you have talked with strong men, whose shoes are worn in a vain search for work and whose brows are knit with worry and despair, you can hardly realize what starvation means."[92]

Time only worsened the cumulative, corrosive effect that other people's suffering had on the workers. Despite their best efforts to be stolid bureaucrats, the human face of their work often overwhelmed the emotional barriers that the workers had erected to guard themselves from the misery that surrounded them. While in theory the relief policies that assessed an applicant's worthiness should have alleviated some of their guilt by bureaucratizing their responsibility, in practice, the burden of triage still had terrible emotional consequences for the humanitarians. In the introduction to his wartime retrospective, Frederick Bliss recalled one such choice almost as a penance for his own inaction, writing, "Was <u>she</u> real, that brave little woman, once tough and wiry, still fighting starvation with incredible energy, who dragged herself to our house and, stabbing me with her dying eyes, said 'I have no one but God and you: don't <u>you</u> let me die.'" Bliss, racked with guilt, openly admitted to his audience that he had failed her.[93]

Even if a form of triage was obviously necessary, this responsibility did not sit well with several of the aid workers, who commented on their discomfort at casting judgments on their fellow human beings, dooming men, women, and children to terrible deaths. Bliss revealed that "it was terrible to assist consciously in the carrying out of the law of the Survival of the Fittest. We felt like Octavius, Antony, and Lepidus 'pricking' those whom we doomed to die by eliminating them from the list of those whom it seemed wise to help."[94] Even McGilvary wrote that despite the logic of the criteria, making choices that privileged one individual over another was "usurping a divine prerogative."[95]

At times, the empathetic burden was so much that the logic of the triage collapsed under its own weight. In one devastating story, a starving mother approached Arthur Dray at the end of a long, difficult day and begged him to take her five children into his Brummana orphanage before she died. Distracted by work and undoubtedly exhausted, Dray initially resisted. He would have fielded that question many times a day and was apparently rushing to conclude his work so he could return home to Beirut. She persisted. Frustrated, he began to negotiate, telling her that the orphanage was full and that he could only accept two of her children. She would have to choose. Panicking, she agonized over the choice until she finally settled on the two she would save. George Doolittle noted that at this point, "a little tot, just old enough to appreciate that he had been left out, clung to her thin skirts and grasped her hand and asked, 'oh mother, take *me!*'"[96] Dray became emotionally distraught once he realized that he had just forced a mother to choose death for three of the only people she had left in the world. He crumbled. He assured the mother that he could take them all, then guiltily handed her a ticket to a shelter in Beirut. On his walk home, he discovered that her premonition about her own condition was tragically correct. She lay dead a few hundred yards down the road.[97]

While Bliss and Dray provide examples of both the hardness that the work demanded and the empathy that it inspired, other reports indicate that the moralization of suffering in the crisis had left the humanitarians emotionally disconnected from those who depended upon them. The once-empathetic William Jessup supplied two such cases. The Sidon Station report from 1917–18 describes Jessup's encounter with a single mother in the mountains who was trying to pry the window shutters off her house. He approached her and asked what she was doing, to which she explained that she going to sell the shutters to buy food for what remained of her starving family. When Jessup inquired why she would disassemble her house when winter was coming, she darkly replied, "What use is a house if we had no food to keep us alive?"[98] His question seemed less earnest than judgmental, and the answer was just as sharp. The deliberate choice of this anecdote for the report is interesting. Certainly, Jessup was not so naive, and the anecdote was chosen to demonstrate the degree of desperation in the mountain for the benefit of those safely back at the Presbyterian Mission Board in America. But we must also confront the nagging question of whether this story was also an unintended demonstration of the missionaries' frustration with those who they dealt with on a daily basis.

This frustration and the moral imperative it provided is evident in a second report featuring Jessup—this one concerning his follow-up visit with one of the few families receiving a weekly $1.50 cash distribution to supplement their income. At the time, the value of the dollar against the lira was roughly $3.50 to one, which would have placed the amount of the stipend at roughly 43 piasters per week, or 2,228 piasters per year. Amid soaring costs in the famine, this was not much, but it would have dramatically improved the quality of life for a family in need.[99] During his interview, Jessup found that the family had spent all of one week's distribution on *kibbeh*,[100] a normally common dish that had been transformed into a luxurious treat by the soaring costs of meat, bulghur, and pine nuts. Scandalized, Jessup scolded the father for his wasteful use of the American Mission's money. Certainly, *kibbeh* was food, but had the family chosen to spend the money on lentils or some bland carbohydrate, their budget would have stretched further. For Jessup, the issue was one of principle. Since the mission's assistance was justified by the family's need and worthiness, to choose to indulge on one meal because it tasted good rather than suffering on a bare-subsistence diet made them seem less needy—perhaps even less worthy.[101]

Both encounters demonstrate the disconnect between Jessup's vicarious experience of famine suffering and how those who actually lived the famine understood it. For Jessup, the famine was horrible, but it was ultimately someone else's problem that he was tasked with solving. Because of this, Jessup saw the shutters and the *kibbeh* only in functional terms—they were mechanisms of survival, and the more the better. However, for a family that had lost so much, the food provided more than just nutrition; it was a source of comfort in a time of fear and uncertainty.[102] To Jessup's paternalistic chagrin, neither the woman with the shutters nor the father was moved by his righteous indignation. Instead, the father replied that "we have longed for *kibbeh* and the Lord will provide."[103] The very fact that the family was receiving aid undoubtedly gave them the security to purchase food that would bring welcome normalcy to their lives. While Jessup's perspective on the issue focused on the practical matter of sustainability, the father was concerned with providing the illusion of the everyday to his family in their time of need. One can see his point: Who could tell if they would survive to see the next payment? Should his family subsist in misery to satisfy the rigid demands of a relatively well-fed foreign missionary?

Whatever their intent, such parables inadvertently highlight the uneven relations of power between those in need and those who had gained the power to decide matters of life or death in the famine. We may find ourselves sympathetic to the suffering of the aid workers but also suspicious about the influence that the famine may have had on their work. Relief documents demonstrate the same noticeable shifts in the ways that poverty and human suffering were perceived across society at the time, but the humanitarians offer acute demonstrations of how attitudes could extend beyond mere abstract concepts. When applied to humanitarianism or government policy, such constructs defined who was to live—and who was left to die.

CONCLUSION

An Uncomfortable Memory

> We have long patched over the "missing things" in our lives with placeholders for an imagined future, when the phrase "This is Lebanon" is no longer spoken in resignation, but with a sense of pride.
> —RIMA RANTISI

TIME, AS IS ITS WONT, has gradually whittled down the number of famine eyewitnesses to zero. Their absence has left us with little more than a collection of fraying documents, secondhand sources, popular mythologies, and familial stories through which to understand a period that was neglected for decades—sometimes deliberately so. As personal memories have been exchanged for collective ones, the shape of the famine as a remembered event has also changed, settling into a timeline of commonly recognized tropes and anecdotes that give the disaster its familiar form in the minds of those who hear and tell about it. At this point, the famine exists as a complex idea—a "sum total" of the components that make up the shared memories of the era.[1] The idea of the famine might vary from person to person based on what they have learned at home and in school, but in general, the narrative of the era follows standard plot lines, includes a consistent cast of characters, and offers similar historical judgments. For many who grew up in Lebanon, the mere mention of the famine summons images of Jamal Pasha, locusts, starvation, and all of the facts and factoids that accompany them. Such memories are not neutral. They carry the meanings that have been given to them, and, like any good narrative, there are often morals and judgments hidden beneath their grim plotlines.

Perhaps nothing has done more for the remembrance of the famine than the centennial of the Great War itself. The rediscovery of the horrors of the crisis led scholars, journalists, and artists to resurrect the disaster for popular and scholarly consumption alike. Public exhibitions brought photo archives and archival documents to the public eye for the first time, and both books and academic conferences have injected needed complexity into the public understanding of the era. Perhaps the most beautiful example of this is Yazan Halwani's stunning *Memory Tree* statue, which he unveiled in central Beirut in 2018 to collectivize the memory of the famine. Halwani's installation is both visually and emotionally arresting, made all the more so because of the symbolic choices he made in its design. Rather than choosing the shape of the famous cedar trees of Mount Lebanon, Halwani fashioned his sculpture after the pines that flank the statue—trees that grow ubiquitously throughout the foothills and peaks of the whole nation, not merely in the isolated upper reaches of the much-afflicted mountain. The tree is adorned with golden calligraphic leaves formed from quotes about the crisis. They are the literal memories of those artists and writers who shared the famine with the world. The words focus not only on the dead, who provide us with the incentive to remember, but also on the living voices that, as Halwani notes, "carried the whispers of the past" to shape the memories of the present.[2] Most important, it is a memorial that all Lebanese are able to share, much like their ancestors shared in suffering and survival a century before.

Certainly, a sober approach to the era is entirely expected and understandable. For many among the nation's Maronite population in particular, the troubled memory of the war is a source of historical trauma that, like a genocide or the tragic famines in nineteenth-century Ireland and India, is both a source of pain and a touchstone of a communal identity. Anything but somber reverence and deference to the victims could easily appear dismissive of the pains of the past or reminiscent of the famine denialism that critics of the French mandate deployed in the war's aftermath. However, there is a curious paradox about even such august and respectful commemorations: sympathetic tributes, too, are inherently extensions of the discourses of decline and victimization that transformed the era from one of collective loss and suffering to one of collective shame in the eyes of social critics.

This is not a new problem for famine commemorations. Youssef Hoyek's original statue dating to 1930 features a Muslim and Christian mother collectively mourning the loss of their children in a decidedly feminized representation of shared suffering and sacrifice. Though the sentiment is unifying and beautiful, the historian Melanie Tanielian cites one critic in particular who objected to the fact that the statue "symbolized tears and resignation rather than courage and heroism," with one writer even opining that the "disgrace" of the era should be collectively forgotten, not commemorated.[3] The statue was eventually targeted by vandals and later replaced by the far more kinetic bronze memorial cast by Italian artist Marino Mazzacurati, which lionizes the political martyrs who were executed in the square by Jamal Pasha in 1916. Mazzacurati's statue does not so much represent loss as it does defiance in the face of oppression, perhaps recalling Muhammad al-Mahmassani's moving repudiation of his Turkish executioners from the very gallows that would end him.[4] This memorial was far more in line with the nation's masculine ideal—perhaps even more so after it was riddled with bullets during the nation's traumatic fifteen-year civil war. (I should note that Hoyek's statue in its exile offers a remarkable example of collective forgetting or forgiveness seeking, as it has found a final home in the Sursuq Palace—the iconic seat of the merchant family that was most associated with wartime profiteering in the collective memory of the era).

Even when the victimhood narrative sought to portray the sufferers of the famine sympathetically, it often spoke for or over those who endured the crisis from within. In doing so, it implicitly (and sometimes explicitly) essentialized the famine and its sufferers, leaving them tainted by the pejorative associations with starvation. Their victimhood marked them, and by extension, the nation, with weakness and shame. However, there is one curious popular work that rejects the usual focus on suffering as the central theme of famine memory—director Henri Barakat's 1967 alternate-history film set in the Great War, *Safar Barlik*.[5] Written by the famed Rahbani brothers as a conduit for Fairuz's white-hot star power in the late 1960s, the film pits the noble protagonist 'Adla and her archetypical Lebanese village against an oppressive Ottoman army unit that threatens their existence while attempting to suppress a local resistance movement. There is little subtlety to the film. From her very name to the actress who portrays her, 'Adla is meant to represent the innocent purity and resilience of the Lebanese people.[6] The resistance group represents local defiance against the forces of oppression and death (a theme that seems so absent in historical accounts of the war), and the oppressive Ottomans represent the . . . oppressive Ottomans—or at least the villainous conception of the Ottomans that dominated the Lebanese popular memory of the era. The Turkish military unit contains a who's-who of bad guy stock characters, including the nefarious mustachioed officer who serves as the main antagonist, a few lumpy naïfs inserted to make the once-fearsome oppressors into fools, and the requisite action-film extras whose sole function is to move about frantically in uniform and fire ineffectually until they are vanquished by the heroes.

The film's plot alludes to many familiar wartime tropes, but with a few creative twists. When the Ottomans occupy the town to target the resistance group, they cut off the transportation of grain—recalling the Ottoman "occupation" of Mount Lebanon and the "blockade" of food coming into the district. Contrary to the historical record, the whole community in the film chooses to collectively resist, defying both death and repression to save the town. For the rebel group, the resistance is overt and violent, but the writers also portray the villagers themselves as clever and resourceful in their ploy to subvert the blockade and smuggle in life-saving grain. To evade the Ottoman cordon, the villagers hold a wedding in the town center to distract the soldiers while a number of the men guide a mule train loaded with wheat through the village rear. When the muleteers find the bridge blocked by a Turkish guard, the sole local conscript, Sleiman, chooses loyalty to his village and nation over duty to his unit and empire, tricking his fellow solider into relinquishing his post and then allowing the smugglers to proceed to their destination. His nobility is rewarded with a fatal bullet from his officer. Sleiman's death launches the film to its climax: a rowdy nine-minute gunfight in which the bravery and marksmanship of the Lebanese rebels stand in stark contrast to their hapless Ottoman foes. In the end, the rebels drive the "Turks" from their village in disgrace. The rebels win, but like the famine itself, the film does not have a happy ending. The finale finds Fairuz's 'Adla bidding farewell to her beloved 'Abdou as he sails away in exile.

Of course, this characterization of the war is pure fantasy. There are some reports of retreating soldiers being attacked by villagers who had grown tired of the banditry of deserters and the corruption of enlisted men during the war, and there is at least one detailed description of a group of men ambushing soldiers as they passed near the town of Choueifat.[7] But these events came at the end of the war when the Ottomans were already on the run and were hardly reflective of anything that happened during the initial conscription campaign. Given the inaccuracies, it might be easy to scoff at such stylized portrayals of violent resistance. However, while the film's timeline is a mess and the events it depicts never happened, it is still an interesting critique of the purported passivity of the Lebanese people in the face of authoritarian domination and starvation during the war. To some extent, the fictional resistance in *Safar Barlik* is just as unfair to those who lived the famine as the standard victimization narrative had been. The credible threat of draconian punishment made open resistance impossible,[8] but many people *did* resist in subtler ways, either via the intermittent bread riots that took place in cities or in the espionage networks for French military intelligence during the war or even simply by defying unenforceable and unpopular wartime laws.[9]

Regardless of its accuracy (or lack thereof), the film's aggressive revisionism has a purpose: to reject the dishonor of an era that is "better forgotten" and to posit an alternative. The film acknowledges the hardship of the war and provides a clear villain in the Ottoman military (and its stand-in for Jamal Pasha), but rather than focusing on the pathos of the famine, the film's plot centers on local agency, using clever deception, sacrifice, heroism, and rebellion to overcome the hated "Anatolian" occupiers. The village's victory, pyrrhic though it is, provides its viewers with a satisfying alternative to the victimization and passivity that defines the era in a historical record written by elite observers. The message that the film sends is clear: the Lebanese did not have to suffer—and when they chose not to, they *won*. In place of the dishonor of rampant starvation and social decline that characterizes the commonly understood famine narrative, the film's portrayal of the struggle gives those who carry its memory a reason to be proud.

Curiously, while there is little evidence of the violent resistance that the film portrays, popular and familial memories of the period do contain subplots of resistance and honor that repudiate the victimization in the dominant narrative. Mayssun Sukarieh and Tarif Khalidi's work on the lore of the notorious bandit from the Biqaʿ Valley, Milhem Qassim, provides a particularly delightful example of this. The wartime myths that Sukarieh and Khalidi unearthed universally laud the rogue's unwillingness to bend the knee to authority, even in the face of a firing squad or, more terrifying still, regional military governor and Ottoman Big Bad himself, Jamal Pasha. In these mostly fictitious tales, Qassim's superheroic acts of valor and brash masculinity provide a compelling foil to the suffering victims of the famine. He represents a Lebanese character who was powerful enough that even Jamal had to respect him. In the story of their first meeting, Qassim was brought to the feared pasha after being captured. When Jamal threatened his head, the brigand burst his restraints and violently pinned the commander to the ground with a chair, submitting him with force. Any member of the audience who was versed in the standard wartime narrative would have known Jamal Pasha's monstrous reputation, so Qassim's defiance would have been understood to represent an act of tremendous valor—which provides the moral of the story in its resolution. Rather than killing Qassim for this grave assault, Jamal respected the bandit's pluck and befriended him before releasing him.[10] In a later story, Qassim was said to have brought a condemned man to Jamal to demand a reprieve. Jamal assented for his new friend's sake, but as the man crawled toward the pasha to thank him for his mercy, Qassim kicked him in the butt and informed the groveling subordinate that he was "here with me" and was thus not to kiss anyone else's hand. The moral of this story is the inverse of that of the first. While Qassim's boldness was rewarded by warm hospitality, the rube of this tale was punished for his obeisance with a shaming blow to the backside.[11]

Qassim's overt and somewhat malicious criminality has left him with a checkered legacy, but as Sukarieh and Khalidi argue, within the broadly understood narrative of the war, he was a hero. Why? According to the authors, his adherence to a strict code of honor and his unrepentant subversion of the hated authorities (despite his apparent friendship with the most hated authority of all) appealed to the "moral inclinations" of those who spread the myths. Like Barakat's fictional protagonists, Qassim's alleged acts of bravery and resistance restored "manliness" to a Shi'i population that had been emasculated by autocratic rule and policies that specifically targeted their community during the war.[12] Even today, many Shi'is in Lebanon remember the war as an era of oppression and devastation. When I once described my work to a man from the southern town of Bint Jbeil, he profanely interjected "kiss ikht al-atrak!" before listing in detail the indignities that his community endured during the war.[13]

As the Qassim mythos and *Safar Barlik* suggest, tales of heroism in this time of oppression and widespread suffering still hold an alluring social cachet. In the case of the film, wishful memory makes for a sharper plot that helped the director evade uncomfortable aspects of the actual event like sickness, poverty, and the misery of public starvation. The Qassim mythos differs in that the stories do not conceal the horrors of the wartime era like the film, but they still rely upon a heroic spirit of defiance that boosts the standing of even the most dubious of characters. However, such heroic reimaginings may also resonate because they reflect the protagonists of *actual* stories of rebellion and reclaimed honor that were conveyed through familial and community memory after the famine. Unlike narratives of victimhood and decline, most of the stories about rebellion originated with those who suffered within the famine itself—in essence, they were survival stories. Suffering was not always prominently discussed, but as with the story of the onion in the introduction, the wartime circumstances and the famine were always present as context, even if the actual misery was happening elsewhere and to others.

One interesting example of this comes from an oral account from the Dakdouk family told to me by the great-granddaughter of the protagonists of the story. The family lived in the coastal foothills just south of Beirut. As landowners with herds of animals, their experience was not necessarily typical of most famine sufferers, but they were still driven to resist the authorities by the circumstances of the war. Given the intense poverty of the mountain during the famine, the yogurt and cheese that they sold to support their family was better marketed in Beirut. Unfortunately, to get it to the market, the family had to pass an Ottoman military checkpoint that divided the mountain from the province of Beirut at a time when transporting food required official permission from the government. After facing harassment and confiscation by the soldiers on the road, the Dakdouks devised schemes to subvert their newfound antagonists. First, the family began traveling with their children and dressing shabbily in order to appear like the migrants who so frequently fled to the coast at this time. By camouflaging themselves in the clothes of the poor, the family was able to take advantage of the social neglect of the era to escape the notice of soldiers and beggars alike. Experience also taught them that the soldiers were far more likely to steal preserved foods like yogurt and cheese than milk, which spoiled rapidly for lack of refrigeration. Eventually, the family traveled only with milk and apparently had far greater success as a result.[14]

Like the tales of Milhem Qassim, the Dakdouk family's story provides a counterexample to the victimhood narrative. What is different about their tale is that it really happened. Through resiliency, cleverness, and resourcefulness, they were able to avoid the common experience of suffering and shame while evading powerful government forces in the process. Although the smuggling operation was ostensibly criminal, the storytellers of subsequent generations remembered the tale of malfeasance as an example of heroism. Indeed, their trickery was such a source of pride for their descendants that they deliberately chose to tell it to me over any of the other stories of the famine that they knew.

It is not surprising that many of those individuals who were canonized in such personal and familial histories were smugglers and muleteers, since their professionally honed ability to skirt the law (or their utter indifference to it) made them perfect protagonists against a state characterized by its corruption, deadly mismanagement, and harsh repression. Amid the misery of the famine, such defiant figures were sources of salvation for their families and, often, their villages, and they have been remembered as such. In his account of survival during the famine, Anis Furayha writes, "The smugglers of our village were courageous heroes. Our children would not die of hunger."[15] In contrast to the stories of suffering, victimhood, and paternal failure, the smugglers in famine narratives protected their vulnerable dependents during the war. By completing their bold missions, they lived up to their masculine obligations to their family and their culture.[16]

Perhaps the most interesting example of such a narrative involves one of Jammul Mahmoud's smuggling expeditions. This story is set during the exceptionally cold winter of 1916–17. While Jammul was still trekking back from the Hawran with his loads of grain, storms battered the region, snowing-in the clandestine mountain routes he normally used to reach his home village of Barouk. With safe smuggling trails rendered impassable by the weather, Jammul was left with only one way home, and it was a bad one: the guarded summit pass of Dhahr al-Baydar on the Beirut-Damascus Highway. The risk that this route posed to the caravan was almost as serious as being stuck on the freezing mountain trails. Not only was Jammul violating laws against smuggling; he was leading valuable animals that could have been confiscated for the war effort. To be stopped would be to be deprived of his livelihood, his expensive cargo, and, possibly, his freedom. If he was arrested, his family would lose its breadwinner, and he might die of hunger in prison. With this in mind, Jammul devised a plan. He began his ascent toward the pass during the bitter cold of night, when he hoped the Ottoman soldiers would seek shelter in their shack and leave the checkpoint unattended. Since only a madman would attempt to cross the mountain in that weather in the dark, he hoped the soldiers would see little reason to stay at their post. When they neared the pass, Jammul paused his team and stealthily approached the checkpoint alone. Luck was on his side: when he arrived at the crossing, he found all of the guards huddled in the building for warmth with the doors shut. In an act of pure audacity, Jammul sneaked up to the entrance of the shack and carefully inserted his staff between the handles of the door, locking them in place. While this would not prevent a concerted effort to escape, the staff would at least slow the exit of any of the soldiers if they happened to walk outside as the mule train was passing by. Once it was secure, Jammul signaled to the party to move, silently leading them home with their freedom and their precious cargo intact.[17] Jammul had defeated the Ottoman cordon—not by violence, but by his courage and wit. His family would survive, and they would also be supplied with a story to commemorate the era of the famine that did not center on starvation, suffering, or loss.

Like any of the stories told in and about the famine, such tales are anecdotal and clearly do not represent universal experience in the war. However, the ways that they are structured and the meaning that the storytellers convey indicate why they are such valuable counternarratives to the standard wartime account. While the difficult circumstances of the famine are important plot elements that provide a sense of urgency for the protagonists, suffering is not the dominant theme of the tales, nor is it even mentioned as a motivation for the characters' actions. Rather, the stories represent implicit repudiations of the passivity of the standard victimhood narrative. The protagonists survive and even thrive. Not because of some deus ex machina or a foreign missionary dispensing gruel, but rather because they refuse to accept victimhood. They will themselves to overcome the challenges of the moment. Such shared narratives from within the crisis ultimately reclaim local honor in the face of the humiliation, starvation, death, and oppression of the wartime years.

Familial narratives like the ones Hayat Mahmoud told of her grandfather Jammul and stories of defiance embedded in popular narratives about figures like Milhem Qassim or in smuggling stories by Afif Tannous and Anis Furayha offer an oblique vindication of the themes of resistance in *Safar Barlik*.[18] Instead of fighting with guns, the characters in the stories resist with weapons of the weak: disobedience, ridicule, and evasion.[19] They succeed through their cleverness and strength of character, and above all through their unwillingness to submit. Though smuggling was hardly a revolutionary act, the subversion of a few Ottoman guards momentarily inverted the power dynamic between the Lebanese and the autocratic state and symbolically contested the fear that the Jamal Pashas, both real and in the narrative, used to reinforce Ottoman dominance over the region.[20] Against the insuperable power of the military, the success of a minor act of social disobedience represented a small victory, enabling those who lacked power to assert it, limited though it was, over an oppressive hegemon.[21] We should be as critical when analyzing such heroic stories as we are with stories of victimization. However, as this book has shown, a narrative that includes individuals playing an active role in their own survival is actually more historically accurate than narratives of victimhood and decline alone. Even when people suffered in the famine, they did so as active participants in their own survival. They strained against the overwhelming force of the crisis to extend their lives—if sometimes in vain.

But why do the stories have value for the families that told them? As the sociologist Maurice Halbwachs has observed, we do not recall the past as a perfect image of the event; instead, it is "reconstructed on the basis of the present" through the memory's instantiations.[22] As the past becomes past, the ways that we remember it are sometimes also the ways that we *want* to remember it. This insight is particularly pertinent to the stories that were recounted to me by the Mahmoud and Dakdouk descendants. When I asked them what their families had told them about life in the famine, my narrators deliberately chose the stories of survival, not ones of misery and victimhood.

In their original contexts, these stories are very unlike *Safar Barlik* or even the general historical narrative of the famine. Popular history and national narratives overtly seek to shape collective memory to bind together those who share a link to that past. The insular nature of familial stories and the close connection between the storyteller and the protagonists of the tales make familial stories the *opposite* of collective. As Najwa al-Qattan has astutely observed about accounts from within the famine, "rather than appeal to an 'imagined community,' the stories they tell are, by and large, neither national nor even communal but, rather, emotive and familial."[23] Unlike the general historical narrative, with its anonymous scenes of an abstract past, those familial stories from within the famine represent slivers of each descendant's personal history. In this sense, they are semiautobiographical, rather than collective, even if they reflect upon the collective memory of the period and its lessons. The general historical narrative of the famine and the collective memory of suffering may provide the setting for such stories, but like the story of the onion or the poverty cosplay that the Dakdouks enacted on each trip to Beirut, the plots of the familial stories are very specific to the histories of the families and to their members. For the descendants of the heroes, the stories that are remembered from their familial histories were retold for a reason. Not only do their heroic plots challenge the shameful sense of powerlessness that had been imposed upon the Lebanese community as a whole in the famine, but they also reveal the traits that the families themselves valued within the crisis. Through this, the tales offer validation of their family's survival amid the widespread death and suffering in the famine world at large. And, perhaps even more important, as pieces of the storytellers' own ancestral histories, they make the narrators feel proud.

Meaning and Crisis in Lebanon's Current Calamity

The trauma woven throughout the popular memory of the famine has made it an archetype of misery in the country's all-too-frequently disastrous modern history. Like the horrors of the civil war, the famine has become a metric to weigh not only the horrors of the past but the mounting calamities of the nation's present as well.[24] I was forced to confront this personally when presenting on the topic of the famine to an audience from the American University of Beirut in June of 2020. At the time, the eventual effects of the state's recent debt default and the growing financial crisis were not fully evident, but the growing social malaise, currency collapse, deadly pandemic, and high prices led one of my audience members to ask me the obvious question: Did I see any parallels between the crises of the past and present? My initial judgment was that the crisis of 2020, as tragic as it was, was a mere shadow of the horrors of the wartime famine. Since then, the situation has become dramatically worse, particularly following the catastrophic blast of August 2020 and the start of the Lebanese lira's real freefall against the dollar. However, even as I write this in mid-2022, the suffering does not (and, I hope with my whole being, will not) approach the horror of a hundred thousand bodies lying dead in the streets.

Still, in the years that followed that talk, I have periodically returned to that question in my mind. Not necessarily to rethink the comparability of the historical cases but rather to ponder the meaning that we attach to the traumas of the past and how they help us derive meaning in the present. What ultimately motivates us to find explanations in the past? Is it to judge the righteous and to punish the villains? Is it to steady ourselves against the problems of today, knowing that even the worst crisis imaginable also did pass? Is it to find solidarity in the shared misery of our ancestors? And does the comparison really make anything better at all? The sociologist and historian Charles Tilly has argued that offering explanations is a form of "social work" that negotiates the relationship between the person explaining and their audience.[25] And indeed, the very act of comparison is rooted in the meaning that we give the memory of the event rather than in the actual historical facts of the event themselves. Certainly, this is not a sentiment that is limited to the Lebanese crises—after all, how many articles on the Spanish flu were written to explain the COVID-19 pandemic?

The reality is that many who analyze crises do so from above or beyond the disaster's immediate effects. Because of this, crises are often portrayed as other people's tragedies, no matter how emotionally connected to them the observer may be. This outside perspective often renders tragedies both past and present as sad curiosities. But these events were and are lived by real people. Any analysis of crisis must remember this, especially when drawing connections to other calamities. Even if there are comparisons to be made with the famine of World War I, it would offer little solace to those struggling to feed their families in Lebanon today to know that their plight is but a milder version of the absolute catastrophe that their ancestors once suffered. As in the crisis of a century ago, life goes on despite the difficulties that mere existence poses. And, as in the crisis of a century ago, many of the personal tragedies of today are suffered in silence as individuals adapt to the ever-multiplying problems that complicate their worlds. Within the crisis, each home faces its own challenges, and each mind confronts and copes with those struggles in different ways. Like in the famine, there are as many crisis worlds in the current Lebanese situation as there are individuals to experience them. And the "missing middle" of the crisis is just as relevant today as it was during the famine.

The nuance of life in the current tragedy was reiterated to me in March 2022 when I returned to Beirut for the first time since 2018, this time to teach again in the same familiar classrooms of my old academic home, the American University of Beirut. Much had changed, of course. In the time since my last visit, the country had experienced a revolution, a pandemic, the largest nonnuclear manmade explosion in history, and an unprecedented financial collapse, but the students and their insights were as incisive as ever. While discussing personal accounts of crisis in a literature class, our conversation turned to the difficulties of conveying complex emotional experiences to one's readers, leading into a discussion of Frederick Bliss's wartime retrospective (which itself was sitting in a file a mere fifty meters away). As the students engaged with Bliss's text, I was moved by how many of them saw themselves in it. The students resonated with Bliss's sad admissions of empathetic failures and guilt over his inability to help those around them in ways that mirrored my own reactions when I first encountered his words years before. Their reactions reiterated the fact that the past's relevance to today may not necessarily be in measuring relative misery but in helping us understand the deeper social and psychological impacts of life in crisis that are often neglected or hidden by those who fear the consequences of revealing them.

Though the day-to-day difficulties of life in Lebanon in 2022 have not approached the morbid scenes of the past, it is clear that coping with the emotional weight of the crisis is just as troubling, even for people who are not themselves facing the worst effects of the situation. In 1917, Edward Nickoley wrote, "There are all about us so many who are suffering so much more intensely that I am ashamed to let anyone know that I too have a regret and a sorrow, that I cherish a hope and a longing the realization and the fulfillment of which is indefinitely deferred."[26] A century later, the writer and social critic Lina Mounzer described her emotional conflict within the present crisis in similar, guilt-stricken terms: "Any avoidance of suffering surrounded by so much suffering feels undeserved, and there is very little joy to be had anymore that doesn't come inflected with the awareness of someone else's misery."[27]

In 2021, Mounzer observed, "We are now in uncharted territory, where so many familiar landscapes have become nightmarish distortions of themselves."[28] Indeed, this is the context in which life must continue, in mundane misery, for everyone within the country for the foreseeable future. And like the famine of the past, the silent suffering of the Lebanese will continue to be obscured by the *grand mal* calamities that have dominated the headlines since the crisis began. Basic coping strategies are more amorphous and not nearly spectacular enough to earn widespread coverage, no matter how prevalent they may be. While it is relatively easy to understand the misery of those living on the streets and eating from dumpsters, or those whose lives were ruined by the blast, or those who took to the street to protest rampant corruption, we are far less likely to hear of those who are forced to dilute baby formula and ration out cheap fast food to ensure their children get some calories each day, or of parents forced to put back bottles of unexpectedly expensive cooking oil, or of students who find themselves priced out of an education or even forced into child labor. We may not read about the troubled debates that individuals have about whether to leave in hopes of a better life for themselves and their families or whether to stay to care for an aging relative. Harsh but necessary decisions are sources of guilt and shame. One does not have to suffer absolute privation to feel the pain of a devalued paycheck or the loss of a business that took a lifetime to build. Certainly, one can avoid starvation while watching one's life savings transform from a nest egg into a hollow shell as black-market exchange rates siphon off its value. The pressure to be strong in the face of crisis can be crippling—and if the sharp rise in suicides in Lebanon since the crisis began is any indication, it can be overwhelming. Many choices made today may be survival strategies, and many may actually work. But these may also not be the things that people will want to remember when pondering over the crisis in the future.

The Illusion of an Ending

We do not know how or when the current crisis in Lebanon will end or what will happen when it does. This is another curious parallel to the famine of the past. It is largely taken for granted that the famine ended when the war ended. Ostensibly, it did. When the blockade and economic embargos were lifted, people returned (often flush with cash) to repay loans and to revive what remained of their families. Behind them, tens of millions of dollars in international aid came pouring into the region to quench the embers of the humanitarian crisis that had been left smoldering by the war. But the war continued to leave its subtle marks on the population for years afterward. Over half a decade after the war ended, poverty remained high and persistent diseases like tuberculosis that had blossomed in the famine continued to erode the margins of society.[29] Ominously, invisible afflictions also gnawed at the minds of survivors who were forced to cope with the residues of the crisis in their own lives. Nearly a century after the war, one of my colleagues mentioned that her grandmother had once grasped her skinny wrist when she was a child, saying, "You never would have lived." The traumas of the famine were not only persistent and contagious; they were apparently hereditary.

What will this mean for those who have to endure the persistent low-level trauma of today's crisis? Those living in the country must, to varying degrees, face the perpetual emotional pressure that the crisis has embedded in their daily lives. They cannot escape its reminders: a corrupt and apparently uncaring political class, skyrocketing inflation and collapsing currency, the incessant hum of generators and the stench of diesel fumes, perpetual discomfort without heat or air conditioning, the inaccessibility of their own wealth and the insulting frustration of "lollars" (depositors' dollars that are trapped by capital control measures, only withdrawable in Lebanese lira at an arbitrarily low value), and even the perpetual questions of whether and when to leave and how long to wait while the country sinks deeper into its current version of hell. This hardly even touches upon those unexpected little quandaries that life in a collapsed country can present. Does one choose to do laundry with the sparse but costly amperes when the generator comes on, or does one try to keep the food in the refrigerator cold and prevent yet another case of food poisoning? The future is just as uncertain. Who knows what years of living in a perpetual cloud of generator exhaust or of rationing medicine will do to people's health, even when the country eventually recovers. Who knows what the emotional impact of constantly coping and learning to cope anew will be as the years drag on. The everyday lives of my friends and colleagues today would have been unfathomable when I left the country in 2015. And they are among the lucky ones.

Rima Rantisi's moving essay on life in the "shattered" city of Beirut after the catastrophic blast of August 4, 2020, grimly points to the deeper challenges of the present and future and to the subtle residues of trauma that remain even after the traumatic event itself fades into the past. In her essay, Rantisi wonders at the chance discovery of a crack that the blast had left in a single drinking glass as it sat tucked safely away in her kitchen cabinet. She surmises that "the shockwaves of such an explosion will play out in our lives in mysterious ways, reminding us of our luck and the burden of their irreversible processes."[30] Suffering is not, as the inevitable platitudes go, a disguised blessing or a source of future strength. Resiliency is a curse if it has to be exercised. If the famine is any indication, even the survivors will retain the scars of trauma. And what will those cracks in the psyche mean? Will they serve as memorials of the years of struggle, loss, and life deferred? Or, like in the famine, will those cracks subtly distort the world that the survivors see around them, behind them, and ahead of them?

Acknowledgments

The list of people to be acknowledged for their help on this project has grown along with the book's timeline. I regret that I can no longer thank Kamal Salibi or my mentor and dear friend Abdulrahim Abu Husayn for their inspiration and support, but you, dear reader, would not be holding this book in your hands were it not for their kindness and their willingness to indulge my fascination with terrible things. This project would not have been possible without the financial support of Patrick McGreevy and the wisdom of Samar Miqati, Kaoukab Chebaro, Carla Chalhoub, and the rest of the incredible team at the American University of Beirut's Nami Jafet Memorial Library. I wish to acknowledge Crystal Safadi's cartographic brilliance and to thank her for sacrificing precious hours of her life making minute adjustments to meet my arbitrary aesthetic preferences. I cannot thank Hayat Mahmoud, Joan Chaker, and Soumar Dakdouk enough for sharing their stories with me.

Over the years, I have been blessed by the support, input, and constructive criticism of colleagues and friends alike. Elizabeth Thompson, Charles D. Smith, Keith David Watenpaugh, Graham Pitts, Stacy Fahrenthold, Ellen Fleischmann, Christine Lindner, Rima Rantisi, Charles Hayek, Melanie Tanielian, and Tarif Khalidi have been particularly generous with their time and wisdom. I am especially indebted to Murat Şiviloğlu, whose masochistic willingness to read drafts and offer more praise than they probably deserved helped me to surmount emotional hurdles several times over the book's intermediate stages. My deepest gratitude and love to my brother Salah and all of my friends in Lebanon, who rescued us from ourselves more than once and gave us a family in our new home. My love and thanks to Tam and Eli, and to Ty, Mel, Jamie, my parents, Violet, and everyone else who has stuck with us through the years, despite it all. I wish to acknowledge the Trinity College Dublin Trust Grant and its Trinity Affinity Credit Card for providing generous funding for map making and final draft preparation. My last and deepest gratitude goes to Kate Wahl at Stanford University Press for all of her faith and work on this project over the years.

Notes

Preface
1. For incisive critical analysis of memoir in the era, see Deringil, *The Ottoman Twilight in the Arab Lands*, xvi–xx.

Introduction
Epigraph taken from Antun Yammine, *Lubnan fil harb* (Beirut: al-matbaʿa al-adabiyya, 1919), 4.
1. See Fawaz, *Land of Aching Hearts*, 23–25.
2. Delightfully, "Before I Forget."
3. Furayha, *Qabl an ansa*, 42.
4. Greater Syria includes the land bounded by the Taurus Mountains in the north, the Mediterranean Sea in the west, the Jazira region in the east, and the southern borders of Palestine to the south.
5. The military favored Turkish soldiers for practical and racial reasons and considered the empire's Christian subjects in particular to be potentially untrustworthy in battle. See Yalman, *Turkey in the World War*, 79, 80; and Beşikçi, *Ottoman Mobilization*, 130–39.
6. Akın, *When the War Came Home*, 111–18.
7. See Beşikçi, *Ottoman Mobilization*, 111. Akın quotes Cavid Bey, who stated, "The state does not have the capacity to keep 800,000 soldiers under arms. They would go hungry and naked." Akın, *When the War Came Home*, 54.
8. The two ships used (the cruiser *Goeben* and the light cruiser *Breslau*) were themselves opportunistic German "donations," manned by German crews, and the attack was unsanctioned by the majority opinion in the Ottoman Parliament. For more on the Ottoman lead-up to the war, see Aksakal, *The Ottoman Road to War*.

9. The ruling triad of Jamal, Enver, and Talaat Pashas was termed the triumvirate.

10. This unfortunately included a number of innocent social critics, intellectuals, and Arab nationalists.

11. On the general logic of British embargo policies, see Offer, *The First World War*.

12. With the exception of American naval vessels, which had access to the port, as the United States remained neutral with the Ottomans even after it declared war against the other Central Powers.

13. Tanielian, *The Charity of War*, 59.

14. For GDP statistics, see Naqqash, "Nadhara fi halat Jabal Lubnan al-iqtisadiyya," 2:472–73. On the effect of the war on the silk industry, see Pitts, "'Make Them Hated,'" 176–78.

15. Rogan, *Fall of the Ottomans*, 57–58.

16. Yammine, *Quatre ans*.

17. Jalal Bey, "Al-ahwal al-ziraʿiyya," 2:469–70.

18. The official title of the governor of the semi-independent district was *mutasarrif*.

19. Yalman, *Turkey in the War*, 80, 83. The American missionary William Miller suggested a literally incredible five hundred thousand deaths by 1916 across the Near East and noted that "the whole Turkish empire is threatened with one of the greatest famines of its history, since all reports indicate that less than fifteen per cent—some say ten per cent—of the arable fields of Turkey are being sown this spring." See Barton, *Story of Near East Relief*, 372.

20. The 1913 harvest totaled 1,238,551 tons. Foster, "The 1915 Locust," 370–71.

21. Ruppin, *Syria*, 14.

22. Akın, *When the War Came Home*, 126, 129.

23. Akın, 118, 126.

24. Al-Maqdisi, *Aʿdham harb fi'l tarikh*, 57.

25. Yammine, *Quatre ans*, 19–22.

26. Yalman, *Turkey in the World War*, 145; Şevket Pamuk, *A Monetary History*, 223.

27. Yalman, *Turkey in the World War*, 144. Some local estimates suggest an even lower value in parts of Syria.

28. Al-Hakim, *Bayrut wa Lubnan*, 255.

29. Brand, "That They May Have Life," 53.

30. Al-Hakim, *Bayrut wa Lubnan*, 251.

31. See Şevket Pamuk's analysis of Ottoman wheat production: Pamuk, "The Ottoman Economy in World War I," 120–21.

32. See Provence, "Druze Shaykhs, Arab Nationalists and Grain Merchants," 143–49. During World War II, the leader of the British occupying forces, Edward Spears, intervened to prevent the French from replicating Ottoman policies, since he had been present in Lebanon in 1918 and was aware of the failures of the previous administrations. He proposed paying traditional middlemen to oversee production and distribution, which ensured a stable flow of food during the war. See Spears, *Fulfilment of a Mission*, 173–86.

33. ʿAwad, *Min ʿahd al-mutasarrifiyya*, 32.

34. See Howe, "Famine Systems," 144–55.

35. The value of the Ottoman piaster fluctuated in Istanbul at roughly the same rate as it did in Beirut. Yalman, *Turkey in the World War*, 144.

36. Williams, "Economy, Environment, and Famine," 150–51.

37. Yammine, *Quatre ans*, 23.

38. Sa'ab, *Stories and Scenes*, 337–38.

39. Jackson, "Compassion and Connections," 90.

40. On this, see Thompson, *How the West Stole Democracy*.

41. Various consequences are noted in Sibley et al., *Social Survey of Syria*.

42. See Fromkin, *A Peace to End All Peace*. See also McMeekin, *The Ottoman Endgame*. For a general overview, see Johnson, "The First World War and the Middle East," 142–51. The region is largely absent from the war's most comprehensive literature overview, Winter and Prost, *The Great War in History*.

43. This originated scholastically with Antonius, *The Arab Awakening*. See also Hitti, *Lebanon in History*; Traboulsi, *A History of Modern Lebanon*; Elizabeth Thompson's excellent *Colonial Citizens* offers a fresh reconsideration of this dynamic. See also Schayegh, *The Middle East and the Making of the Modern World*; Çiçek, *War and State Formation in Syria*; Provence, *The Last Ottoman Generation*; and Kayalı, *Imperial Resilience*.

44. Excellent recent integrated histories include Fawaz, *Land of Aching Hearts*; and Rogan, *Fall of the Ottomans*. See also the incomplete set by Shaw, *The Ottoman Empire in World War I*.

Several edited volumes have also emerged in recent years to add greater texture to our understanding of the war. Notably: Qassis, *Lubnan fi l harb al-'alamiyya al-ula*; and Frazier, *The First World War*.

45. Winter and Robert, *Capital Cities at War*; Procter, *Civilians in a World at War*; and Grayzel and Proctor, *Gender and the Great War*.

46. Without even touching on the vast literature of the Armenian genocide, this would include Akın, *When the War Came Home*; Tanielian, *The Charity of War*; Metinsoy, *Ottoman Women during World War I*; Ajay, "Mount Lebanon"; Pitts, "Fallow Fields"; Pitts, "Hungry Population," 217–36; Rose, "Implications of the Spanish Influenza Pandemic," 655–84; Watenpaugh, *Bread from Stones*; Schilcher, "The Famine of 1915–1918 in Greater Syria"; Jacobson, "Negotiating Ottomanism in Times of War," 69–88; al-Qattan, "When Mothers Ate Their Children," 731–32; Nakhul, "Bilad al-Batrun," 2: 795–867; al-Khuri, *Maja'a*; Pitts, "'Make them Hated,'" 175–90; and Williams, *Economy, Environment, and Famine*.

47. For an excellent literature review, see Abi Fadil, "Bibliographi al-harb al-'alamiyya al-ula fi Lubnan," 83–116.

48. An oft-neglected example would be the Iranian famine; see Majd, *Great Famine*. However, reports of famine conditions ranged from Anatolia to the Arabian Gulf and, to a lesser extent, Greece and Egypt.

49. The most prominent of these sources include Yammine, *Quatre ans*; Yammine, *Lubnan fi l harb*; McGilvary, *Dawn of a New Era*; Doolittle, "Pathos and Humor in Wartime Syria"; al-Maqdisi, *A'dham harb*; Khuwayri, *Al-rihla al-suriyya*; and Dhahir, *Jabal 'Amil*.

50. The Maronites are a Uniate Catholic sect who formed a majority population in

the territory of Mount Lebanon in 1918. See Huwayek, *Les Revendications du Liban*. The translated text of the patriarch's speech appears in Zamir, *Formation of Modern Lebanon*, 269–78.

51. See von Sanders, *Five Years in Turkey*, 140; Khuwayri, *Al-rihla al-suriyya*, 91; Yammine, *Quatre ans*, 39; and Yammine, *Lubnan fil harb*. Henri Lammens's postwar account of Syrian history, dedicated to conquering French general Gouraud, amplified such notions: Lammens, *La Syrie précis historique*. For the American perspective, see McGilvary, *Dawn of a New Era*, 25; and Doolittle, "Pathos and Humor." For more contemporary analysis, see al-Khuri, *Maja'a*, 32–43; Schumann, "Individual and Collective Memories," 247–263; Moawad, "Jamal Pasha en une version libanaise," 425–46; and Walker, "Clericist Catholic Authors," 91–128.

52. Foster, "The 1915 Locust Attack," 370–71.

53. Pitts, "Was Capitalism the Crisis?"

54. This story was told to me during an interview with Hayat Mahmud conducted on January 24, 2014. I have structured and edited the narrative for clarity but have kept its plot intact.

55. Nickoley, "Historic Diary," 19.

56. Anderson, *Encountering Affect*, 13–14.

Chapter 1

Epigraph taken from Anis Furayha, *Qabl an ansa* (Beirut: Dar al-nahar, 1989), 48.

1. Lebanist scholars have accused the Ottoman Empire, and specifically regional commander Jamal Pasha, of deliberately initiating the famine. This was a commonly held belief during the war and is reflected in Yammine, *Lubnan fil harb*; Yammine, *Quatre ans*; Khuwayri, *Al-rihla al-suriyya*; McGilvary, *Dawn of a New Era*; Lammens, *La Syrie précis historique*; Antonius, *The Arab Awakening*; and Hitti, *Lebanon in History*. Recent popular works like the film *Safar Barlik* (1968) and Dominique Baudis's *Passion des Chrétiens du Liban* (1979) echo such sentiments. In recent years, historians have revisited this debate more critically. Al-Khuri, in *Maja'a*, has faulted the Ottomans but with more nuance. Schumann, in "Individual and Collective Memories"; Moawad, in "Jamal Pasha en une version libanaise"; and in Walker, "Clericist Catholic Authors," have approached the issue as one of collective memory. Foster, in "The 1915 Locust Attack," has found famine roots with the locust plague of 1915, and Pitts, in "Was Capitalism the Crisis?," has blamed it on capitalism and elite manipulation, while Thompson, in *Colonial Citizens*, has found increasing fault in the Entente blockade. Most others have argued that the famine was a product of a variety of factors that influenced market prices; see Ajay, "Mount Lebanon"; Schilcher, "The Famine of 1915-1918"; and Tanielian, *The Charity of War*.

2. See O Grada, *Eating People Is Wrong*, 1.

3. Each of these examples is taken from an actual case mentioned anecdotally in the famine literature.

4. For a good overview of famine causality, see de Waal, "The End of Famine?," 185.

5. This analysis is rooted in Howe's famine system theory. See Howe, "Famine Systems," 145–49.

6. Sorokin, *Man and Society in Calamity*, 14.

7. Carbonnier, *Humanitarian Economics*, 152.

8. Oversimplified, *wasta* is a transactional social asset that allows a person to get things done. It could be the ability to call in a favor from a powerful person, help someone through their social position, move bureaucracy, or even get oneself out of a political bind. On its applications, see Johnson, *Class and Client in Beirut*, 97–99.

9. O Grada, *Famine*, 109.

10. The winters of 1915–16 and 1916–17 were reputed to be bitterly cold, and in 1920 it actually snowed on the coast.

11. On regional weather patterns, see Bruin, *Lee Observatory*; Mazloum, *De la variabilité des pluies*; and Plassard, "Notice explicative."

12. Doolittle, "Pathos and Humor," 96.

13. Sen, *Poverty and Famines*; Devereux, *Theories of Famine*; and de Waal, *Famine That Kills*.

14. Butterly and Shepherd, *Hunger*, 57–58.

15. Butterly and Shepherd, 33.

16. Muhieddine, "Grafik al-wafayat."

17. On this issue, see Appleby, "Epidemics and Famine in the Little Ice Age," 654; and Post, "Nutritional Status and Mortality," 267.

18. George Doolittle, "Report of Sidon Station 1916–1917," Presbyterian Historical Society Archives (hereafter PHS Archives), RG 115-17-19: Sidon Station Reports 1907–35, 1.

19. Bayard Dodge, "Report of the Abeih and Suk al-Gharb Soup Kitchens 1914–1918," 1919, Howard Bliss Collection: AUB President 1902–1920, archive AA:2.3.2, box 18, file 3, p. 4, American University of Beirut/Library Archives, Beirut, Lebanon.

20. Ira Harris, "Medical Work—Tripoli Station—Syrian Mission—1902," PHS Archives, RG 115-19-16: Tripoli—Medical Reports 1895–1914, 1.

21. Ira Harris, "Medical Report of the Tripoli Station—Syria Mission: for 1907," PHS Archives, RG 115-19-16: Tripoli—Medical Reports 1895–1914, 1.

22. McGilvary, *Dawn of a New Era*, 266.

23. McGilvary, 94.

24. Nickoley, "Historic Diary,"4; Doolittle, "Pathos and Humor," 114.

25. Baba, *Tarablus fi l tarikh*, 280.

26. Metinsoy, *Ottoman Women during World War I*, 34.

27. O Grada describes the consensus as "overwhelming" in O Grada, *Famine*, 100. On metabolism and famine, see Svedberg, *Poverty and Undernutrition*, 115–22.

28. Robert Byerly, "Report of Sidon Station, 1917 to 1918," PHS Archives, RG 115-17-19: Sidon Station Reports 1907–35, 5.

29. The shelter managed to devise workarounds for some of the men whose work supported it. See McGilvary, *Dawn of a New Era*, 215.

30. Bahjat and Tamimi, *Wilayat Bayrut*, 1:297.

31. Chalabi, *Shi'is of Jabal 'Amil*, 47–48.

32. Sami, "Gender Differentials in Famine Mortality," 2593.

33. On death in the Syrian famine, see the anonymous report of Sidon Station from

1916–1917: Anonymous, "Report of Sidon Station 1916–1917," PHS Archives, RG 115-17-19: Sidon Station Reports 1907–35, 1. See also Nickoley, "Historic Diary," 3.

34. Metinsoy, *Ottoman Women*, 70.

35. See ʿAwad, *Min ʿahd al-mutasarrifiyya*, 31; Ziadeh, "First-Person Account," 265–77.

36. Khater, *Inventing Home*, 31–34.

37. Nakhul, "Bilad al-Batrun," 2:821.

38. For a map of syphilis centers, see Muhieddine, "Al-umur al-sihiyya," 2:641.

39. Orfalea, *Arab Americans*, 69–70.

40. Metinsoy, *Ottoman Women*, 99.

41. Muhieddine, "Jadwal al-amrad al-sariyya."

42. Muhieddine, "Al-umur al-sihiyya," 2:658.

43. Paul Erdman, "Letter from Paul Erdman to Charles Dana, October 31, 1917," PHS Archives, RG 115-16-11: Relief Work 1915–1917, 2.

44. Al-Maqdisi, *Aʿdham harb*, 69.

45. Ajay, "Mount Lebanon," 1:279.

46. Sen, *Poverty and Famines* is a seminal work, but Sen's initial assessment has been amended and critiqued over time. See Devereux, *Theories of Famine*; Devereux, "Sen's Entitlement Approach," 245–246; de Waal, "The End of Famine?," 184–95; Edkins, "Legality with a Vengeance,'" 547–75.

47. On the economy of Bhamdoun, see Salibi, *Bhamdoun*, 6.

48. Provence, "Druze Shaykhs, Arab Nationalists and Grain Merchants," 144.

49. Schilcher, "The Famine of 1915–1918 in Greater Syria," 239–41.

50. Barton, *Story of Near East Relief*, 372.

51. Gilsenan, *Lords of the Lebanese Marches*, 150–51.

52. Bahjat and Tamimi, *Wilayat Bayrut*, 2:276.

53. Yalman, *Turkey in the World War*, 128–130; Doolittle, "Pathos and Humor," 93.

54. Pamuk, "The Ottoman Economy in World War I," 120.

55. See Saliqa, *Tarikh Hasbaya*, 117.

56. Owen, *The Middle East in the World Economy*, 254–60.

57. Latron, *La vie rurale*, 46, 50, 55.

58. George Doolittle, "Report of Sidon Station 1916–1917," PHS Archives, RG 115-17-19: Sidon Station Reports 1907–35, 5–6.

59. Latron, *La vie rurale*, 46.

60. Saliqa, *Tarikh Hasbaya*, 117.

61. For a broad regional discussion, see Horden and Purcell, *Corrupting Sea*, 115–22.

62. Though sericulture was the dominant industry in the mountain, many areas that focused on silk production also engaged in other forms of farming, including the cultivation of cereal and other agricultural products like citrus and olives, which were generally sold for sale in the cities or shipped abroad. See al-Mir, *Batha fil tarikh al-hadith wa al-muʿasir*, 33–46. On agriculture in Mount Lebanon, see al-Asfar, "Al-ziraʿa fi Lubnan," 390–400.

63. A notable case was the likely fraudulent diary of "Aziz Bey," *Suriyya wa Lubnan fil-harb al-ʿalamiyya*, 59. See also Arslan, *Sira dhatiyya*.

64. See Ajay, "Mount Lebanon," 1:302.
65. Bahjat and Tamimi, *Wilayat Bayrut*, 1: 289.
66. Naqqash, "Nadhara fi halat Jabal Lubnan al-iqtisadiyya," 2:472–73. For a detailed discussion of remittances, see Pitts, "Ecology of Migration," 107–9.
67. Doolittle, "Pathos and Humor," 83–85.
68. Estimates of suffering for several districts are provided in George Doolittle's unpublished retrospective. See Doolittle, "Pathos and Humor," 78, 110.
69. Sen, *Poverty and Famines*, 1.
70. George Doolittle, "Report of Sidon Station, Syria Mission, Summer 1915, to Summer 1916," PHS Archives, RG 115-17-19: Sidon Station Reports 1907–35.
71. Ajay, "Mount Lebanon," 1:293.
72. Sa'id, "Tatawwur harakat al-as'ar wa al-ujur," 1:412.
73. Bahjat and Tamimi, *Wilayat Bayrut*, 2:276–77.
74. This salary is calculated at the normal exchange rate of roughly $4.5 to the lira and at the prewar exchange rate of 108 piasters to the lira—though local exchange rates were 124:1. Paul Erdman, "Letter from Paul Erdman to Charles Dana, May 2, 1917," PHS Archives, RG 115-16-11: Relief Work 1915–1917.
75. Yalman, *Turkey in the World War*, 151–53.
76. On the compelling lives of the porters, see Johnson, *Class and Client in Beirut*.
77. Tanielian, "The War of Famine," 120.
78. Yalman, *Turkey in the War*, 152–53.
79. Al-Hakim, *Bayrut wa Lubnan*, 255.
80. Paul Erdman, "Letter from Paul Erdman to Charles Dana, May 2, 1917," PHS Archives, RG 115-16-11: Relief Work 1915–1917.
81. George Doolittle, "Letter from George Doolittle to Charles Dana, May 22, 1917," PHS Archives, RG 115-16-10: Relief Work 1915–1917.
82. William Fredinger, "School Report: Lebanon School for Boys—1915–1916," PHS Archives, RG 115-18-2: Suk-ul-Gharb Lebanon School for Boys Reports 1909–1927, 2.
83. This request may have been a clever negotiating tactic because the high price of wheat at the time and the weakening of the Ottoman lira would have meant that the leftover food may have actually had more value than the money. See Affeffi Saba', "Letter to Anna Jessup regarding a Servant, July 8, 1916," PHS Archives, RG 115-8-16: Hamlin Memorial Sanatorium Correspondence 1916–27.
84. Affeffi Saba', "Letter to Anna Jessup August 25, 1916," PHS Archives, RG 115-8-16: Hamlin Memorial Sanatorium Correspondence 1916–27.
85. Affeffi Saba', "Letter to Anna Jessup, September 18, 1916," PHS Archives, RG 115-8-16: Hamlin Memorial Sanatorium Correspondence 1916–27.
86. Affeffi Saba', "Letter to Anna Jessup September 1, 1916," PHS Archives, RG 115-8-16: Hamlin Memorial Sanatorium Correspondence 1916–27.
87. Sa'id, "Tatawwur harakat al-as'ar," 397. In 1914, a *fallaha* averaged 33.35 piasters per day, whereas an unskilled laborer might have made 6 piasters per day. The latter is close to the base pay of 6–7 piasters per day for an agricultural laborer in Mount Lebanon in 1910, as recorded by Issawi in *The Fertile Crescent*, 90.

88. Saʻid, "Tatawwur harakat al-asʻar," 412. Nakhul, "Bilad al-Batrun," 2:821.

89. Nickoley, "Historic Diary," 32.

90. Howard Bliss, "Letter, November 27, 1916," in "Correspondence on Food Supplies, 24 July 1916–1917, November 1918," Howard Bliss Collection: AUB President 1902–1920, archive AA:2.3.2, box 16, file 7, p. 3.

91. Al-Hakim, *Bayrut wa Lubnan*, 251.

92. Emphasis in original. Nickoley, "Historic Diary," 32.

93. These cases are drawn from an interview conducted with Hayat Mahmud on January 24, 2014.

Chapter 2

Epigraph taken from Nickoley, "Historic Diary," 44. Reprinted with the permission of the American University of Beirut Archives.

1. The Shiʻi in particular were targeted by Ottoman conscription policies. See chapter 1.

2. On this policy, see Tanielian, *The Charity of War*, 104; Metinsoy, *Ottoman Women during World War I*, 31; and Akın, *When the War Came Home*, 69, 114–18.

3. Doolittle, "Pathos and Humor," 89–90, 92–93.

4. Doolittle, 95–96.

5. For a discussion of numbers and famine classification, see de Waal, "The End of Famine?," 185.

6. Schilcher, "The Famine of 1915–1918 in Greater Syria," 229.

7. Yammine, *Quatre ans*, 51.

8. *L'Asie Française*, no. 199, 1922.

9. *Lisan al-Hal*, no. 7223, August 30, 1918, 2.

10. Adib, *Lubnan baʻd al-harb*, 52.

11. Nickoley, "Historic Diary," 8.

12. Doolittle, "Pathos and Humor," 87, 110.

13. Khuwayri, *Al-rihla al-suriyya*, 91.

14. Al-Baʻini, *Dhikrayat al-Amir Shakib Arslan*, 43. Arslan has been maligned as a famine denier in certain circles on account of a few dismissive quotes. See Havemann, "Impact of the First World War," 213–21.

15. The population declined from 798,389 to 748,128. See McCarthy, *Population of Palestine*, 26.

16. Bayard Dodge, "Relief Work in Syria During the Period of the War," 1919, Howard Bliss Collection: AUB President 1902–1920, archive AA:2.3.2, box 18, file 3, p. 13, American University of Beirut/Library Archives, Beirut, Lebanon.

17. Dodge, *The American University of Beirut*, 46.

18. In 1938, George Antonius estimated that the famine caused 300,000–350,000 deaths across Syria as a whole, a number that Albert Hourani repeats in his book *Syria and Lebanon*. See Antonius, *The Arab Awakening*, 241; and Hourani, *Syria and Lebanon*, 59. Stephen Longrigg ventures that a fifth of the mountain died and a significant but proportionately smaller number died along the coast. See Longrigg, *Syria and Lebanon*

under French Mandate, 49. Philip Hitti suggests a death toll of 100,000 out of 450,000 inhabitants in Mount Lebanon. See Hitti, *Lebanon in History*, 486. Nicholas Ajay agonizes over wartime mortality before eventually settling on an estimate that 24 percent of the combined population of Lebanon and the province of Beirut died, reduced to 20 percent to account for the effects of migration. See Ajay, "Mount Lebanon," 1:432–33. More recent historians have regarded the issue of numbers with skepticism. Elizabeth Thompson in *Colonial Citizens* notes the broad range of death tolls without trusting any of them. Fawwaz Traboulsi suggests that 100,000 died, while Graham Pitts has estimated that potentially 200,000 died between Mount Lebanon and the Beirut province. See Traboulsi, *A History of Modern Lebanon*, 72; and Pitts, "Fallow Fields," 38. Zachary Foster places the regional death tolls at 11–16 percent of the total inhabitants of greater Syria. See Foster, "The 1915 Locust Attack," 1. Tanielian has remained somewhat agnostic about the matter, but she has used local analysis to make excellent specific observations. See Tanielian, *The Charity of War*, 6; and Tanielian, "The War of Famine," 55–57. John Nakhul similarly has shown the variability of famine mortality in great detail in Nakhul, "Bilad al-Batrun," 2:795–867. It is easier to get totals from Christian communities because the churches kept records of births and deaths. For examples, see al-Najjar, *Masarat fi tarikh baladat al-Mtein*, 321–23. The most specific estimate comes from Istifan Ibrahim al-Khuri, who tallies 185,722 dead by parsing prewar statistics and wartime mortality estimates and adjusting for the impacts of migration. Al-Khuri uses the 414,800 figure cited in the *Mabahith* rather than the migration-adjusted figure as the baseline population, though he later removes migrants. In his statistical analysis, al-Khuri subtracts the figures provided in the *Mabahith* from 1918 population statistics, leaving a gap of 129,300 individuals. See al-Khuri, *Maja'a*, 259–71.

19. Contemporary estimates suggested that a third of the population of Mount Lebanon (around 120,000 people) had migrated prior to the war. See Jalal Bey, "Al-ahwal al-zira'iyya," 2: 469–70; and Fahrenthold, *Between the Ottomans and the Entente*, 6. Kamal Karpat estimates that an incredible 600,000 Lebanese and Syrians migrated from 1881 to 1914. See Karpat, "The Syrian Emigration from the Ottoman State," 294. See also Maktabi, "The Lebanese Census of 1932 Revisited," 225–26.

20. I have excluded Syrians and foreigners from this total since they would not have been tallied in the Ottoman census. See Ministère des Affaires Étrangères, "Rapport sur la situation de la Syrie et du Liban," 9.

21. For Lebanese census data, see Faour, "The Demography of Lebanon," 632. This total was reached by combining the lower range of the population estimates in the *Mabahith* with the region estimates for the district of Beirut (from within the province): Beirut's subdistrict contained a (low) 50,000, since many residents would have been registered in Mount Lebanon; 54,000 in Sidon; 41,240 in Tyre; 31,110 in Marjayoun; and 172,525 across the districts of Tripoli, for a total of 348,875. The population of the district of Ba'albek, which was included in Greater Lebanon after 1920, was roughly 33,000. See Bahjat and Tamimi, *Wilayat Bayrut*, 2:23; Naqqash, "Nadhara fi halat Jabal Lubnan al-iqtisadiyya," 2:472; and Aluf, *A History of Baalbek*, 10.

22. Sibley et al., *Social Survey of Syria*, 11–12.

23. Bahjat and Tamimi, *Wilayat Bayrut*. See also Baylan, "Jadwal Ihsa' Ahali Jabal Lubnan 'an Sana 1329."

24. See Jalal Bey, "Al-ahwal al-zira'aiyya," 470; and Naqqash, "Nadhara fi halat Jabal Lubnan al-iqtisadiyya," 472.

25. Fahrenthold, *Between the Ottomans and the Entente*, 17–19; Karpat, "The Syrian Emigration," 289–94.

26. See Fahrenthold, *Between the Ottomans and the Entente*, 154–155; Harris, *Lebanon*, 178.

27. See Ozdemir, *The Ottoman Army*, 119–122; Beşikçi, *Ottoman Mobilization*, 114.

28. Muhieddine, "Grafik yahtawi 'ala muqdar al-wafayat."

29. Muhieddine, "Jadwal al-tawalidat wa wafayat."

30. See Tomkins, "Nutrition and Maternal Morbidity and Mortality," S97.

31. See Schocken, Holloway, and Powers, "Weight Loss and the Heart," 877–81.

32. Sparén et al., "Long Term Mortality," 3–4.

33. See Sen, "Ingredients of Famine Analysis," 441, 447; and O Grada, *Famine*, 21.

34. Nakhul, "Bilad al-Batrun," 2:858–59.

35. Yammine, *Quatre ans*, 46.

36. George Doolittle, "Report of Sidon Station, Syria Mission, Summer 1915, to Summer 1916," PHS Archives, RG 115-17-19: Sidon Station Reports 1907–35, 2.

37. Dodge, "Relief Work," Howard Bliss Collection, archive AA:2.3.2, box 18, file 3, p. 13.

38. Harriet LaGrange, "Tripoli Girl's School Report 1916–1917," PHS Archives, RG 115-19-8: Tripoli Girls' School 1885–1964, 3.

39. Al-Maqdisi, *A'dham harb fil tarikh*, 70.

40. Butler, *Frames of War*, xix.

41. See also Sayyad, *The Suffering of the Immigrant*.

42. Butler, *Frames of War*, 31.

43. George Doolittle, "Report of Sidon Station, 1916," PHS Archives, RG 115-17-19: Sidon Station Reports 1907–35, 9–10.

44. This has been observed in other areas with high child mortality. See Scheper-Hughes, *Death Without Weeping*; Masterman, "Hygiene and Disease in Palestine," 71.

45. Sibley et al., *Social Survey*, 79–81.

46. Hertz, *Death and the Right Hand*, 54.

47. See Khayat, *Lebanon*, 119–27.

48. Taylor, *The Buried Soul*, 123.

49. Tanielian makes a similar observation in "The War of Famine," 61.

50. Nickoley, "Historic Diary," 44.

51. Hertz, *Death and the Right Hand*, 81.

52. Nickoley, "Historic Diary," 19.

53. Dodge, "Relief Work, Howard Bliss Collection, archive AA:2.3.2, box 18, file 3, p. 13.

54. Doolittle, "Pathos and Humor," 103.

55. Bulus 'Aqil, "Intelligence Report to Allied Agent, 19 October, 1916," in Ajay, "Mount Lebanon," 2:194–95.

56. McGilvary, *Dawn of a New Era*, 220–21.
57. Doolittle, "Pathos and Humor," 34.
58. Dodge, "Relief Work," Howard Bliss Collection, archive AA:2.3.2, box 18, file 3, p. 13.
59. Bahjat and Tamimi, *Wilayat Bayrut*, 1:290.
60. Doolittle, "Pathos and Humor," 110, 116.
61. Bahjat and Tamimi, *Wilayat Bayrut*, 1:296.
62. McGilvary, *Dawn of a New Era*, 204.
63. Ajay, "Mount Lebanon," 1:431. The location of said "sands" is vague, but they were likely located in Ras Beirut or in the patches of land south of Sana'aya, labeled "the sands" on contemporary maps. I have found little mention of mass grave discoveries as the city developed southward, but since such finds would have to be reported, it would not surprise me if the bodies were simply paved over to avoid construction delays.
64. Anonymous, "Tripoli Station Report 1917–1918," PHS Archives, RG: 115-19-18, Tripoli Station Reports 1891–1919, 4.
65. Orfalea, *Arab Americans*, 70.
66. Nickoley, "Historic Diary," 44.
67. Ajay, "Mount Lebanon," 1:399.
68. Nickoley, "Historic Diary," 44.
69. Doolittle, "Pathos and Humor," 34.
70. Al-Amin, *Autobiographie*, 164.
71. Doolittle, "Pathos and Humor," 87.
72. There were a few reported cases of starving individuals disinterring and eating corpses. None are verifiable—unlike a few of the cannibalism stories—but it is not unthinkable that this did occur.
73. Taylor, *The Buried Soul*, 222.
74. Doolittle, "Pathos and Humor," 86–88.
75. Brand, "Years of Horror," 179.
76. Nickoley, "Historic Diary," 2. Emphasis in the original.
77. Nickoley, 3.
78. Nickoley, 17.
79. Nickoley, 50.
80. See Tanielian, *The Charity of War*, 5.

Chapter 3

Epigraph taken from Al-Amin, *Autobiographie*, 167. Reprinted with the permission of Sabrina Mervin.

1. On this, see Carbonnier, *Humanitarian Economics*, 151–52, 187.
2. Al-Amin, *Autobiographie*, 164.
3. Al-Amin, 164.
4. Dhahir, *Jabal 'Amil*, 44–45.
5. Al-Amin, *Autobiographie*, 167.
6. Camporesi, *Bread of Dreams*, 122.
7. See Fawaz, *Land of Aching Hearts*, 1–4.

8. Additional discussion of this can be found in Brand, "Years of Horror," 179; Tanielian, "The War of Famine," 58–63; and, beautifully, in al-Qattan, "Eating Grass in WWI Syria."

9. Doolittle, "Pathos and Humor," 96.

10. See also al-Qattan, "When Mothers Ate Their Children," 721–22.

11. Sorokin, *Man and Society in Calamity*, 17–21.

12. Al-Maqdisi, *Aʿdham harb fi tarikh*, 68; Saʿad, *Jabal ʿAmil*, 47.

13. Nicholas Ajay, "Interview with George Ashqar" in Ajay, "Mount Lebanon," 2:78.

14. Nicholas Ajay, "Interview with Shehadi Salim Muʿallim" in Ajay, "Mount Lebanon," 2:397.

15. ʿAwad, *Min ʿahd al-mutasarrifiyya*, 44.

16. Doolittle, "Pathos and Humor," 114.

17. Appleby, "Grain Prices and Subsistence Crises," 868–69.

18. Affeffi Sabaʾ, "Letter to Anna Jessup September 1, 1916," PHS Archives, RG 115-8-16: Hamlin Memorial Sanatorium Correspondence 1916–27.

19. Nakhul, "Bilad al-Batrun," 2:814.

20. Yalman, *Turkey in the World War*, 144.

21. Ajay, "Mount Lebanon," 2:328.

22. Tannous, *Village Roots and Beyond*, 41; Gulick, *Social Structure*, 40.

23. Antun Yammine claims that villagers in the Biqaʿ pelted the caravan bearing Enver Pasha to express their disgust with their Turkish overlords. See Yammine, *Quatre ans*, 39.

24. Hayat Mahmud, interview by the author, January 24, 2014.

25. Brand, "Some Eat to Remember."

26. Riyashi, *Tarikh Zahle*, 157.

27. Orange prices had actually fallen due to the loss of an export market for major producers like Sidon and Jaffa. Nicholas Ajay, "Interview with Dr. Nabih Shab," in Ajay, "Mount Lebanon," 2:54.

28. Doolittle, "Pathos and Humor," 32.

29. Hayat Mahmoud, interview by the author, January 24, 2014.

30. Al-Amin, *Autobiographie*, 166.

31. Doolittle, "Pathos and Humor," 84.

32. Ira Harris, "Medical Report of the Tripoli Station—Syria Mission: for 1907," PHS Archives, RG 115-19-16: Tripoli—Medical Reports 1895–1914; Ira Harris, "Medical Work—Tripoli Station—Syrian Mission—1902," PHS Archives, RG 115-19-16: Tripoli—Medical Reports 1895–1914.

33. Nickoley, "Historic Diary," 4. In the Great Irish Famine, fodder maize acquired the epithet "Peel's brimstone" for its impacts on the human gut. See Keneally, *Three Famines*, 72.

34. Nickoley, "Historic Diary," 45.

35. Farhat, "Analysis of Indigenous Nutritional Knowledge," table 4. See also Khayat, *Lebanon*, 143–46.

36. Farhat, "Analysis of Indigenous Nutritional Knowledge," 62–63.

37. See Yammine, *Quatre ans*, 5, 46.

38. Doolittle, "Pathos and Humor," 103.
39. Al-Amin, *Autobiographie*, 168.
40. On the mune, see Massaad, *Mouneh*; and Kanafani-Zahar, *Mune*, 1–5.
41. Soumar Dakdouk, interview by the author, October 13, 2013.
42. Furayha, *Qabl an ansa*, 45–46.
43. Tannous, *Village Roots and Beyond*, 40–41.
44. ʿAwad, *Min ʿahd al-mutasarrifiyya*, 33–35.
45. ʿAwad, 44.
46. Riyashi lists the weight in *mudd*, which is a unit of volume roughly equivalent to 18 liters—13.5 kilograms of wheat. For a thorough analysis of weights and measures, see Issawi, *The Fertile Crescent*, 478–79; and Latron, *La vie rurale*, appendix 1.
47. Riyashi, *Tarikh Zahle*, 149, 174.
48. Owen, *The Middle East in the World Economy*, 254–60; Latron, *La vie rurale*.
49. Al-Amin, *Autobiographie*, 167; Dhahir, *Jabal ʿAmil*, 44.
50. Bahjat and Tamimi, *Wilayat Bayrut*, 2:276. See also Gilsenan, *Lords of the Lebanese Marches*, 148–50.
51. Riyashi, *Tarikh Zahle*, 155.
52. Latron, *La vie rurale*, 45.
53. Doolittle, "Pathos and Humor," 96.
54. Darwaza, *Mudhakkirat*, 1:288.
55. Darwaza's math may be questionable, but the point remains valid. Darwaza, 1:288.
56. Latron, *La vie rurale*, 46.
57. See Sen, *Poverty and Famines*, 102.
58. Sen, 161.
59. On lending, see Yammine, *Quatre ans*, 37; and Nickoley, "Historic Diary," 32–36.
60. The cartel, like other government distribution schemes, became a magnet for corruption. See Yammine, *Qatre ans*, 43, 73.
61. For figures on municipal tax revenues, see Bahjat and Tamimi, *Wilayat Bayrut*, 1:216, 306.
62. On the Beirut municipality's efforts, see Tanielian, "Feeding the City," 742–49.
63. Bahjat and Tamimi, *Wilayat Bayrut*, 1:306.
64. Bahjat and Tamimi, 1:290.
65. Anonymous, "Tripoli Station Report 1917–1918," PHS Archives, RG 115-19-18: Tripoli Station Reports 1891–1919, 4.
66. McGilvary, *Dawn of a New Era*, 135–36.
67. Statistics compiled by Gulick, *Tripoli*, 31.
68. Bahjat and Tamimi, *Wilayat Bayrut*, 1:196.
69. Riyashi, *Tarikh Zahle*, 144. See also Pitts, "Ecology of Migration," 116–18, for a short analysis of Zahle.
70. Furayha, *Qabl an ansa*, 42.
71. O Grada, *Famine*, 82.
72. ʿAwad, *Min ʿahd al-mutasarrifiyya*, 32; Hayak, *ʿAyn ʿAlaq bayn al-qarn al-sabiʿ wa al-qarn al-hadi wa al-ʿishrin*; Riyashi, *Tarikh Zahle*, 144; Furayha, *Qabl an ansa*, 42.
73. Doolittle, "Pathos and Humor," 87.

74. Bahjat and Tamimi, *Wilayat Bayrut*, 2:215–219.
75. Nickoley, "Historic Diary," 35.
76. Darwaza, *Mudhakkirat*, 1:288.
77. For a critique of the demoralization concept, see Solnit, *Paradise Built in Hell*, 6–10; and Carbonnier, *Humanitarian Economics*, 161.
78. See 'Awad, *Min 'ahd al-mutasarrifiyya*, 31–45.
79. Gulick, "Conservatism and Change," 303.
80. Tannous, "Group Behavior," 233.
81. Tannous, "The Village," 158.
82. Tannous, 28.
83. Sa'ab, *Stories and Scenes*, 337–38.
84. It may give pause that this anecdote was taken from a report to exonerate the Mission Press for its own much-critiqued lending practices. See Unknown (presumed Margaret McGilvary), "Relief Work and Loans to Syrians during the War," in *The American Press, Beirut Syria*, PHS Archives, RG 115-16-11: Relief Work 1915–1917, 6.
85. Doolittle, "Pathos and Humor," 114.
86. Ziadeh, "First-Person Account," 268.
87. Tanielian, *The Charity of War*, 6.

Chapter 4

Epigraph taken from Frederick Bliss, "The Question of Syria: Retrospect or Prospect," 1920, Howard Bliss Collection: AUB President 1902–1920, archive AA:2.3.2, box 18, file 3, p. 20, American University of Beirut/Library Archives, Beirut, Lebanon. Reprinted with the permission of the American University of Beirut Archives.

1. Bliss, 2.
2. Bliss, 8.
3. Bliss, 2.
4. Bliss, 20.
5. For a theoretical analysis of bearing witness and the audience-centric "rhetorical witnessing," see Allen, "Rhetorical Witnessing," 62.
6. Nicholas Ajay, "Interview with Salwa Salibi," in Ajay, "Mount Lebanon," 2:90.
7. Bulus 'Aqil, "Letter of Father 'Aqil to Allied Agent, October 3, 1916," in Ajay, "Mount Lebanon," 2:181.
8. LaCapra, *Writing History, Writing Trauma*, ix–x.
9. On trauma as an analytical field, see Craps, "Wor(l)ds of Grief," 52–59; and Craps and Beulens, "Introduction: Postcolonial Trauma Novels," 1–12.
10. LaCapra, *Writing History, Writing Trauma*, xi.
11. On time and history, see Kidambi, "Time, Temporality and History," 220–37.
12. See Jansen, "Time, Narrative, and Fiction," 16–18; Flaherty, *A Watched Pot*, 29–34.
13. "Tarikh al-inqilab," *Lisan al-Hal*, October 14, 1918, 2.
14. With some variation: areas like southern Iraq and Palestine that were conquered earlier would have naturally differed from areas like Syria and Anatolia, which remained part of the empire until the end. Likewise for the area around Mosul, which was captured after the armistice.

15. With the exception of the leap year of 1916.
16. Bliss, "The Question of Syria," Howard Bliss Collection, archive AA:2.3.2, box 18, file 3, p. 1.
17. W. S. Nelson, "Letter from W. S. Nelson to Charles Dana, April 25, 1916," PHS Archives, RG 115-16-10: Relief Work 1915–1917.
18. George Doolittle, "Second Letter from George Doolittle to Charles Dana, August 1, 1917," PHS Archives, RG 115-16-10: Relief Work 1915–1917.
19. McGilvary, *Dawn of a New Era*, 71.
20. William Nimeh, "War Annals of the College Part 4: 1915–1916," *al-Kulliyah* 6, no. 5, March 15, 1920, 37. On Nimeh's personal history, see Pastor, *The Mexican Mahjar*, 179–80.
21. See Brand, "Some Eat to Remember."
22. Bliss, "The Question of Syria," Howard Bliss Collection, archive AA:2.3.2, box 18, file 3, p. 1
23. McGilvary, *Dawn of a New Era*, 183.
24. Nickoley, "Historic Diary," 58. According to Ahmed Emin Yalman, the Ottoman lira's value in July of 1917 stood at 381 piasters to the lira, up from 100:1 when it was issued in July 1915. See Yalman, *Turkey in the World War*, 144.
25. Yammine, *Lubnan fil harb*.
26. Edib, *Memoirs of Halidé Edib*, 401.
27. Pitts, "Fallow Fields."
28. On the controversy over the Aziz "memoir," see Bordewitch, "Diaries of an Ottoman Spymaster," 112–134; and Aziz Bey, *Suriyya wa Lubnan fil harb al-'alamiyya*, 149. While the authorship and veracity of Aziz's memoir is in dispute, some events he noted are not, and in some cases, he shows a striking knowledge of intimate information.
29. De Nogales, *Four Years Beneath the Crescent*, 158.
30. See Salibi, "Beirut under the Young Turks," 211–15.
31. Khalidi, *Memoirs*, 64–71.
32. Ajay, "Mount Lebanon," 1:360.
33. For these descriptions, see 'Awad, *Min 'ahd al-mutasarrifiyya*, 34–36.
34. Nickoley, "Historic Diary," 55.
35. I experienced something like this while living in Beirut from 2012 until 2015 during the Syrian refugee crisis, and psychologists observed similar effects during the 2020 COVID-19 pandemic. Kalaichandran, "We're Not Ready for This Kind of Grief."
36. W. S. Nelson, "Tripoli Station Report, 1917," PHS Archives, RG: 115-19-18, Tripoli Station Reports 1891–1919, 1.
37. Bulus 'Aqil, "General Report on the Situation in Lebanon," in Ajay, "Mount Lebanon," 2:195.
38. Anonymous, "Report of Sidon Station 1916–1917," PHS Archives, RG 115-17-19: Sidon Station Reports 1907–35, 1.
39. Al-Maqdisi, *A'dham harb*, 69.
40. Ajay, "Mount Lebanon," 1:424.
41. Al-Maqdisi, *A'dham harb*, 69.
42. Dodge, "Report of the Abeih and Suk al-Gharb Soup Kitchens 1914–1918," Howard Bliss Collection, archive AA:2.3.2, box 18, file 3, p. 2.

43. Herman, *Trauma and Recovery*, 140.
44. Ajay, "Mount Lebanon," 1:397.
45. McGilvary, *Dawn of a New Era*, 206.
46. Bliss, "The Question of Syria," Howard Bliss Collection, archive AA:2.3.2, box 18, file 3, p. 1.
47. McGilvary, *Dawn of a New Era*, 206.
48. Al-Maqdisi, *A'dham harb*, 97.
49. Bliss, "The Question of Syria," Howard Bliss Collection, archive AA:2.3.2, box 18, file 3, p. 1.
50. Al-Maqdisi, *A'dham harb*, 69.
51. Nickoley, "Historic Diary," 44.
52. Al-Maqdisi, *A'dham harb*, 68.
53. For additional analysis of the seminary, see Fleischmann, "Living in 'An Isle of Safety'"; and Dora Eddy, "Report of Sidon Seminary, 1915–1916," PHS Archives, RG 115-17-18: Sidon Girls' School Reports 1906–1955.
54. Dora Eddy, "Report of Sidon Seminary, 1915–1916," PHS Archives, RG 115-17-18: Sidon Girls' School Reports 1906–1955, 3.
55. Charlotte Brown, "Report of the Sidon Seminary Oct. 1917-Oct. 1918" (this report was incorrectly labeled as 1918–1919 in the handwritten copy that followed), PHS Archives, RG 115-17-18: Sidon Girls' School Reports 1906–1955, 3.
56. Brown, 3.
57. Nickoley, "Historic Diary," 5.
58. Nickoley, 4–5.
59. Slovic et al., "Psychic Numbing and Mass Atrocity," 129.
60. Nickoley, "Historic Diary," 19.

Chapter 5
Epigraph taken from Al-Maqdisi, *A'dham harb*, 70.
1. Nicholas Ajay, "Interview with Yusuf Rufayil" in Ajay, "Mount Lebanon," 2:427.
2. Ajay, "Interview with Yusuf Rufayil," in Ajay, "Mount Lebanon," 2:61.
3. *Inhitat* is a loaded concept in historiography that has often been used to internally critique Islamic, Arab, or Ottoman society, either as an indication of internal spiritual failings or in relation to the rise of Europe. For a brief discussion, see Sacks, "Futures of Literature," 32.
4. Dodge, "Relief Work," Howard Bliss Collection, archive AA:2.3.2, box 18, file 3, p. 12.
5. Nickoley estimated that it would take generations for the country to morally recover from the disaster. See Nickoley, "Historic Diary," 6.
6. Tanielian, *The Charity of War*, 5.
7. On forms of narrative in history, see White, *Metahistory*, 7–11.
8. Dodge, "Report of the Abeih and Suk al-Gharb Soup Kitchens," Howard Bliss Collection, archive AA:2.3.2, box 18, file 3, p. 9.
9. Al-Maqdisi, *A'dham harb*, 58, 69; Dhahir, *Jabal 'Amil*, 43.

10. Sorokin, *Man and Society in Calamity*, 156.

11. This is itself not completely confirmed by data. The one study on this topic is Hablas, "Hadith al-maja'a," 1:209.

12. Nickoley, "Historic Diary," 6.

13. Doolittle, "Pathos and Humor," 33.

14. W. S. Nelson, "Tripoli Station Report, 1917," PHS Archives, RG 115-19-18: Tripoli Station Reports 1891–1919, 2.

15. Dhahir, *Jabal 'Amil*, 45–46; Sa'ab, *Stories and Scenes*, 163–68; Edib, *Memoirs of Halidé Edib*, 462; Anonymous, "Report of Tripoli Station, 1918–1919," PHS Archives, RG 115-19-18: Tripoli Station Reports 1891–1919.

16. Yammine, *Lubnan fil harb*, 5.

17. Nickoley, "Historic Diary," 32.

18. McGilvary, *Dawn of a New Era*, 69.

19. On prostitution in the Anatolian context, see Metinsoy, *Ottoman Women*, 101–2.

20. Tamari, *Year of the Locust*, 54.

21. Bliss, "The Question of Syria," Howard Bliss Collection, archive AA:2.3.2, box 18, file 3, p. 5.

22. Ajay, "Mount Lebanon," 1:394.

23. Yilmaz, "Threats to Public Order and Health," 233–37.

24. Douglas, *Purity and Danger*, 3–4.

25. See al-Qattan, "When Mothers Ate Their Children," 721–22.

26. Doolittle, "Pathos and Humor," 95.

27. Ajay, "Interview with Yusuf Rufayil," in Ajay, "Mount Lebanon," 2:60, 62.

28. Robert Byerly, "Report of Sidon Station, 1917 to 1918," PHS Archives, RG 115-17-19: Sidon Station Reports 1907–35, 3.

29. Nickoley, "Historic Diary," 17.

30. *Ptomaine* is an antiquated term for food poisoning (probably botulism). Nickoley, "Historic Diary," 4.

31. Doolittle, "Pathos and Humor," 114.

32. Nickoley, "Historic Diary," 17.

33. Nickoley, 17.

34. Nickoley, 4.

35. Yammine, *Quatre ans*, 46.

36. Grave robbing for food was treated with revulsion but less so than cannibalism resulting from premeditated murder. The topic of cannibalism in famine in general is controversial.

37. The police found a liver removed and apparently ready for cooking, as well as minced human flesh. Dhahir, *Jabal 'Amil*, 45–46.

38. Dhahir, 46.

39. Dhahir, 46.

40. O Grada, *Eating People Is Wrong*, 14–24.

41. The story of the girls who murdered boys near Tripoli can be found in a number of sources, and the tale of the man from Damour appears in at least three sources, includ-

ing Nickoley, "Historic Diary"; Dhahir, *Jabal Amil*; and Doolittle, "Pathos and Humor."

42. Lahd Khatir, *'Ahd al-mutasarrifiyyin fi Lubnan: 1861–1918* (Beirut: Dar Lahd Khatir, 1982), 207. Anonymous, "Tripoli Station Report 1917–1918," PHS Archives, RG 115-19-18: Tripoli Station Reports 1891–1919, 4.

43. Nickoley, "Historic Diary," 6.

44. Al-Maqdisi, *A'dham harb*, 69.

45. Fassin, *Humanitarian Reason*, 41.

46. Thompson, "Ontology of Disaster," 502.

47. A large collection of the photos is available at *L'Orient Le Jour*: "Famine au Mont Liban (1915–1918): Images de l'horreur," *L'Orient Le Jour*, accessed May 15, 2022, https://www.lorientlejour.com/multimedia/702-famine-au-mont-liban-1915-1918-images-de-lhorreur.

48. On the topic of innocence in crisis portrayals, see O Grada, *Famine*, 99. See also Moeller, *Compassion Fatigue*, 68; and McKinney, "Breaking the Conspiracy of Silence," 289.

49. Butler, *Frames of War*, 71.

50. Melanie Tanielian makes this observation in *The Charity of War*, 246–47.

51. Recuber, "Disaster Porn!," 28.

52. Nickoley, "Historic Diary," 4.

53. Nickoley, 4.

54. Brand, "Years of Horror," 179.

55. See Adriana Cavarero for a theoretical assessment of horror: Cavarero, *Horrorism*, 42–44.

56. On this point, I disagree with Talal Asad's assessment that horror is an intransitive thing—to experience the feeling of horror, which he defines (via Stanley Cavell) as the "feeling of precariousness of human identity," you need to be horrified by or at something. Asad, *On Suicide Bombing*, 68.

57. Douglas, *Purity and Danger*, 95.

58. Nickoley, "Historic Diary," 4.

59. Nickoley, 19.

60. Al-Maqdisi, *A'dham harb*, 69.

61. Doolittle, "Pathos and Humor," 31.

62. The passage is from Lamentations 4: 8. Al-Maqdisi, *A'dham harb*, 70.

63. Al-Maqdisi, 68–69.

64. Nickoley, "Historic Diary," 17.

65. Qattan, "When Mothers Ate Their Children," 720.

66. Sa'ab, *Stories and Scenes*, 209. Ajay, "Interview with Salwa Salibi," in Ajay, "Mount Lebanon," 2:91.

67. Khalidi, *Memoirs of an Early Arab Feminist*, 68.

68. Nickoley, "Historic Diary," 17.

69. Yammine, *Lubnan fi l harb*, 115.

70. Dhahir, *Jabal 'Amil*, 45.

71. Camporesi, *Bread of Dreams*, 26.

72. Douglas, *Purity and Danger*, 35.

73. Ajay, "Political Intrigue and Suppression," 142–46.

74. See Ajay, 150–53; and Fawaz, *Land of Aching Hearts*, 248–49. A detailed account of wartime information and control is provided in the potentially fabricated memoir of Aziz Bey, *Suriyya wa Lubnan fil-harb al-ʿalamiyya*, 197–229. Though "Aziz's" account is suspect, whoever wrote it reflected the state's attitudes during the war.

75. Akın, *When the War Came Home*, 66.

76. Furayha, *Qabl an ansa*, 42–43.

77. Pitirim Sorokin argues that this is a common feature of disaster. See Sorokin, *Man and Society in Calamity*, 30.

78. LaCapra, *Writing History, Writing Trauma*, 35.

79. Recuber, *Consuming Catastrophe*, 9.

80. Tilly, "Reasons Why," 447.

81. See Douglas, Sutton, and Cichocka, "The Psychology of Conspiracy Theories," 538–42.

82. Information gathering is a common response to crisis. See Thompson, "Ontology of Disaster," 501–2. Charles Rosenberg's concept of dramaturgy makes a similar point; see Rosenberg, "What Is an Epidemic?," 282–83.

83. Sorokin, *Man and Society in Calamity*, 28.

84. Sorokin, 33. In this respect, we can view the gossip networks as analogs of the "doomscrolling" (obsessively checking the news for updates during dark times) that has become so common in our present calamities.

85. McGilvary, *Dawn of a New Era*, 180.

86. This is not to be confused with the current trend of internet memes, though the concept is related. In this sense, a meme is a piece of information, a message, a story, etc., that is replicated through social transmission, spreading through the population like a trait through a gene pool (accumulating slight variations, i.e., mutations, along the way). This concept is articulated in an early phase decades ago by Richard Dawkins in *The Selfish Gene* (Oxford: Oxford University Press, 2006), 192–201.

87. Harriet LaGrange, "Tripoli Girl's School Report 1916–1917," PHS Archives, RG 115-19-8: Tripoli Girls' School 1885–1964, 2.

88. Nickoley, "Historic Diary," 3.

89. Nickoley, "Historic Diary," 7–8.

90. Nickoley, 17.

91. Howard Bliss, "Letter, November 23, 1916," in "Correspondence on Food Supplies, 24 July 1916–1917, November 1918," Howard Bliss Collection: AUB President 1902–1920, archive AA:2.3.2, box 16, file 7, p. 1.

92. On this idea, see Butler, *Frames of War*, 41.

93. On trauma and bearing witness, see Zelizer, "Finding Aids to the Past," 697–99. See also Tait, "Bearing Witness, Journalism and Moral Responsibility," 1221–22.

94. This is an inversion of the normal understanding of the role of media in identity formation most famously postulated by Benedict Anderson's *Imagined Communities*, which assert that the creation of such collective identities depends on mass media to convey uniform concepts of place and identification. See also Fritz, "Disasters and Mental Health," 28.

95. Alex de Waal notes that the re-narration of famine through the subjective lenses of observers was common in late twentieth-century famines as well. See de Waal, *Famine That Kills*, 23.

96. Fassin, *Humanitarian Reason*, 37.

97. Camporesi, *Bread of Dreams*, 26.

Chapter 6

Epigraph taken from Al-Maqdisi, *Aʿdham harb*, 75.

1. Al-Maqdisi, 75.
2. Doolittle, "Pathos and Humor," 103.
3. Yammine, *Quatre ans*, 42, 48.
4. Rosenberg, "What Is an Epidemic?," 292.
5. The idea of disease as construct has elicited a variety of strong opinions. See Foucault, *Birth of the Clinic*; and Foucault, *Discipline and Punish*. For criticism, see Rosenberg, "Disease in History," 1–3; and Anderson, "Disease, Culture and History," 30–33. For a more recent sociological defense, see Conrad and Barker, "Social Construction of Illness," 67–79. For Middle Eastern contexts, see Watts, *Epidemics and History*.
6. Hayes, *Burdens of Disease*, 3.
7. Even Melanie Tanielian's generally solid discussion of disease is introduced by the plague story; see Tanielian, *The Charity of War*, 141–43. For other good analyses, see Pitts, "Fallow Fields"; and Ajay, "Mount Lebanon."
8. There were only two recorded cases of plague during the war. In Husni Bey Muhieddine's report on the health situation in Lebanon during the truncated year of 1917, there were merely 33 cholera cases, while dysentery and typhoid struck 245 and 292 individuals, respectively, with exceptionally high case fatality rates of 33 percent and 18 percent, respectively. See Muhieddine, "Jadwal al-amrad al-sariyya."
9. The malarial crisis during the war was blamed by some contemporaries on the lack of access to quinine. See Dodge, "Report of the Abeih and Suk al-Gharb Soup Kitchens 1914–1918," Howard Bliss Collection, archive AA:2.3.2, box 18, file 3.
10. Masterman, "Hygiene and Disease in Palestine," 61–67.
11. The surveyors of the province of Beirut reported no smallpox cases in ʿAkkar in 1916 (1332) due to the vaccination of sixty thousand individuals in the region; see Bahjat and Tamimi, *Wilayat Bayrut*, 2:287. However, there were regional variations. Husni Bey Muhieddine reported a high incidence of the disease in the district of the Matn, likely due to the large number of unvaccinated Armenian refugees in terrible conditions in Bourj Hammoud. See Muhieddine, "Jadwal al-amrad al-sariyya." See also Tanielian, *The Charity of War*, 158–61.
12. CFR is the percentage of those infected who die as a result of the disease. For statistics, see Muhieddine, "Jadwal al-amrad al-sariyya."
13. Ira Harris, "Medical Report for 1911, Syria Mission," PHS Archives, RG115-19-10: Tripoli Kennedy Memorial Hospital 1914–1963, 6. On applications of biopower in the Middle East and the implications of state application, see Khaled Fahmy, *In Quest of Justice*, 16–21; and Fahmy, "Medicine and Power," 38–50.

14. Adams, "Ulcus Epidemicum," 605–8.

15. Syphilis was called *al-zuhari* (a term confusingly also applied to other sexually transmitted diseases like gonorrhea) and the more etymologically suggestive name of *al-ifranji*, which indicated that the disease was associated with the "Franks," a term denoting any Europeans. See Shahbandar, *Kitab al-wiqayya*, 80–83. See also Boyer, *Conditions hygiéniques*, 97; and Hasselmann, "Syphilis among Arabs in the Near East," 841–45. Syphilis was also a scourge during Ibrahim Pasha's 1831 invasion of Ottoman Syria. Khaled Fahmy writes that the number of syphilis infections equaled that of all other infections *combined* during the campaign. See Fahmy, "Women, Medicine, and Power," 43.

16. Muhieddine, "Grafik al-wafayat."

17. Brabin, "Malaria's Contribution," 9–10.

18. Malaria afflicted the Ottoman and British armies alike in Palestine. See Ozdemir, *The Ottoman Army*, 100–102; and Dolev, *Allenby's Military Medicine*.

19. Muhieddine, "Al-umur al-sihiyya," 649–50.

20. See Brand, "Lives Darkened by Calamity," 83–91; Gratien, "The Ottoman Quagmire," 583–85; and Pitts, "Fallow Fields," 186–209.

21. George Doolittle, "Report of Sidon Station 1916–1917," PHS Archives, RG 115-17-19: Sidon Station Reports 1907–35, 8.

22. Ozdemir, *The Ottoman Army*, 100.

23. Impressively, the sample size was 7,771. Masterman, "Hygiene and Disease," 62.

24. Boyer, *Conditions hygiéniques*, 98.

25. Timing varied by parasite. The "tropical" or malignant variety, *Plasmodium falciparum*, prefers warmer weather. See Masterman, "Hygiene and Disease," 63.

26. Horsfall, *Medical Entomology*, 341.

27. See Kliger, "Movements of Anopheles," 75.

28. Kliger, "Notes on the Hibernation of Anopheles Mosquitos," 404.

29. Bahjat and Tamimi, *Wilayat Bayrut*, 1:296.

30. Edema is inflammation.

31. Snowden, *The Conquest of Malaria*, 13–14; and Masterman, "Hygiene and Disease," 63.

32. See Butterly and Shepherd, *Hunger*, 166. Such symptoms are described by Khalidi, *Memoirs of an Early Arab Feminist*, 68.

33. For an approachable discussion of malarial symptoms, see Snowden, *The Conquest of Malaria*, 13–14. For more technical descriptions, see Bloland and Williams, *Malaria Control*; and Horsfall, *Medical Entomology*, 337–39.

34. Horsfall, *Medical Entomology*, 340.

35. Masterman, "Hygiene and Disease," 63.

36. Butterly and Shepherd, *Hunger*, 214–17.

37. Svedberg, *Poverty and Undernutrition*, 201–2.

38. As calculated from Muhieddine, "Jadwal al-amrad al-sariyya."

39. Carmichael, "Infection," 53.

40. Carmichael, "Infection," 65.

41. Bloland and Williams, *Malaria Control*, 20–21.

42. See Conferees, "Relationship of Nutrition, Disease and Social Conditions," 308.

43. Carmichael, "Infection," 63.

44. Bahjat and Tamimi, *Wilayat Bayrut*, 2:296. On Ottoman attempts to regulate men, see Yilmaz, "Threats to Public Order and Health," 234.

45. Muhieddine, "Al-umur al-sihiyya," 651.

46. Philippe and Mansi, "Nonlinearity"; Koopman and Longini, "Ecological Effects"; and Waldman, "Infectious Diseases," 310.

47. Bloland and Williams, *Malaria Control*, 4, 14, 17.

48. Zinsser, *Rats, Lice and History*, 283.

49. Zinsser, 296.

50. Tanielian, *The Charity of War*, 152.

51. Muhieddine, "Al-umur al-sihiyya," 658.

52. Zinsser suggests that typhus was better established in the "East" than in Western Europe prior to the continental wars of the sixteenth and seventeenth centuries. See Zinsser, *Rats, Lice and History*, 246–48.

53. Boyer, *Conditions hygiéniques*, 104; and Hanssen, "Colonial Anxiety," 53.

54. Corbett, "Typhus Fever in Palestine," 887–88. See also Masterman, "Hygiene and Disease," 64.

55. Muhieddine, "Jadwal al-asabat wa wafayat."

56. Refugees were drawn to larger local towns like 'Amioun and Jazzine but in smaller numbers than to the major cities. For information on 'Amioun and other towns in Koura, see al-Hakim, *Bayrut wa Lubnan*.

57. For analysis of the road systems in Mount Lebanon, see Sami Bey, "Tarikh ahwal al-turuqat fi Jabal Lubnan," 2:600–615.

58. Doolittle, "Pathos and Humor," 103.

59. Nicholas Ajay, "Interview with Dr. Joseph Hitti" in Ajay, "Mount Lebanon," 2:83.

60. Bahjat and Tamimi, *Wilayat Bayrut*, 1:296.

61. Muhieddine, "Jadwal al-asabat wa wafayat."

62. Anonymous, "Report Lebanon Station 1918, Syria Mission," PHS Archives, RG 115-10-10: Lebanon Station Reports 1911–29, 1.

63. Ajay, "Mount Lebanon," 1:416.

64. Yammine, *Quatre ans*, 48. For mistaken figures, see Nantet, *Histoire du Liban*, 233.

65. One caveat: this rate was calculated in the 1917 epidemic. Dr. Joseph Hitti's low estimate was that typhus had a 30 percent CFR, but mortality statistics taken from Muhieddine's "Al-umur al-sihiyya" put the rate at 19.3 percent across Mount Lebanon—this may be an underestimation due to the neglect of nonclinical cases, but the benefit of the state's numbers is that they give mortality figures for *known* infections.

66. The population of Beirut was estimated to be 120,000–150,000 and the population of Mount Lebanon to be 414,800 (see Baylan, "Jadwal Ihsa' Ahali Jabal Lubnan 'an Sana 1329"). The latter figure was likely closer to 350,000 if one accounts for the massive migration that took place prior to the war.

67. Typhus does confer immunity to survivors, so this is not out of the question.
68. Muhieddine, "Jadwal al-amrad al-sariyya."
69. See Tanielian, "The War of Famine," 89.
70. Arzuni, *Tarikh Shuhur al-ijtima'i*, 264.
71. Bahjat and Tamimi, *Wilayat Bayrut*, 1:296.
72. Bahjat and Tamimi, 1:137.
73. Bahjat and Tamimi, 2:25.
74. Ajay, "Mount Lebanon," 1:432.
75. Statistics from Muhieddine, "Jadwal al-asabat wa wafayat."
76. Moeller, *Compassion Fatigue*, 62.
77. For comparison, CDC statistics estimate that the 2014–16 Ebola outbreak, which fixated the globe and restricted travel from central Africa, had a CFR of 39.5 percent. See Center for Disease Control and Prevention, "2014–2016 Ebola Outbreak in West Africa."
78. Rosenberg, "What Is an Epidemic?," 282–84.
79. Masterman, "Hygiene and Disease," 17.
80. Perhaps the most famous authority on the topic of lice and typhus fever (and certainly the most entertaining) was Hans Zinsser, who expressed a surprisingly tender appreciation of the creatures in his monumental work *Rats, Lice and History*. Zinsser notes that while lice have been demonized as vectors of typhus and plague, the disease is in fact 100 percent fatal for them. He writes, "If lice can dread, the nightmare of their lives is the fear of some day inhabiting an infected rat or human being. . . . In eight days he sickens, in ten days he is *in extremis*, on the eleventh or twelfth his tiny body turns red with blood extravasated from his bowel, and he gives up his little ghost." Zinsser, *Rats, Lice and History*, 168.
81. Ajay, "Mount Lebanon," 2:82
82. Ozdemir, *The Ottoman Army*, 56–57.
83. Arthur Fowler, "Tripoli Station Report 1915–1916," PHS Archives, RG 115-19-18: Tripoli Station Reports 1891–1919, 3.
84. McGilvary, *Dawn of a New Era*, 92.
85. Doolittle, "Pathos and Humor," 63.
86. Harriet LaGrange, "Tripoli Girl's School Report 1916–1917," PHS Archives, RG 115-19-8: Tripoli Girls' School 1885–1964, 3.
87. Doolittle, "Pathos and Humor," 85.
88. Nickoley, "Historic Diary," 43.
89. Nickoley, 43.
90. Nickoley, 4.
91. Al-Maqdisi, *A'dham harb*, 58.
92. Doolittle, "Pathos and Humor," 126.
93. Charlotte Brown, "Report of the Sidon Seminary Oct. 1917–Oct. 1918" (incorrectly labeled as 1918–1919 in the handwritten copy that followed), PHS Archives, RG 115-17-18: Sidon Girls' School Reports 1906–1955, 3.
94. Nickoley, "Historic Diary," 3.

Chapter 7

Epigraph taken from McGilvary, *Dawn of a New Era*, 110.

1. McGilvary, *Story of Our Syria Mission*, 1.

2. Much of the aid was channeled through the Presbyterian-backed Near East Relief foundation, which spent $12,527,957.39 on relief work in Syria alone from its inception in 1915 as a rescue fund for survivors of the Armenian genocide until 1929 (the rough equivalent $217 million in 2022 dollars). At the time, this was an enormous sum for a private organization, even one with fingers in the bottomless pockets of American aristocrats like John D. Rockefeller and Cleveland Dodge. See Barton, *Story of Near East Relief*, 439, and Tejirian, "Faith of Our Fathers."

3. For recent work on this, see Ouhanes, "'Machine Age Humanitarianism,'" 184, 192–95.

4. Doolittle, "Pathos and Humor," 122.

5. Mark Bristol to Force Commander, "Data about the Near East Relief in General and in the Syria-Palestine Area, 1920" in Bayard Dodge Collection, Personal Letters 1917–1919, archive AA:2.3.4, box 7, file 1, American University of Beirut/Library Archives, Beirut, Lebanon.

6. This ethos is laid out clearly by Bliss in *The Modern Missionary*.

7. George Doolittle, "Report of Sidon Station, Syria Mission, Summer 1915, to Summer 1916," PHS Archives, RG 115-17-19: Sidon Station Reports 1907–35, 2.

8. William Jessup, "Report of Beirut Station, 1914–1915," PHS Archives, RG 115-4-17: Beirut Station Reports 1902–1916, 1.

9. Doolittle, "Pathos and Humor," 122.

10. On aid, see Watenpaugh, *Bread from Stones*; al-Khuri, *Majaʿa*, 199–240; Tanielian, *The Charity of War*; Brand, "That They May Have Life," 51–62; Jackson, "Compassion and Connections"; Jacobson, "A City Living through Crisis," 80–82; and Barton, *Story of Near East Relief*. See also the work on charity in Muslim societies by Singer, *Charity in Islamic Societies*.

11. The relationship between categorization and death is discussed as an extension of biopower in Achille Mbembe's *Necropolitics*. Mbembe and Foucault intend to show how sovereignty and power related to innate identities like race, but the concept is also relevant to the power dynamic between the humanitarian and the impoverished supplicant for aid. See Mbembe, *Necropolitics*, 71.

12. McGilvary, *Dawn of a New Era*, 209–34; and Cortas, *A World I Loved*.

13. On this, see Tanielian, *The Charity of War*, chapter 6.

14. For a description of the negotiation process, see Khalidi, *Memoirs of an Early Arab Feminist*, 68–72. In addition to Tanielian, *The Charity of War*, see also Jacobson, "A City Living through Crisis," 80–82.

15. Tanielian, *The Charity of War*, 226–29.

16. See Brand, "That They May Have Life." 55.

17. Jackson, "Compassion and Connections, 90.

18. McGilvary, *Dawn of a New Era*, 92.

19. Watenpaugh, *Bread from Stones*, 18–19.

20. Anonymous, "War Annals of the College Part 4: 1915–1916," *al-Kulliyah* 5, no. 6 (1915): 35–37.

21. Some were not particularly well hidden, like the soup kitchen in the Khayat's building across the street from the college.

22. Anonymous, "War Annals of the College," 36.

23. Nickoley, "Historic Diary," 5.

24. Nickoley, 5.

25. McGilvary, *Dawn of a New Era*, 91.

26. Doolittle, "Pathos and Humor," 73.

27. McGilvary, *Dawn of a New Era*, 92.

28. Several sources accuse the mutasarrif himself of looting the wheat company with Lebanon's general health inspector, Najib al-Asfar, whose participation in the project nearly caused Abu 'Izzedine Effendi to quit before it even started. Antun Yammine also accuses Georges Mezher of stealing five thousand liras from the Hadath distribution center. See Yammine, *Quatre ans*, 22; and Doolittle, "Pathos and Humor," 73.

29. McGilvary, *Dawn of a New Era*, 210–11; and Ajay, "Mount Lebanon," 1:460.

30. See Lindner, "From George Tom," 59–61.

31. Paul Erdman, "The Press Report for the Year 1918," 1918, PHS Archives, RG 115-2-1: American Press Annual Reports 1918–30, 4.

32. Oscar Gunkel, "Letter #113 from Oscar Gunkel (Standard Oil) to Charles Dana, January 6, 1916," PHS Archives, RG 115-16-10: Relief Work 1915–1917; Oscar Gunkel, "Letter #120 from Oscar Gunkel (Standard Oil) to Charles Dana, January 20, 1916," PHS Archives, RG 115-16-10: Relief Work 1915–1917.

33. Lindner, "From George Tom," 61.

34. Paul Erdman, "The Press Report for the Year 1918," 1918, PHS Archives, RG 115-2-1: American Press Annual Reports 1918–30, 8.

35. Anonymous, "Relief Work and Loans to Syrians during the War," PHS Archives, RG 115-16-11: Relief Work 1915–1917, 4.

36. Anonymous, "Tripoli Station Report 1917–1918," PHS Archives, RG 115-19-18: Tripoli Station Reports 1891–1919, 12.

37. George Doolittle, "Report of Sidon Station, Syria Mission, Summer 1915, to Summer 1916," PHS Archives, RG 115-17-19: Sidon Station Reports 1907–35, 4.

38. McGilvary, *Dawn of a New Era*, 192–93.

39. Paul Erdman, "The Press Report for the Year 1918," 1918, PHS Archives, RG 115-2-1: American Press Annual Reports 1918–30, 8.

40. Doolittle, "Pathos and Humor," 7–11.

41. The metric equivalent of nine *qantars*. W. S. Nelson, "Letter #153 from W. S. Nelson to Charles Dana, August 18, 1917," PHS Archives, RG 115-16-10: Relief Work 1915–1917, 1.

42. W. S. Nelson, "Letter #153 from W. S. Nelson to Charles Dana, August 18, 1917," PHS Archives, RG 115-16-10: Relief Work 1915–1917, 6.

43. Paul Erdman, "Letter from Paul Erdman to Charles Dana, January 15, 1917," PHS Archives, RG 115-16-11: Relief Work 1915–1917, 1.

218   Notes to Chapter 7

44. George Doolittle, "Communication from American Press to George Doolittle, November 2, 1916," PHS Archives, RG 115-16-10: Relief Work 1915–1917, 1.

45. W. S. Nelson, "Letter from W. S. Nelson to Charles Dana, March 30, 1916," PHS Archives, RG 115-16-10: Relief Work 1915–1917, 1.

46. W. S. Nelson, "Letter from W. S. Nelson to Charles Dana, March 31, 1916," PHS Archives, RG 115-16-10: Relief Work 1915–1917, 1.

47. Paul Erdman, "Letter from Paul Erdman to Charles Dana, February 5, 1916," PHS Archives, RG 115-16-11: Relief Work 1915–1917, 1; Paul Erdman, "Letter from Paul Erdman to Charles Dana, March 27, 1916," PHS Archives, RG 115-16-11: Relief Work 1915–1917, 1; Paul Erdman, "Letter from Paul Erdman to Charles Dana, May 8, 1916," PHS Archives, RG 115-16-11: Relief Work 1915–1917, 1.

48. George Doolittle, "Letter from George Doolittle to Charles Dana, November 8, 1917," PHS Archives, RG 115-16-10: Relief Work 1915–1917, 1.

49. William S. Nelson, "Letter # 170 from W. S. Nelson to Charles Dana, November 20, 1917," PHS Archives, RG 115-16-10: Relief Work 1915–1917. See also Doolittle, "Pathos and Humor," 123.

50. Paul Erdman, "The Press Report for the Year 1918," 1918, PHS Archives, RG 115-2-1: American Press Annual Reports 1918–30, 7.

51. W. S. Nelson, "Letter from W. S. Nelson to Charles Dana, March 30, 1916," PHS Archives, RG 115-16-10: Relief Work 1915–1917, 1.

52. George Doolittle, "Letter from George Doolittle to Charles Dana, May 22, 1917," PHS Archives, RG 115-16-10: Relief Work 1915–1917, 1.

53. Affeffi Saba, "Letter to Anna Jessup," August 25, 1916, PHS Archives, RG 115-8-16: Hamlin Memorial San. Corres, 1916–27, 1.

54. Nickoley, "Historic Diary," 33.

55. Anonymous, "Relief Work and Loans to Syrians during the War," PHS Archives, RG 115-16-11: Relief Work 1915–1917, 3–6.

56. George Doolittle, "Pathos and Humor," 33.

57. De Waal, "The End of Famine?," 192.

58. Paul Erdman, "Letter from Paul Erdman to Charles Dana, October 31, 1917," PHS Archives, RG 115-16-11: Relief Work 1915–1917, 2.

59. McGilvary, *Dawn of a New Era*, 104; and Lindner, "From George Tom," 61.

60. George Scherer, "Annual Report of Sidon Station, Syria Mission for the year 1914–1915," PHS Archives, RG 115-17-19: Sidon Station Reports 1907–35, 9.

61. Robert Byerly, "Report of Sidon Station, 1917 to 1918," PHS Archives, RG 115-17-19: Sidon Station Reports 1907–35, 6.

62. Arthur Fowler, "Tripoli Station Report for 1914–1915," PHS Archives, RG 115-19-18: Tripoli Station Reports 1891–1919, 5.

63. Fowler, 5.

64. Fowler, 7.

65. Anonymous, "Report Lebanon Station 1918, Syria Mission," PHS Archives, RG 115-10-10: Lebanon Station Reports 1911–29, 3.

66. W. S. Nelson, "Tripoli Station Report, 1917," PHS Archives, RG 115-19-18: Tripoli Station Reports 1891–1919, 2.

67. Nelson, 7.
68. Anonymous, "Report of Lebanon Station 1917, Syria Mission," PHS Archives, RG 115-10-10: Lebanon Station Reports 1911–29, 3.
69. Anonymous, 3.
70. Anonymous, "Report of Tripoli Station, 1918–1919," PHS Archives, RG 115-19-18: Tripoli Station Reports 1891–1919, 2.
71. Anonymous, "Report of Beirut Station 1917 & 1918, Syria Mission," PHS Archives, RG 115-4-17: Beirut Station Reports 1902–1916, 3.
72. Tripoli bishop Antun 'Arida and Greek Orthodox patriarch Gregorios Haddad in Damascus are excellent examples of this. See al-Hakim, *Bayrut wa Lubnan*, 254.
73. Bayard Dodge, "The Near East Relief in Syria," Howard Bliss Collection, AUB Archives AA.7.5, box 2, file 4, p. 2.
74. McGilvary, *Dawn of a New Era*, 224.
75. Paul Erdman, "Letter from Erdman to Dana, October 31, 1917," PHS Archives, RG 115-16-11: Relief Work 1915–1917, 2.
76. Arthur Fowler, "Tripoli Station Report for 1914–1915," PHS Archives, RG 115-19-18: Tripoli Station Reports 1891–1919, 4.
77. Watenpaugh, *Bread from Stones*, 33.
78. For more details, see Paul Erdman, "Letter from Paul Erdman to Charles Dana, October 31, 1917," PHS Archives, RG 115-16-11: Relief Work 1915–1917.
79. All points but the first paraphrased from Robert Byerly, "Report of Sidon Station, 1917 to 1918," PHS Archives, RG 115-17-19: Sidon Station Reports 1907–35. See also Paul Erdman, "Letter from Paul Erdman to Charles Dana, October 31, 1917," PHS Archives, RG 115-16-11: Relief Work 1915–1917.
80. Robert Byerly, "Report of Sidon Station, 1917 to 1918," PHS Archives, RG 115-17-19: Sidon Station Reports 1907–35, 1.
81. Byerly, 1.
82. Carbonnier, *Humanitarian Economics*, 171–74; and UNHCR, "Cash Assistance and Protection," 1–7. See also Harvey, "Cash-Based Responses," 1–3.
83. Butler, *Frames of War*, 53.
84. Aloudat, "The Damage Aid Workers Can Do."
85. See Bayard Dodge, "Report of the Abeih and Suk al-Gharb Soup Kitchens," Howard Bliss Collection, archive AA:2.3.2, box 18, file 3. Tanielian has written on this issue as well; see Tanielian, *The Charity of War*, 222–23.
86. MacKay, "The Mendicity Society," 42.
87. Carbonnier, *Humanitarian Economics*, 34.
88. Cardozo et al. "Psychological Distress," 2–3. See also Daubman, Black, and Goodman, "Recognizing Moral Distress," 696–98.
89. Doolittle, "Pathos and Humor," 122.
90. Anonymous, "Report of Beirut Station 1917 & 1918, Syria Mission," PHS Archives, RG 115-4-17: Beirut Station Reports 1902–1916, 1.
91. Nickoley, "Historic Diary," 5.
92. Dodge, "Report of the Abeih and Suk al-Gharb Soup Kitchens," Howard Bliss Collection, archive AA:2.3.2, box 18, file 3, p. 3.

93. Bliss, "The Question of Syria," Howard Bliss Collection, archive AA:2.3.2, box 18, file 3, p. 2.
94. Bliss, "The Question of Syria," Howard Bliss Collection, archive AA:2.3.2, box 18, file 3, pp. 2–3.
95. McGilvary, *Dawn of a New Era*, 199.
96. Emphasis in the original.
97. Doolittle, "Pathos and Humor," 133.
98. Robert Byerly, "Report of Sidon Station, 1917 to 1918," PHS Archives, RG 115-17-19: Sidon Station Reports 1907–35, 5.
99. This is calculated at the official Ottoman exchange rate used by the mission of 100 piasters to a pound, though with inflation, the value was significantly less, since the stipend was generally paid in paper.
100. *Kibbeh* is a mixture of spiced minced meat, pine nuts, and burghul
101. Robert Byerly, "Report of Sidon Station, 1917 to 1918," PHS Archives, RG 115-17-19: Sidon Station Reports 1907–35, 3.
102. A version of this analysis appears in Brand, "Some Eat to Remember."
103. Robert Byerly, "Report of Sidon Station, 1917 to 1918," PHS Archives, RG 115-17-19: Sidon Station Reports 1907–35, 3.

Conclusion

Epigraph taken from Rantisi, "The Murderer Inside Me (Us)." Reprinted with her permission.

1. Fawaz, *Land of Aching Hearts*, 279.
2. Halwani, "The Memory Tree."
3. Tanielian, *The Charity of War*, 5; al-Qattan, "Historicizing Hunger," 111.
4. For the text of Mahmassani's speech, see Ajay, "Political Intrigue and Suppression," 155.
5. Barakat, *Safar Barlik*.
6. Stone, *Popular Culture and Nationalism*, 144–52.
7. Sa'ab, *Stories and Scenes*, 73–76.
8. See Thompson, *Colonial Citizens*, 22–23.
9. On grain riots, see Fawaz, "Family and Famine in Beirut," 250; and Khalidi, "The Arab World," 298. On spies, see Ajay, "Political Intrigue and Suppression," 140–60.
10. Sukarieh and Khalidi, "Near Eastern Banditry," 280.
11. Sukarieh and Khalidi, 280.
12. Sukarieh and Khalidi, 274, 281.
13. Essentially, "Fuck the Turks!"
14. Soumar Dakdouk, interview by the author, October 13, 2013.
15. Furayha, *Qabl an ansa*, 41.
16. Thompson, *Colonial Citizens*, 24–28.
17. Hayat Mahmud, interview by the author, January 24, 2014.
18. See Tannous, *Village Roots and Beyond*, 40–41.
19. Scott, *Weapons of the Weak*, 37–38.

20. See Chalcraft, *Popular Politics*, 38–39.
21. On defiance and resistance, see Tripp, *The Power and the People*, 72–73. See also Ismail, *The Rule of Violence*, 16–17.
22. Halbwachs, *On Collective Memory*, 39–40.
23. Al-Qattan, "Fragments of Wartime Memories," 133.
24. See Azhari, "An Abandoned Village."
25. Tilly, "Reasons Why," *Sociological Theory*, 447.
26. Nickoley, "Historic Diary," 55.
27. Mounzer, "The Phantom Pain."
28. Mounzer, "The Phantom Pain."
29. Sibley et al., *Social Survey of Syria*.
30. Rantisi, "Losing Beirut."

Bibliography

Secondary Sources, Film, and Literature

Abi Fadil, Michel. "Bibliographi al-harb al-ʿalamiyya al-ula fi Lubnan." In Qassis, *Lubnan fil harb al-ʿalamiyya al-ula*, 1:83–116.

Abu Husayn, Abdulrahim, Tarif Khalidi, and Suleiman Mourad, eds. *In the House of Understanding: Histories in Memory of Kamal Salibi*. Beirut: American University of Beirut Press, 2017.

Afana, Abdul Hamid, Douglas Pedersen, Henrik Ronsbo, and Laurence J. Kirmeyer. "Endurance Is to Be Shown at the First Blow: Social Representations and Reactions to Trauma in the Gaza Strip." *Traumatology* 16, no. 4 (December 2010): 73–84.

Ajay, Nicholas. "Mount Lebanon and the Wilayah of Beirut, 1914–1918: The War Years." 2 vols. PhD diss., Georgetown University, 1973.

———. "Political Intrigue and Suppression in Lebanon during World War I." *International Journal of Middle Eastern Studies* 5 (1974): 140–60.

Akın, Yiğit. *When the War Came Home: The Ottomans' Great War and the Devastation of an Empire*. Stanford: Stanford University Press, 2018.

Aksakal, Mustafa. *The Ottoman Road to War in 1914: The Ottoman Empire and the First World War*. New York: Cambridge University Press, 2008.

Allen, Ira. "Rhetorical Witnessing and Unconcluded War: For Becoming-in-Loss." *Journal of Contemporary Rhetoric* 11, no.1/2 (2021): 55–77.

Aloudat, Tammam. "The Damage Aid Workers Can Do—with Just Their Words." *National News*, March 26, 2021. https://www.thenationalnews.com/opinion/comment/the-damage-aid-workers-can-do-with-just-their-words-1.1190907.

Amirkhan, James. "A Factor Analytically Derived Measure of Coping: The Coping Strategy Indicator." *Journal of Personality and Social Psychology* 59, no. 5 (1990): 1066–74.

Anderson, Ben. *Encountering Affect: Capacities, Apparatuses, Conditions*. London: Routledge, 2016.
Anderson, Benedict. *Imagined Communities: Reflections on the Origin and Spread of Nationalism*. Revised and extended edition. London: Verso, 1991.
Anderson, Warwick. "Disease, Culture and History." *Health and History* 1, no. 1 (1998): 30–34.
Antonius, George. *The Arab Awakening: The Story of the Arab National Movement*. Beirut: Khayat's College Book Cooperative, 1938.
Appleby, Andrew. "Epidemics and Famine in the Little Ice Age." *Journal of Interdisciplinary History* 10, no. 4 (Spring 1980): 643–63.
——— "Grain Prices and Subsistence Crises in England and France, 1590–1740." *Journal of Economic History* 39, no. 4 (1979): 865–87.
Argyle, Michael, and Benjamin Beit-Hallahmi. *The Social Psychology of Religion*. Oxford: Routledge & Kegan Paul, 1975.
Arnold, David. *Famine: Social Crisis and Historical Change*. Oxford: Basil Blackwell, 1988.
Arzuni, Khalil. *Tarikh Shuhur al-ijtimaʿi, 1900–2000*. Dar al-insaniyya, 2001.
Asad, Talal. *On Suicide Bombing*. New York: Columbia University Press, 2007.
Awad, Tawfiq Yusuf al-. *Al-Raghif*. Beirut: Maktabat Lubnan, 1984.
Ayalon, Yaʾaron. "Plagues, Famines, Earthquakes: The Jews of Ottoman Syria and Natural Disasters." PhD diss., Princeton University, 2009.
Azhari, Timur. "An Abandoned Village Bears Witness to Lebanon's Famines—Old and New." *Newlines Magazine*, February 15, 2021. https://newlinesmag.com/reportage/lebanons-famines-old-and-new/.
Baba, Muhammad Kamil. *Tarablus fi tarikh*. Tripoli: Jarouss Press, 1995.
Baʿini, Najib al-. *Dhikrayyat al-Amir Shakib Arslan*. Beirut: Dar Nawfal, 2001.
Barakat, Henri. *Safar Barlik*. Beirut: Phenicia Films, 1967.
Baudis, Dominique. *La passion des Chrétiens du Liban*. Paris: Editions France Empire, 1979.
Beşikçi, Mehmet. *The Ottoman Mobilization of Manpower in the First World War: Between Voluntarism and Resistance*. Leiden: Brill, 2012.
Blanford, J. S., R. G. Crane, M. Mann, K. Paaijmans, K. Schreiber, M. Thomas. "Implications of Temperature Variation for Malaria Parasite Development across Africa." *Scientific Reports* 3, no. 1300 (2013).
Bloch, Marc. *Feudal Society*. Chicago: University of Chicago Press, 1974.
Bloland, Peter, and Holly A. Williams. *Malaria Control during Mass Population Movements and Natural Disasters*. Washington: The National Academies Press, 2001.
Bloxham, Donald. *The Great Game of Genocide: Imperialism, Nationalism, and the Destruction of the Ottoman Armenians*. Oxford: Oxford University Press, 2009.
Bolaños, Isacar A. "The Ottomans during the Global Crises of Cholera and Plague: The View from Iraq and the Gulf." *International Journal of Middle East Studies* 51, no. 4 (2019): 603–20.
Bordewitch, Cloe. "Diaries of an Ottoman Spymaster? Treason, Slander, and the Afterlife of Memoir in Empire's Long Shadow." *Jerusalem Quarterly* 78 (2019): 112–34.

Bowbrick, Peter. *A Refutation of Professor Sen's Theory of Famines.* Oxford: Agricultural Economics Research Institute, 1988.

Brabin, Bernard. "Malaria's Contribution to World War I—the Unexpected Adversary." *Malaria Journal* 12, no. 497 (2014): 1–22.

Brand, Tylor. "Lives Darkened by Calamity: Enduring the Famine of World War I in Lebanon and Western Syria." PhD diss., American University of Beirut, 2014.

———. "Some Eat to Remember, Some to Forget: Starving, Eating, and Coping in the Syrian Famine of World War I." In *Insatiable Appetite: Food as a Cultural Signifier in the Middle East and Beyond*, edited by Kirill Dimitriev, Julia Hauser, and Bilal Orfali. Leiden, Brill: 2019. https://doi.org/10.1163/9789004409552_016.

———. "That They May Have Life: The Syrian Protestant College and Emergency Relief during World War I." In *One Hundred and Fifty*, edited by Nadia el-Cheikh, Bilal Orfali, and Lina Choueiri, 51–62. Beirut: American University of Beirut Press, 2016.

———. "Years of Horror: The American Experience of the Famine of World War I in Lebanon and Western Syria." In *Southern Horrors: Northern Visions of the Mediterranean World*, edited by Gilbert Bonifas and Martine Monacelli, 173–85. Newcastle upon Tyne: Cambridge Scholars, 2013.

Braudel, Fernand. *The Mediterranean and the Mediterranean World in the Age of Philip II.* 2 vols. New York: Harper and Row, 1972–73.

Bruin, Frans. *Lee Observatory, The American University of Beirut Meteorological Summary, 1876–1967.* Beirut: American University of Beirut, 1967.

Burroughs, William James. *Does the Weather Really Matter? The Social Implications of Climate Change.* Cambridge: Cambridge University Press, 1997.

Butler, Judith. "Foucault and the Paradox of Bodily Inscriptions." Eighty-Sixth Annual Meeting American Philosophical Association, Eastern Division, *Journal of Philosophy* 86, no. 11 (1989): 601–7.

———. *Frames of War: When is Life Grievable?* London: Verso, 2009.

Butterly, John R., and Jack Shepherd. *Hunger: The Biology and Politics of Starvation.* Hanover, NH: University Press of New England, 2010.

Camporesi, Piero. *Bread of Dreams: Food and Fantasy in Early Modern Europe.* Translated by David Gentilcore. Cambridge: Polity Press, 1989.

Carbonnier, Gilles. *Humanitarian Economics: War, Disaster and the Global Aid Market.* Oxford: Oxford University Press, 2015.

Cardozo, Barbara, Carol Crawford, Cynthia Eriksson, Julia Zhu, Miriam Sabin, Alastair Ager, Leslie Snider, et al. "Psychological Distress, Depression, Anxiety, and Burnout among International Humanitarian Aid Workers: A Longitudinal Study." *PLoS One* 7, no. 9 (2012): 1–13.

Carmichael, Ann. "Infection, Hidden Hunger, and History." In Rotberg and Rabb, *Hunger and History*, 51–66.

Cavarero, Adriana. *Horrorism: Naming Contemporary Violence.* New York: Columbia University Press: 2008.

Center for Disease Control and Prevention. "2014–2016 Ebola Outbreak in West Africa." Last updated March 8, 2019. https://www.cdc.gov/vhf/ebola/history/2014-2016-outbreak/index.html

Chaker, Joane. "Mule Drivers in Nineteenth-Century Lebanon: From Local Social History towards Global History." *Almanack Guarulhos* no. 14 (2016): 27–51.
Chalabi, Tamara. *The Shiʿis of Jabal ʿAmil and the New Lebanon: Community and Nation State, 1918–1943*. New York: Palgrave Macmillan, 2006.
Chalcraft, John. *Popular Politics in the Making of the Modern Middle East*. Cambridge: Cambridge University Press, 2016.
Çiçek, Talha, ed. *Syria in World War I: Politics, Economics, and Society*. New York: Routledge, 2016.
———. *War and State Formation in Syria: Cemal Pasha's Governate during World War I, 1914–1917*. New York: Routledge, 2014.
Collinge, Sharon, and Chris Ray. "Community Epidemiology." In *Community Structures and Pathogen Dynamics*, edited by Sharon Collinge and Chris Ray, 1–5. New York: Oxford University Press, 2006.
Committee on Herbal Medicinal Product. "Assessment Report on *Centaurium erythraea* Rafn. S. L. FINAL, Including *C. Majus* (H. et L.), Zeltner, and *C. Suffruticosum* (Griseb.) Ronn., Herba, for the Development of a Community Herbal Monograph." European Medicines Agency, Evaluation of Medicines for Human Use. London: November 2015.
Conferees. "The Relationship of Nutrition, Disease, and Social Conditions: A Graphical Presentation." In Rotberg and Rabb, *Hunger and History*, 305–8.
Conrad, Lawrence. "Arabic Plague Chronologies and Treatises: Social and Historical Factors in the Formation of a Literary Genre." *Studia Islamica*, no. 54 (1981): 51–93.
———. "'Taʿun and Wabaʾ': Conceptions of Plague and Pestilence in Early Islam." *Journal of the Economic and Social History of the Orient* 25, no. 3 (1982): 268–307.
Conrad, Peter, and Kristin K. Barker. "The Social Construction of Illness: Key Insights and Policy Implications." *Journal of Health and Social Behavior* 51 (2010): 67–79.
Craps, Stef. "Wor(l)ds of Grief: Traumatic Memory and Literary Witnessing in Crosscultural Perspective." *Textual Practice* 24, no. 1 (2010): 51–68.
Craps, Stef, and Gert Beulens. "Introduction: Postcolonial Trauma Novels." *Studies in the Novel* 40, no. 1/2 (2008): 1–12.
Curtin, Philip D. "Nutrition in African History." In Rotberg and Rabb, *Hunger and History*, 173–84.
Dando, William. *The Geography of Famine*. London: Edward Arnold, 1980.
Daoudy, Marwa. *Origins of the Syrian Conflict: Climate Change and Human Security*. Cambridge: Cambridge University Press, 2020.
Daubman, Bethany Rose, Lynn Black, Annekathryn Goodman. "Recognizing Moral Distress in the COVID-19 Pandemic: Lessons From Global Disaster Response." *Journal of Hospital Medicine* 11 (2020): 696–98.
Deringil, Selim. *The Ottoman Twilight in the Arab Lands: Turkish Memoirs and Testimonies of the Great War*. Brighton: Academic Studies Press, 2018.
de Terra, Helmut. "Rainfall Periodicity in Relation to Agriculture and Malaria in the Near East." *Science* 101, no. 2634 (1945): 629–31.
Devereux, Stephen. "Sen's Entitlement Approach: Critiques and Counter-critiques." *Oxford Development Studies* 29, no. 3 (2001): 245–63.

———. *Theories of Famine*. New York: Harvester Wheatsheaf, 1993.
Devi, Sharmila. "Lebanon Faces Humanitarian Emergency after Blast." *Lancet* 336 (2020): 456.
De Waal, Alex. "The End of Famine? Prospects for Eliminating Mass Starvation by Political Action." *Political Geography* 62 (2018): 184–95.
———. *Famine That Kills: Darfur, Sudan, 1984–1985*. Oxford: Oxford University Press, 1989.
Dodge, Bayard. *The American University of Beirut: A Brief History of the University and the Lands Which It Serves*. Beirut: Khayat's, 1958.
Dolev, Eran. *Allenby's Military Medicine: Life and Death in World War I Palestine*. London: I. B. Tauris, 2007.
Douglas, Karen M., Robbie M. Sutton, and Aleksandra Cichocka. "The Psychology of Conspiracy Theories." *Current Directions in Psychological Science* 26, no. 6 (December 2017): 538–42. https://doi.org/10.1177/0963721417718261.
Douglas, Mary. *Purity and Danger: An Analysis of the Concepts of Pollution and Taboo*. New York: Routledge, 1992.
Edkins, Jenny. "Legality with a Vengeance: Famines and Humanitarian Relief in 'Complex Emergencies.'" *Journal of International Studies* 25 (1996): 547–75.
Ergene, Boğaç A. "On Ottoman Justice: Interpretations in Conflict (1600–1800)." *Islamic Law and Society* 8, no. 1 (2001): 52–87.
Fahmy, Khaled. *In Quest of Justice: Islamic Law and Forensic Medicine in Modern Egypt*. Berkeley: University of California Press, 2018.
———. "Medicine and Power: Towards a Social History of Medicine in Nineteenth Century Egypt." *Cairo Papers in the Social Sciences* 23, no. 2 (2000): 38–50.
———. "Women, Medicine, and Power in Nineteenth-Century Egypt." In *Remaking Women: Feminism and Modernity in the Middle East*, edited by Lila Abu-Lughod, 35–72. Princeton, NJ: Princeton University Press, 1998.
Fahrenthold, Stacy. *Between the Ottomans and the Entente: The First World War in the Syrian and Lebanese Diaspora, 1908–1925*. Oxford: Oxford University Press, 2019.
Faour, Muhammad. "The Demography of Lebanon: A Reappraisal." *Middle Eastern Studies* 27, no. 4 (1991): 631–41.
Farhat, Cynthia Chaker. "Analysis of Indigenous Nutritional Knowledge, Cultural Importance and Nutritional Content of Wild Edible Plants." Master's thesis, American University of Beirut, 2006.
Farschid, Olaf, Manfred Kropp, and Stephan Dahne. *The First World War as Remembered in the Countries of the Eastern Mediterranean*. Beirut: The Orient Institute, 2006.
Fassin, Didier. *Humanitarian Reason: A Moral History of the Present*. Berkley: University of California Press, 2011.
Fawaz, Leila. "Family and Famine in Beirut and Mount Lebanon in World War I." In Abu Husayn, Khalidi, and Mourad, *In the House of Understanding*, 239–52.
———. *A Land of Aching Hearts*. Cambridge: Harvard University Press, 2015.
Figley, Charles. "Compassion Fatigue as Secondary Traumatic Stress Disorder: An Overview." In *Compassion Fatigue: Coping with Secondary Traumatic Stress Disorder in Those Who Treat the Traumatized*, edited by Charles Figley, 1–20. London: Brunner Routledge, 1995.

Firro, Kais. "Silk and Agrarian Changes in Lebanon, 1860–1914." *International Journal of Middle Eastern Studies* 22 (1990): 151–69.

Flaherty, Michael D. *A Watched Pot: How We Experience Time.* New York: New York University Press, 1999.

Fleischmann, Ellen. "Living in 'An Isle of Safety': The Sidon Female Seminary in World War I and the Constraints of Compassion." *Jerusalem Quarterly* 56 (2014): 40–51.

Foster, Zachary. "The 1915 Locust Attack in Syria and Palestine and Its Role in the Famine during the First World War." *Middle Eastern Studies* 51, no. 3 (December 2014): 370–94. https://doi.org/10.1080/00263206.2014.976624.

Foucault, Michel. *The Archaeology of Knowledge and the Discourse on Language.* Translated by A. M. Sheridan Smith. New York: Pantheon Books, 1972.

———. *The Birth of the Clinic: An Archaeology of Medical Perception.* New York: Vintage Books, 1975.

———. *Discipline and Punish: The Birth of the Prison.* New York: Vintage Books, 1995.

Frazier, T.G., ed. *The First World War and Its Aftermath.* London: Gingko Press, 2016.

Fritz, Charles E. "Disasters and Mental Health: Therapeutic Principles Drawn from Disaster Studies." In University of Delaware Disaster Research Center Historical and Comparative Disaster Series 10. Newark, DE: University of Delaware, 1996.

Fromkin, David. *A Peace to End All Peace: The Fall of the Ottoman Empire and the Creation of the Modern Middle East.* New York: Henry Holt, 1989.

Gilsenan, Michael. *Lords of the Lebanese Marches: Violence and Narrative in an Arab Society.* London: I. B. Tauris, 1996.

Gotz, Norbert. "'Moral Economy,' Its Conceptual History and Analytical Prospects." *Journal of Global Ethics* 11, no. 2 (2015): 147–62.

Gratien, Chris. "The Ottoman Quagmire: Malaria, Swamps, and Settlement in the Late Ottoman Mediterranean." *International Journal of Middle Eastern Studies* 49, no. 4 (2017): 583–604.

Grayzel, Susan, and Tammy Proctor, eds. *Gender and the Great War.* Oxford: Oxford University Press, 2017.

Gulick, John. "Conservatism and Change in a Lebanese Village." *Middle East Journal* 8, no. 3 (1954): 295–307.

———. *Social Structure and Culture Change in a Lebanese Village.* New York: Wenner Gren Foundation for Anthropological Research, 1955.

———. *Tripoli: A Modern Arab City.* Cambridge: Harvard University Press, 1967.

Hablas, Faruq. "Hadith al-maja'a fi safar barlik bayn al-watha'iq al-rasmiyya wa al-dhakira al sha'biyya." In Qassis, *Lubnan fil harb al-'alamiyya al-ula*, 1:191–218.

Halbwachs, Maurice. *On Collective Memory.* Translated by Lewis Coser. Chicago: University of Chicago Press, 1992.

Halwani, Yazan. "The Memory Tree—Memorial for the Great Famine of Lebanon (1915–1918)—Artwork by Yazan Halwani." Uploaded May 31, 2020. YouTube video, 1:40. https://www.youtube.com/watch?v=c7DVXq5ipoI.

Hanssen, Jens. "Colonial Anxiety, Scientific Missionaries, and Social Containment in Fin de Siècle Beirut." *Archaeology and History in the Lebanon* 22 (2005): 52–61.

———. "Public Morality and Marginality in *Fin-de-Siècle* Beirut." In *Outside In: On the Margins of the Modern Middle East*, edited by Eugene Rogan, 183–211. London: I. B. Tauris, 2002.

Harris, William. *Lebanon: A History, 600–2011*. Oxford: Oxford University Press, 2012.

Harvey, Paul. "Cash-Based Responses in Emergencies." *IDS Bulletin* 38, no. 3 (2007): 1–3.

Hasselmann, C. M. "Syphilis among Arabs in the Near East." *Archives of Dermatology and Siphology* 38, no. 6 (1938): 841–45.

Havemann, Axel. "The Impact of the First World War on Lebanon's History and Memory: The Case of Shakib Arslan (1869–1946)." In Farschid, Kropp, and Dahn, *The First World War as Remembered in the Countries of the Eastern Mediterranean*, 213–21.

Hayak, Marun. *'Ayn 'Alaq bayn al-qarn al-sabi' wa al-qarn al-hadi wa al-'ishrin*. Beirut: Mia Press, 2005.

Hayes, J. N. *The Burdens of Disease: Epidemics and Human Response in Western History*. 2nd ed. New Brunswick, NJ: Rutgers University Press, 2009.

Herman, Judith. *Trauma and Recovery*. New York: Basic, 1992.

Hertz, Robert. *Death and the Right Hand*. Abingdon: Routledge, 2004.

Hitti, Philip. *Lebanon in History*. 3rd ed. London: Macmillan, 1967.

Hobsbawm, Eric. *Bandits*. New York: Delacorte Press, 1969.

Horsfall, William. *Medical Entomology: Arthropods and Human Disease*. New York: Ronald Press, 1962.

Hourani, Albert. *Syria and Lebanon: A Political Essay*. London: Oxford University Press, 1946.

Horden, Peregrine, and Nicholas Purcell. *The Corrupting Sea: A Study of Mediterranean History*. Oxford: Blackwell, 2000.

Howe, Paul. "Famine Systems: A New Model for Understanding the Development of Famines." *World Development* 105 (2018): 144–55.

Hufton, Olwen. "Conflict and Grain Supplies." In Rotberg and Rabb, *Hunger and History*, 105–34.

Ismail, Salwa. *The Rule of Violence: Subjectivity, Memory, and Government in Syria*. Cambridge: Cambridge University Press, 2018.

Issawi, Charles. *The Fertile Crescent, 1800–1914: A Documentary Economic History*. New York: Oxford University Press, 1988.

Ja'ja', Ghazi. *Tarikh Bsharri al-hadith: 1415–1920*. Bsharri: Bsharri lil nushr, 1990.

Jackson, Simon. "Compassion and Connections: Feeding Beirut and Assembling Mandate Rule in 1919." In *The Routledge Handbook of the History of the Middle East Mandates*, edited by Cyrus Schayegh and Andrew Arsan, 87–101. Abingdon: Routledge, 2015.

Jacobson, Abigail. "A City Living through Crisis: Jerusalem during World War I." *British Journal of Middle Eastern Studies* 36, no. 1: 73–92.

———. "Negotiating Ottomanism in Times of War: Jerusalem during World War I through the Eyes of a Local Muslim Resident." *International Journal of Middle East Studies* 40 (2008): 69–88.

Jansen, Harry. "Time, Narrative, and Fiction: The Uneasy Relationship between Ricoeur and a Heterogeneous Temporality." *History and Theory* 54 (2015): 1–24.

Johnson, Michael. *Class and Client in Beirut: The Sunni Muslim Community and the Lebanese State, 1840–1985*. London: Ithaca Press, 1986.

Johnson, Rob. "The First World War and the Middle East: A Literature Review of Recent Scholarship." *Middle East Studies* 54, no. 1 (2018): 142–51.

Kalaichandran, Amitha. "We're Not Ready for This Kind of Grief: The Coronavirus Pandemic Will Leave Lasting Emotional Scars." *Atlantic*, April 13, 2020. https://www.theatlantic.com/ideas/archive/2020/04/were-not-ready-for-this-kind-of-grief/609856/.

Kanifani-Zahar, Aida. *Mune: La conservation alimentaire traditionnelle au Liban*. Paris: Maison des sciences de l'homme, 1994.

Karamursel, Ceyda. "Shiny Things and Sovereign Legalities: Expropriation of Dynastic Property in the Late Ottoman Empire and Early Turkish Republic." *International Journal of Middle Eastern Studies* 51, no. 3 (2019): 445–63.

Karpat, Kamal. "The Syrian Emigration from the Ottoman State, 1870–1914." *Revue d'histoire maghrebine*, vol. 31/32 (1983): 285–98.

Kayalı, Hasan. *Arabs and Young Turks: Ottomanism, Arabism, and Islamism in the Ottoman Empire, 1908–1918*. Berkeley: University of California Press, 1997.

———. *Imperial Resilience: The Great War's End, Ottoman Longevity, and Incidental Nations*. Oakland: University of California Press, 2021.

———. "The Ottoman Experience of World War I: Historiographical Problems and Trends." *Journal of Modern History* 89, no. 4 (2017): 875–907.

Keneally, Thomas. *Three Famines: Starvation and Politics*. New York: Public Affairs, 2011.

Khalidi, Tarif. "The Arab World." In *The People's Experience*, edited by John Bourne, Peter Liddle, and Ian Whitefield, 291–308. Vol. 2 of *The Great World War 1914–45*. London: Harper Collins, 2001.

Khater, Akram Fouad. *Inventing Home: Emigration, Gender, and the Middle Class in Lebanon, 1870–1920*. Berkeley: University of California Press, 2001.

Khatir, Lahd. *'Ahd al-mutasarrifiyyin fi Lubnan: 1861–1918*. Beirut: Dar Lahd Khatir, 1986.

Khayat, Marie. *Lebanon: Land of the Cedars*. Beirut: Khayat's, 1960.

Khuri, Istifan Ibrahim al-. *Maja'a: Ahalil Jabal Lubnan khilal al-harb al-kawniyya al-ula, 1914–1918*. Zuq Mikayil: Al-markaz al-maruni lil tawthiq wa al-abhath, 2016.

Khuri, Robert M. *La médecine au Liban: De la Phénicie jusqu'à nos jours*. Beyrouth: Éditions ABCD, 1988.

Kidambi, Prashant. "Time, Temporality and History." In *Research Methods for History*, edited by Simon Gunn and Lucy Faire, 220–37. 2nd ed. Edinburgh: Edinburgh University Press, 2016.

Koopman, J. S., and I. M. Longini. "The Ecological Effects of Individual Exposures and Nonlinear Disease Dynamics in Populations." *American Journal of Public Health* 84, no. 5 (1994): 836–42.

LaCapra, Dominick. *Writing History, Writing Trauma*. Baltimore: Johns Hopkins University Press, 2014.

Latron, Andre. *La vie rurale en Syrie et au Liban*. Beirut: L'Institut Français de Damas, 1936.
Lindner, Christine. "From George Tom in Cleveland, Ohio, to His Father Tannous Gergis, Mt. Lebanon, Syria: Remittances as Transnational Relief in World War I." In *An International Rediscovery of World War I: Distant Fronts*, edited by Robert B. McCormick, Araceli Hernández-Laroche, Catherine G. Canino, 55–78. London: Routledge, 2020.
Loheac-Ammoun, Blanche. *History of Lebanon*. Translated by Wilton Wynn. Beirut: Systeco, 1972.
Longrigg, Stephen H. *Syria and Lebanon under French Mandate*. London: Oxford University Press, 1958.
MacKay, Lynn. "The Mendicity Society and Its Clients: A Cautionary Tale." *Left History* 5, no. 1 (1997): 39–64.
Majd, Mohammad Gholi. *The Great Famine and Genocide in Iran: 1917–1919*. 2nd ed. Lanham, MD: University Press of America, 2013.
Maktabi, Rania. "The Lebanese Census of 1932 Revisited: Who Are the Lebanese?" *British Journal of Middle Eastern Studies* 26, no. 2 (1999): 219–41.
Malthus, Thomas. *An Essay on the Principle of Population*. 2 vols. London: J. M. Dent, 1983.
Maruwwa, Ali. *Tarikh Jubba', madhiha wa hadharuha: al-qariya al-lubnaniyya wa al-janna al-dha'i'a alleti 'utlaq minha al-fikr al-'amili washa'fi Lubnan wa al-aqtar al-sharqiyya*. Beirut: Dar al-Andalus, 1967.
Massaad, Barbara Abdeni. *Mouneh: Preserving Foods for the Lebanese Pantry*. Beirut: Barbara Massaad, 2010.
Mayer, Kenneth, and H. F. Pizer. "Introduction: What Constitutes the Social Ecology of Infectious Diseases?" In Mayer and Pizer, *The Social Ecology of Infectious Diseases*, 1–15.
———, eds. *The Social Ecology of Infectious Diseases*. London: Academic Press, 2007.
Mazloum, Subhi. *De la variabilité des pluies dans le bassin oriental de la Méditerranée*. Publications techniques et scientifiques de l'école française d'ingénieurs de Beyrouth, no. 5. Beirut: L'école française d'ingénieurs, 1944.
Mbembe, Achille. *Necropolitics*. Durham, NC: Duke University Press, 2019.
McCarthy, Justin. *The Population of Palestine: Population History and Statistics from the Late Ottoman Period and the Mandate*. New York: Columbia University Press.
McKinney, Kelly. "Breaking the Conspiracy of Silence: Testimony, Traumatic Memory, and Psychotherapy with Survivors of Political Violence." *Ethos* 35, no. 3 (2007): 265–99.
McMeekin, Sean. *The Ottoman Endgame: War, Revolution, and the Making of the Modern Middle East, 1908–1923*. London: Allen Lane, 2015.
McNeill, John. *Mosquito Empires: Ecology and War in the Greater Caribbean, 1620–1914*. Cambridge: Cambridge University Press, 2010
McNeill, William. *The Human Condition: An Ecological and Historical View*. Princeton, NJ: Princeton University Press, 1980.
Metinsoy, Elif Mahir. *Ottoman Women during World War I: Everyday Experiences, Politics, and Conflict*. Cambridge: Cambridge University Press, 2017.

Mikhail, Alan. *Nature and Empire in Ottoman Egypt*. New York: Cambridge University Press, 2011.

———, ed. *Water on Sand: Environmental Histories of the Middle East and North Africa*. New York: Oxford University Press, 2013.

Mir, Maher Zakhiyya al-. *Batha fil tarikh al-hadith wa al-muʿasir*. Lebanon: Self-published, 2003.

Moawad, Yusuf. "Jamal Pasha en une version libanaise, l'usage positif de un legend noir." In Farschid, Kropp, and Dahne, *The First World War as Remembered in the Countries of the Eastern Mediterranean*, 425–46.

Moeller, Susan. *Compassion Fatigue: How the Media Sell Disease, Famine, War and Death*. New York: Routledge, 1999.

Monahon, Cynthia. *Children and Trauma*. New York: Lexington Books, 1993.

Mounzer, Lina. "The Phantom Pain." *L'Orient Today*, May 5, 2021. https://today.lorientlejour.com/article/1260721/the-phantom-pain.html.

Najjar, Charbel Simaʿan al-. *Masarat fi tarikh baladat al-Mtein, 1830–1918*. Al-Mahdiyya, Tunisia: Matabʿa Harun, 2014.

Nakhul, John. "Bilad al-Batrun fil harb al-ʿalamiyya al-ula: Al-jarad, al-ghalaʾ, al-majaʿa, al wafayat." In Qassis, *Lubnan fil harb al-ʿalamiyya al-ula*, 2:795–867.

Nantet, Jacques. *Histoire du Liban*. Paris: Les éditions de minuit, 1963.

Noden, B. H., M. D. Kent, J. C. Beier. "The Impact of Variations in Temperature on Early Plasmodium Falciparum Development in Anopheles Stephensi." *Parasitology* 111, pt. 5 (1995): 539–45.

Offer, Avner. *The First World War: An Agrarian Interpretation*. Oxford: Clarendon Press, 1989.

O Grada, Cormac. *Eating People Is Wrong, and Other Essays on Famine, Its Past, and Its Future*. Princeton, NJ: Princeton University Press, 2015.

———. *Famine: A Short History*. Princeton, NJ: Princeton University Press, 2009.

Ouhanes, Idir. "'Machine Age Humanitarianism': American Humanitarianism in Early-20th Century Syria and Lebanon." In *Christian Missions and Humanitarianism in the Middle East, 1850–1950*, edited by Inger Marie Okkenhaug and Karène Sanchez Summerer, 183–208. Leiden: Brill, 2020. https://doi.org/10.1163/9789004434530_010.

Owen, Roger. *The Middle East in the World Economy, 1800–1914*. London: I. B. Tauris, 2002.

Ozdemir, Hikmet. *The Ottoman Army 1914–1918: Disease and Death on the Battlefield*. Salt Lake City: University of Utah Press, 2008.

Pamuk, Şevket. *A Monetary History of the Ottoman Empire*. Cambridge: Cambridge University Press, 2000.

———. "The Ottoman Economy in World War I." In *The Economics of World War I*, edited by. S. N. Broadberry and Mark Harrison, 112–36. New York: Cambridge University Press, 2005.

Panian, Karnig. *Goodbye Antoura: A Memoir of the Armenian Genocide*. Translated by Simon Beukegian. Stanford, CA: Stanford University Press, 2015.

Pargament, Kenneth. *The Psychology of Religion and Coping: Theory, Research, Practice*. New York: Guilford Press, 2001.

Pastor, Camilla. *The Mexican Mahjar: Transnational Maronites, Jews, and Arabs under the French Mandate*. Austin: University of Texas Press, 2017.
Penrose, Stephen. *That They May Have Life: The Story of the American University of Beirut, 1866–1941*. Beirut: American University of Beirut, 1970.
Philippe, P., and O. Mansi. "Nonlinearity in the Epidemiology of Complex Health and Disease Processes." *Theoretical Medicine and Bioethics* 19, no. 6 (1998): 591–607.
Pitts, Graham. "The Ecology of Migration: Remittances in World War I Mount Lebanon." *Arab Studies Journal* 26, no. 2 (Fall 2018): 88–112.
———. "Fallow Fields: Famine and the Making of Lebanon," PhD diss., Georgetown University, 2016.
———. "A Hungry Population Stops Thinking About Resistance: Class, Famine, and Lebanon's World War I Legacy." *Journal of the Ottoman and Turkish Studies Association* 7, no. 2 (2021): 217–36.
———. "'Make Them Hated in All the Arab Countries': France, Famine, and the Making of Lebanon." In *Environmental Histories of World War I*, edited by Richard P. Tucker, Tait Keller, J. R. McNeill, and Martin Schmid, 175–90. Cambridge: Cambridge University Press, 2018.
———. "Was Capitalism the Crisis? Mount Lebanon's World War I Famine." Environment & Society Portal, *Arcadia*, no. 3. Rachel Carson Center for Environment and Society (2021). https://doi.org/10.5282/rcc/8801.
Plassard, Jacques. "Notice explicative de la carte pluviométrique du Liban." Beirut: Service Météorologique du Liban, 1972.
Post, John D. "Climatic Variability and the European Mortality Wave of the Early 1740s." *Journal of Interdisciplinary History* 15, no. 1 (Summer 1984): 1–30.
———. "Nutritional Status and Mortality in Eighteenth-Century Europe." In *Hunger in History: Food Shortage, Poverty, and Deprivation*, edited by Lucille Newman, 241–80. Oxford: Oxford University Press, 1990.
Pozzi, Lucia, and Diego Ramiro Fariñas. "Infant and Child Mortality in the Past." *Annales de démographie historique* 1, no. 129 (2015): 55–75.
Procter, Tammy M. *Civilians in a World at War, 1914–1918*. New York: New York University Press, 2010.
Provence, Michael. "Druze Shaykhs, Arab Nationalists and Grain Merchants." In *The Druze: Realities and Perceptions*, edited by Kamal Salibi, 139–53. London: Druze Heritage Foundation, 2005.
———. *The Last Ottoman Generation and the Making of the Modern Middle East*. Cambridge: Cambridge University Press, 2017.
Qassis, Antoine, ed. *Lubnan fi l harb al-ʿalamiyya al-ula*. 2 vols. Beirut: Manshurat al-jamiʿa al lubnaniyya, 2011.
Qattan, Najwa, al-. "Eating Grass in WWI Syria: Animals and Identity in the Discourses of the Famine." Presented at the annual meeting of the Middle East Studies Association, New Orleans, October 11, 2013.
———. "Fragments of Wartime Memories from Syria and Lebanon." In Çiçek, *Syria in World War I*, 130–49.

———. "Historicizing Hunger: The Famine in Wartime Lebanon and Syria." In Frazier, *The First World War*, 112–26.

———. "When Mothers Ate Their Children: Wartime Memory and the Language of Food in Syria and Lebanon." *International Journal of Middle Eastern Studies* 46 (2014): 719–36.

Rantisi, Rima. "Inside the Seismic Shift." *Slag Glass City* 7 (June 2021). http://www.slagglasscity.org/dispatches/special-issue-this-blissful-city-2021/inside-the-seismic-shift/.

———. "Losing Beirut: On Life in a Shattered City." *Literary Hub*, August 11, 2020. https://lithub.com/losing-beirut-on-life-in-a-shattered-city/.

———. "The Murderer Inside Me (Us)." *Rusted Radishes*, 2022. http://www.rustedradishes.com/the-murderer-inside-me-us/.

Recuber, Timothy. *Consuming Catastrophe: Mass Culture in America's Decade of Disaster*. Philadelphia, PA: Temple University Press, 2016.

———. "Disaster Porn!" *Contexts* 12, no. 2 (2013): 28–33.

Riyashi, Liza Wadiaʻ. *Tarikh Zahle al-ʻam, 4000 Q.M.—1986M: Wa nukhba min ʻalamiha al-wataniyyin fi matlaʻ al-qarn al-ʻishrin*. Beirut: Dar Ishtar, 1986.

Rogan, Eugene. *The Fall of the Ottomans: The Great War in the Middle East*. New York: Basic Books, 2015.

Rose, Christopher. "Implications of the Spanish Influenza Pandemic (1918–1920) for the History of Early Twentieth-Century Egypt." *Journal of World History* 32, no. 4 (2021): 655–84.

Rosenberg, Charles. "Disease in History: Frames and Framers." *Milbank Quarterly* 67 (1989): 1–15.

———. "What Is an Epidemic? AIDS in Historical Perspective." In *Explaining Epidemics and Other Studies in the History of Medicine*. Cambridge: Cambridge University Press, 1992.

Rotberg, Robert, and Theodore Rabb, eds. *Hunger and History: The Impact of Changing Food Production and Consumption Patterns on Society*. Cambridge: Cambridge University Press, 1983.

Saʻad, Hassan Muhammad. *Jabal ʻAmil bayn al-atrak wa al-faransiyyin 1914–1920*. Beirut: Dar al-kitab, 1980.

Sacks, Jeffrey. "Futures of Literature: Inhitat, Adab, Naqd." *Diacritics* 37, no. 4 (2007): 32–43.

Saʻid, Abdallah. "Tatawwur harakat al-asʻar wa al-ujur." In Qassis, *Lubnan fi l harb al-ʻalamiyya al-ula*, 1:373–416.

Salibi, Kamal. "Beirut under the Young Turks: As Depicted in the Political Memoirs of Salim Ali Salam (1868–1938)." In *Les Arabes par leur archives XVIe-XXe siècles*, edited by Jacque Berque and Dominique Chevallier, 193–215. Paris: Editions du Centre National de la Recherche Scientifique, 1976.

———. *Bhamdoun: Historical Portrait of a Lebanese Mountain Village*. Oxford: Center for Lebanese Studies, 1997.

———. *A House of Many Mansions: The History of Lebanon Reconsidered*. London: I. B. Tauris, 1988.

Saliqa, Ghalib. *Tarikh Hasbaya: Imara wa turatha wa maqamat hatta nihayat al-harb al-kawniyya al thaniyya.* Sidon: Al-matbʿa al-ʿasriyya, 1997.
Sami, Leela. "Gender Differentials in Famine Mortality: Madras (1876–78) and Punjab (1896–97)." *Economic and Political Weekly* 37, no. 26 (2002): 2593–600.
Sayyad, Abdulmalek. *The Suffering of the Immigrant.* Hoboken, NJ: Wiley, 2004.
Schayegh, Cyrus. *The Middle East and the Making of the Modern World.* Cambridge: Harvard University Press, 2017.
Scheper-Hughes, Nancy. *Death without Weeping: The Violence of Everyday Life in Brazil.* Berkeley: University of California Press, 1993.
Schilcher, Linda Schatkowski. "The Famine of 1915–1918 in Greater Syria." In *Problems of the Middle East in Historical Perspective: Essays in Honour of Albert Hourani*, edited by John P. Spagnolo and Albert Hourani, 229–58. Reading: Ithaca Press, 1992.
Schocken, D. D., J. D. Holloway, and P. S. Powers. "Weight Loss and the Heart: Effects of Anorexia Nervosa and Starvation." *Archives of Internal Medicine* 149, no. 4 (1989): 877–81.
Schull, Kent. "Ottoman Criminal Justice and the Transformation of Islamic Criminal Law and Punishment in the Age of Modernity, 1839–1922." In *Prisons in the Late Ottoman Empire: Microcosms of Modernity*, 28–35. Edinburgh: Edinburgh University Press, 2014.
Schumann, Christoph. "Individual and Collective Memories of the First World War." In Farschid, Kropp, and Dahne, *The First World War as Remembered in the Countries of the Eastern Mediterranean*, 247–63.
Scott, James C. *Weapons of the Weak: Everyday Forms of Peasant Resistance.* New Haven, CT: Yale University Press, 1985.
Sen, Amartya. "The Ingredients of Famine Analysis: Availability and Entitlements." *Quarterly Journal of Economics* 96, no. 3 (1981): 433–64.
———. *Poverty and Famines: An Essay on Entitlement and Deprivation.* Oxford: Oxford University Press, 1981.
———. "Wars and Famines: On Divisions and Incentives." *Peace Economics, Peace Science and Public Policy* 6, no. 2 (2000): 10–26.
Shaw, Stanford. *The Ottoman Empire in World War I.* Ankara: Turkish Historical Society, 2006.
Shoshan, Boaz. "Grain Riots and the 'Moral Economy': Cairo, 1370–1517." *Journal of Interdisciplinary History* 10, no. 3 (1980): 459–78.
Singer, Amy. *Charity in Islamic Societies.* Cambridge: Cambridge University Press, 2008.
———. "Serving up Charity: The Ottoman Public Kitchen." *Journal of Interdisciplinary History* 35, no. 3 (2005): 481–500.
Slovic, Paul, David Zionts, Andrew K. Woods, Ryan Goodman, and Derek Jinks. "Psychic Numbing and Mass Atrocity." In *The Behavioral Foundations of Public Policy*, edited by E. Shafir, 126–42. Princeton, NJ: Princeton University Press. 2013.
Snowden, Frank. *The Conquest of Malaria: Italy, 1900–1962.* New Haven, CT: Yale University Press, 2006.
Solnit, Rebecca. *A Paradise Built in Hell: Extraordinary Communities That Arise in Disaster.* New York: Viking, 2009.

Sorokin, Pitirim. *Man and Society in Calamity.* New York: E. P. Dutton, 1942.
Sparén, Pär, Denny Vågerö, Dmitri B Shestov, Svetlana Plavinskaja, Nina Parfenova, Valeri Hoptiar, Dominique Paturot, and Maria Rosaria Galanti. "Long Term Mortality after Severe Starvation during the Siege of Leningrad: Prospective Cohort Study." *British Medical Journal* 328, no. 7430 (2004): 1–5.
Speece, Mark. "Children's Concepts of Death." *Michigan Family Review* 1, no.1 (1995).
Stacey, Jonathan, ed. *A History of the American Community School at Beirut.* Beirut: Alumni Association of the American Community School, 1998.
Stone, Christopher. *Popular Culture and Nationalism in Lebanon: The Fairouz and Rahbani Nation.* New York: Routledge, 2008.
Sukarieh, Mayssun, and Tarif Khalidi. "Near Eastern Banditry: A Study in History and Folklore." In Abu Husayn, Khalidi, and Mourad, *In the House of Understanding*, 271–82.
Svedberg, Peter. *Poverty and Undernutrition: Theory, Measurement and Policy.* Oxford: Oxford University Press, 2000.
Tait, Sue. "Bearing Witness, Journalism and Moral Responsibility." *Media, Culture & Society* 33, no. 8 (2011): 1220–35.
Tamari, Salim. *The Great War and the Remaking of Palestine.* Oakland: University of California Press, 2017.
———. *Year of the Locust: A Soldier's Diary and the Erasure of Palestine's Ottoman Past.* Berkeley: University of California Press, 2011.
Tanielian, Melanie Schulze. *The Charity of War: Famine, Humanitarian Aid, and World War I in the Middle East.* Stanford, CA: Stanford University Press, 2018.
———. "Feeding the City: The Beirut Municipality and the Politics of Food during World War I." *International Journal of Middle Eastern Studies*, 46 (2014): 737–58.
———. "The War of Famine: Everyday Life in Wartime Beirut and Mount Lebanon." PhD diss., University of California Berkeley, 2013.
Tannous, Afif I. "Group Behavior in the Village Community of Lebanon." *American Journal of Sociology* 48, no. 2 (1942): 231–39.
———. "The Village in the National Life of Lebanon." *Middle East Journal* 3, no. 2 (1949): 151–63.
Taylor, Timothy. *The Buried Soul: How Humans Invented Death.* London: Fourth Estate, 2002.
Tejirian, Eleanor. "Faith of Our Fathers: Near East Relief and the Near East Foundation From Mission to NGO." Presented at Altruism and Imperialism: The Western Religious and Cultural Missionary Enterprise in the Middle East, Bellagio, 2000.
Thompson, Elizabeth. *Colonial Citizens: Republican Rights, Paternal Privilege, and Gender in French Syria and Lebanon.* New York: Columbia University Press, 2000.
———. *How the West Stole Democracy from the Arabs: The Destruction of the Syrian Arab Kingdom in 1920 and the Rise of Anti-Liberal Islamism.* New York: Atlantic Monthly Press, 2020.
Thompson, Neil. "The Ontology of Disaster." *Death Studies* 19 (1995): 501–10.
Tilly, Charles. "Reasons Why." *Sociological Theory* 22, no. 3 (2004): 445–54.

Tomkins, Andrew. "Nutrition and Maternal Morbidity and Mortality." *British Journal of Nutrition* 85 (2001): S93–S99.
Traboulsi, Fawwaz. *A History of Modern Lebanon*. London: Pluto Press, 2007.
Tripp, Charles. *The Power and the People: Paths of Resistance in the Middle East*. Cambridge: Cambridge University Press, 2013.
UNHCR. "Cash Assistance and Protection: What, Why and How." United Nations High Commission for Refugees (2021): 1–7.
Waldman, Ronald. "Infectious Diseases in the Context of War, Civil Strife, and Social Dislocation." In Mayer and Pizer, *The Social Ecology of Infectious Diseases*, 300–315.
Walker, Dennis. "Clericist Catholic Authors and the Crystallization of Historical Memory in Lebanonist-Particularlist Discourse, 1918–1922." In Farschid, Kropp, and Dahne, *The First World War as Remembered in the Countries of the Eastern Mediterranean*, 91–128.
Walter, John, and Roger Schofield. "Famine, Disease and Crisis Mortality in Early Modern Society." In Walter and Schofield, *Famine, Disease and the Social Order in Early Modern Society*, 1–74.
Walter, John, and Roger Schofield. *Famine, Disease and the Social Order in Early Modern Society*. Cambridge: Cambridge University Press, 1989.
Watenpaugh, Keith David. *Bread from Stones: The Middle East and the Making of Modern Humanitarianism*. Oakland: University of California Press, 2015.
Watts, Sheldon. *Epidemics and History: Disease, Power and Imperialism*. New Haven, CT: Yale University Press, 1997.
Weulersse, Jacques. *Paysans de Syrie et du Proche-Orient*. Paris: Gallimard, 1946.
White, Hayden. *Metahistory: The Historical Imagination in Nineteenth-Century Europe*. Baltimore, MD: Johns Hopkins University Press, 1973.
White, Sam. *The Climate of Rebellion in the Early Modern Ottoman Empire*. Cambridge: Cambridge University Press, 2011.
———. "Rethinking Disease in Ottoman History." *International Journal of Middle Eastern Studies* 42 (2010): 549–67.
Wilcox, Bruce A., Duane J. Gubler, and H. F. Pizer. "Urbanization and the Social Ecology of Emerging Infectious Diseases." In Mayer and Pizer, *The Social Ecology of Infectious Diseases*, 113–37.
Williams, Elizabeth. "Economy, Environment, and Famine: World War I from the Perspective of the Syrian Interior." In Çiçek, *Syria in World War I*, 150–68.
———. *Economy, Environment, and Famine: World War I from the Perspective of the Syrian Interior*. London: Routledge, 2015.
Winter, Jay, and Antoine Prost. *The Great War in History: Debates and Controversies, 1914 to the Present*. Cambridge: Cambridge University Press, 2005.
Winter, Jay, and Jean-Louis Robert, eds. *Capital Cities at War: Paris, London, Berlin 1914–1919*. New York: Cambridge University Press, 2007.
Wrigley, E. A. "Some Reflections on Corn Yields and Prices in Pre-Industrial Economies." In Walter and Schofield, *Famine, Disease and the Social Order in Early Modern Society*, 235–78.

Yilmaz, Seçil. "Threats to Public Order and Health: Mobile Men as Syphilis Vectors in Late Ottoman Medical Discourse and Practice." *Journal of Middle East Women's Studies* 13, no. 2 (2017): 222–43.

Zamir, Meir. *The Formation of Modern Lebanon*. London: Croom Helm, 1985.

Zelizer, Barbie. "Finding Aids to the Past: Bearing Personal Witness to Traumatic Public Events." *Media, Culture & Society* 24, no. 5 (2002): 697–714.

Zembylas, Michalinos. *Emotion and Traumatic Conflict: Reclaiming Healing in Education*. Oxford: Oxford University Press, 2015.

Zinsser, Hans. *Rats, Lice and History*. Boston: Little & Brown for Atlantic Monthly Publications, 1935.

Primary Sources, Contemporary Sources, and Memoirs

Adams, Walter. "Ulcus Epidemicum: A Preliminary Report." *Archives of Dermatology and Siphilology* 7, no. 5 (1922): 605–8.

Adib, Augustus. *Lubnan ba'd al-harb*. Cairo: Matb'at al-ma'arif, 1919.

Aluf, Mikha'il. *A History of Baalbek by One of Its Inhabitants*. 12th ed. Beirut: Catholic Printing Press, 1914.

Amin, Muhsin al-. *Autobiographie d'un clerc chiite du Gabal 'Amil, tiré de: Les notables chiites*. Translated and annotated by Sabrina Mervin and Haitham al-Amin. Damascus: Institute Français de Damas, 1998.

Arslan, Shakib. *Sira dhatiyya*. Beirut: Dar al-taliyya'a, 1967.

Asfar, Salim al-. "Al-zira'a fi Lubnan." In Bustani, *Lubnan*, 2: 380–420.

'Awad, Ibrahim Khalil. *Min 'ahd al-mutasarrifiyya ila 'ahd al-istiqlal: Mudhakkirat*. Bharsaf: Matb'a Hayak wa Kamil, 1981.

Aziz Bey. *Suriyya wa Lubnan fil harb al-'alamiyya*. Translated by Fu'ad Maydani. Beirut: Al-ahrar, 1933.

Bahjat, Muhammad, and Muhammad Rafiq Tamimi. *Wilayat Bayrut*. 2 vols. Beirut: Dar Lahd Khatir, 1987.

Barton, James L. *The Story of Near East Relief (1915–1930): An Interpretation*. New York: Macmillan, 1930.

Baylan, Salim. "Al-nufus fi Lubnan." In Bustani, *Lubnan*, 2:643.

Bliss, Howard. *The Modern Missionary*. Beirut: American Press, 1920.

Boyer, Benoit. *Les conditions hygiéniques actuelles de Beyrouth (Syrie) et de ses environs immédiats*. Lyon: Imprimerie Alexandre Rey, 1897.

Bristol, Mark. Commander US Naval Detachment in Turkish Waters Mark Bristol to Force Commander, November 22, 1920, USS Scorpion Flagship, Constantinople, Turkey. Subject: Correspondence relative to damaging reports concerning Near East Relief. "Data about the Near East Relief in General and in the Syria-Palestine Area, 1920." In Bayard Dodge Collection, Personal Letters 1917–1919. Archive AA:2.3.4. Box 7, file 1. American University of Beirut/Library Archives, Beirut, Lebanon

Bustani, Fu'ad Ifram. *Lubnan: Mabahith 'ilmiyya wa ijtima'iyya*. 2 vols. Beirut: Manshurat al-Jami'a al-Lubnaniyya, 1969.

Combier, Charles. "La Climatologie de la Syrie et du Liban." *Revue de Géographie de Physic* 6, no. 4 (1933).

Corbett, C. H. "Typhus Fever in Palestine, 1913–1914." *British Medical Journal* 1, no. 2838 (1915): 887–88.
Cortas, Wadad Maqdisi. *A World I Loved: A Story of an Arab Woman.* New York: Nation Books: 2009.
Cropper, J. "Mosquitos and Malarial Fever in Palestine." *Palestine Exploration Quarterly* 34, no. 3 (1902): 305–6.
Darwaza, Muhammad 'Izzat. *Mudhakkirat Muhammad 'Izzat Darwaza: Sijjil hafil bi masarat al- haraka al-'arabiyya wa al-qadhiya al-filastiniyya khilal qarn min al-zaman: 1305–1404 (1887–1984)*, vol. 1. Beirut: Dar al-gharb al-islami, 1993.
de Nogales, Rafael. *Four Years beneath the Crescent.* London: Sterndale Classics, 2003.
Dhahir, Sulayman. *Jabal 'Amil fil harb al-kawniyya.* Beirut: Dar al-matbu'at al-sharqiyya, 1986.
Djemal Pasha. *Memories of a Turkish Statesman, 1913–1919.* London: Hutchinson, 1922.
Doolittle, George Curtis. "Pathos and Humor of the War Years in Syria: A Book of Personal Experiences." Unpublished manuscript, 1920.
Edib, Halidé. *Memoirs of Halidé Edib.* New York: The Century Co., 1926.
Furayha, Anis. *Qabl an ansa.* Beirut: Dar al-nahar, 1989.
Hakim, Yusuf al-. *Bayrut wa Lubnan fi 'ahd âl-'uthman.* Beirut: Dar al-nahar, 1991.
Howard Bliss Collection: AUB President, 1902–1920. Archive AA:2.3.2. Box 18, file 3. American University of Beirut/Library Archives, Beirut, Lebanon.
Huwayek, Elias. *Les Revendications du Liban memoire de la delegacion libanaise a la conference de la paix.* Paris Peace Conference, October 25, 1919.
Ismail, Adel. *Documents diplomatiques et consulaires relatifs à l'histoire du Liban et des pays du proche orient du XVII siècle à nos jours*, vol. 18. Beirut: Editions des Œuvres Politiques et Historiques, 1979.
Jalal Bey. "Al-ahwal al-zira'iyya wa al-tijariyya wa al-sana'iyya wa al-iqtisadiyya fi Jabal Lubnan." In Bustani, *Lubnan*, 2:456–71.
Khalidi, Anbara Salam. *Memoirs of an Early Arab Feminist: The Life and Activism of Anbara Salam Khalidi.* Translated by Tarif Khalidi. London: Pluto Press, 2013.
Khuri, Shakir al-. *Majama' al-masarat.* Beirut: Al-matb'a al-ijtihad, 1908.
Khuwayri, Butrus. *Al-rihla al-suriyya fil harb al-'umumiyya: Akhtar wa ahwal wa 'aja'ib.* Cairo: Al maktab al-'arab, 1921.
Kliger, I. J. "The Movements of Anopheles at Various Seasons of the Year with Special Reference to Infected Mosquitos." *Transactions of the Royal Society of Tropical Medicine and Hygiene* 26, no. 1 (1932): 73–88.
———. "Notes on the Hibernation of Anopheles Mosquitos in Palestine." *Bulletin of Entomological Research* 14, no. 4 (April 1924): 403–7.
———. "Quinine Prophylaxis and Latent Malaria Infection." *Transactions of the Royal Society of Tropical Medicine and Hygiene* 17, no. 4 (1923): 259–62.
Kuyumjian Pasha, Ohannes. *Le Liban à la veille et au début de la grande guerre: Mémoirs d'un gouverneur, 1913–1915.* Paris: Centre d'Histoire Arménienne Contemporaine, 2003.
Lammens, Henri. *La Syrie précis historique.* Beirut: Imprimerie Catholique, 1921.
Maqdisi, Jirjis Khuri al-. *A'dham harb fil tarikh.* Beirut: Al-matba'a al-'ilmiyya, 1927.

Masterman, E. W. G. "Hygiene and Disease in Palestine in Modern and in Biblical Times." *Palestine Exploration Quarterly* 50, no. 2 (1918): 56–71.

McGilvary, Margaret. *The Dawn of a New Era in Syria*. New York: Fleming H. Revell, 1920.

———. *A Story of Our Syria Mission*. New York: Presbyterian Church in the USA Board of Foreign Missions, 1920.

Muhieddine, Husni Bey. "Al-umur al-sihiyya fi Jabal Lubnan." In Bustani, *Lubnan*, 2:644–66.

Naqqash, Albert. "Nadhara fi halat Jabal Lubnan al-iqtisadiyya." In Bustani, *Lubnan*, 2:472–530.

Nickoley, Edward. "Historic Diary." 1917. Edward F. Nickoley Collection, 1873–1937. Archive AA:2.3.3. Box 1, file 2. American University of Beirut/Library Archives, Beirut, Lebanon.

Orfalea, Gregory. *The Arab Americans: A History*. Northampton: Olive Branch Press, 2006.

Ruppin, Arthur. *Syria: An Economic Survey*. Translated by Nellie Strauss. New York: Provisional Zionist Committee, 1918.

Saʻab, Mahmud Khalil. *Stories and Scenes from Mount Lebanon*. Translated by Tamam Abushakra. London: Saqi, 2004.

Sami Bey. "Tarikh ahwal al-turuqat fi Jabal Lubnan." In Bustani, *Lubnan*, 2:600–615.

Shahbandar, Abd al-Ghani. *Kitab al-wiqayya min al-amrad al-muʻadiyya*. Beirut: Al-matbʻa al wataniyya, 1929.

Sibley, Frank, et al. *Social Survey of Syria Compiled under the Auspices of the Near East Relief, the United Missionary Council of Syria and Palestine, the American University of Beirut*. Beirut: American University of Beirut Press, 1925.

Spears, Edward. *Fulfilment of a Mission: The Spears Mission to Syria and Lebanon, 1941–1944*. London: Leo Cooper, 1977.

Tannous, Afif. *Village Roots and Beyond*. Lebanon: Dar Nelson, 2004.

von Sanders, Liman. *Five Years in Turkey*. Baltimore: Williams and Wilkins, 1928.

Wortabet, John. "Cessation of Cholera in Northern Syria." *Lancet* 137, no. 3532 (May 9, 1891): 1036–37.

Yalman, Ahmed Emin. *Turkey in the World War*. New Haven, CT: Yale University Press, 1930.

Yammine, Antun. *Lubnan fil harb*. Beirut: Al-matbaʻa al-adabiyya, 1919.

———. *Quatre ans de misère*. Cairo: Imprimerie Emin Hindie, 1922.

Ziadeh, Nicola. "A First-Person Account of the First World War in Greater Syria." In Farschid, Kropp, and Dahne, *The First World War as Remembered in the Countries of the Eastern Mediterranean*, 265–77.

Journalistic Sources

L'Asie Française
al-Kulliyah (alt. al-Kulliyeh)
Lisan al-Hal

Consular and Diplomatic Documents

Despatches from United States Consul in Beirut

Ministère des Affaires Étrangères. "Rapport sur la situation de la Syrie et du Liban, Julliet 1922 Julliet 1923." Paris: Imprimerie Nationale, 1923.

PHS: Presbyterian Historical Society Archives

RG 115-17-19: Sidon Station Reports 1907–35

RG 115-19-18: Tripoli Station Reports 1891–1919

RG 115-16-10: Relief Work 1915–1917

RG 115-16-11: Relief Work 1915–1917

RG 115-4-17: Beirut Station Reports 1902–1916

RG 115-17-18: Sidon Girls' School Reports 1906–1955

RG 115-3-1: American School for Girls, reports, 1838–1955

RG 115-10-10: Lebanon Station Reports 1911–29

RG 115-8-16: Hamlin Memorial Sanatorium Correspondence 1916–27

RG 115-18-2: Suk-ul-Gharb Lebanon School for Boys Reports 1909–1927

RG 115-19-8: Tripoli Girls' School 1885–1964

RG 115-19-10: Tripoli Kennedy Memorial Hospital 1914–1963

RG 115-19-16: Tripoli—Medical Reports 1895–1914

RG 90-2-12: Station Reports 1915–1920

Interviews

Hayat Mahmud, interview by the author, conducted January 24, 2014.

Soumar Dakdouk, interview by the author, conducted October 13, 2013.

The Institutional Review Board (IRB) of the American University of Beirut deemed the collection of anecdotes from these interviews to be outside of the scope of their oversight and permitted me to collect and use them to enhance my research.

Charts

Baylan, Salim. "Jadwal Ihsa' Ahali Jabal Lubnan 'an Sana 1329." Chart pullout from Baylan, "Al-nufus fi Lubnan," in Bustani, *Lubnan*, vol. 2.

Muhieddine, Husni Bey. "Grafik al-wafayat fi liwa' Jabal Lubnan min ibtida' mart hata ghayat kanun al-awwal wa al-asbab al-ra'isiyya lil wafa' wa nisbatuha bil mi'a bi i'tibar al-sin wa muqayisatuha ma' ba'd musatahan." Chart pullout from Muhieddine, "Al-umur al-sihiyya fi Jabal Lubnan," in Bustani, *Lubnan*, vol. 2.

———. "Grafik yahtawi 'ala muqdar al-wafayat fi liwa' Jabal Lubnan min ibtid'a mart 1333 li ghayat kanun al-awwal wa muqayisatiha bi ba'diha bi sura musataha." Chart pullout from Muhieddine, "Al-umur al-sihiyya fi Jabal Lubnan," in Bustani, *Lubnan*, vol. 2.

———. "Jadwal al-amrad al-sariyya fi liwa' Jabal Lubnan min awwal mart li ghayat kanun al-awwal 333." Chart pullout from Muhieddine, "Al-umur al-sihiyya fi Jabal Lubnan," in Bustani, *Lubnan*, vol. 2.

———. "Jadwal al-asabat wa wafayat al-hama al-namashiyya al-yawmiyya fi liwa' Jabal Lubnan 'itibaran min awwal mart li ghayat kanun al-awwal 1333." Chart pullout from Muhieddine, "Al-umur al-sihiyya fi Jabal Lubnan," in Bustani, *Lubnan*, vol. 2.

———. "Jadwal al-tawalidat wa wafayat fi liwa' Jabal Lubnan min awwal mart li ghayat kanun al-awwal [1]333." Chart pullout from Muhieddine, "Al-umur al-sihiyya fi Jabal Lubnan," in Bustani, *Lubnan*, vol. 2.

Index

'Abeih, 97, 154, 159
Abu 'Izzedine, Muhammad Effendi, 144, 153, 217n28
adaptation. *See* surviving and coping
Adib Pasha, Augustus, 41
age, as vulnerability factor, 25–26. *See also* children; elderly
agency, adaptation as, 82
agricultural labor: camels, rumor about slaughter of, 123; conscription of women and elderly as, 38; effects of war on, 33–34; salaries for, 32, 34–35; shortages of, 8, 28, 38; skilled versus unskilled, 35, 199n87
agriculture and animal husbandry: land tenure and landlord servitude, 28–29, 72; as survival/coping strategy, 62, 71–72. *See also* food; grain and grain production
'Ainab, 154
Ajay, Nicholas, 26, 32, 201n18
'Akkar, 5, 28, 32, 72, 212n11
Alam al-Din, Dr., 144
Aleppo, 73
'Aley, 53, 134, 154

'Alma, 70, 130
Aloudat, Tammam, 166
American Mission, charitable work by, 149, 152, 153, 154–60, 163
American Mission Press, 33, 147, 154, 155, 157, 160, 206n84. *See also* Dana, Charles; McGilvary, Margaret
American Mission schools: employees at, 32, 33; Sidon Girls' School, 99; Sidon Seminary, 145; Tripoli Girls' School, 47, 122
American neutrality with Ottomans during WWI, 151–52, 194n12
American Red Cross. *See* Red Cross
American Relief Committee, 158, 164
American University of Beirut, xi, 42, 84, 158, 184, 185
al-Amin, Muhsin, 54, 61, 62–64, 68, 70, 71, 72, 78, 82
'Amioun, 214n56
Anatolia, 5, 11, 28, 30, 195n48, 206n14, 209n19
Anderson, Benedict, 211n94
animal fodder, human consumption of, 69, 204n33

243

animals/beasts, dehumanization of sufferers as, 117–19
anonymizing of death and the dead, 47–48
Antelias, 129, 131
Antonius, George, 200n18
'Antoura, 151
'Aqil, Bulus, 85, 96
Arab Revolt (1918), 11, 27
Arab Spring, xi
'Arida, Antun, 219n72
Armenians/Armenian refugees, 11, 12, 137, 147, 212n11, 216n2
Arslan, Emir Shakib, 42, 200n14
Asad, Talal, 210n56
al-Asfar, Najib, 217n28
L'Asie Française, 41
'Awad, Ibrahim Kahlil, 8, 71–72, 78–81
Aziz Bey, 93, 198n63, 207n28, 211n74
'Azmi Bey, 8, 81, 151–53

Bahjat, Muhammad, 32, 52, 53, 76, 77, 140
Barakat, Henri, 175, 178
Barouk, 10, 14, 36, 181
Batroun, 52, 67, 132, 137
Baudis, Dominique, 196n1
Ba'abda, 153
Ba'albek, 10, 43, 201n21
Ba'qlin, 36
begging and beggars, xi–xii, 92, 97, 98, 105, 117, 128, 145, 164, 169, 180
Beirut: charitable aid and relief programs in, 8, 75, 76, 148, 152, 162, 168; deaths from famine in, 41, 42, 201n18; declensionist discourse about, 111; flour crises and flour cartels in, 4–5, 75, 93, 205n60; food prices in, 66; funerary practice in, 54; impact of WWI and famine in, 4, 5, 6, 8, 10, 30, 31; Italian shelling of customs house (1912), 1; malaria, prevalence of, 131, 132; *Memory Tree* (Halwani), 174; migration to, 74, 75; modern Syrian refugees in, xi–xiii; population estimates for, 201n21; population of, 214n66; sale of possessions in, 73; summer retreat to mountains, availability of, 91–92; typhus in, 137, 139, 144–45; work and wages in, 32, 33
Beyhum, Ahmad Mukhtar, 81, 93
Bhamdoun, 27, 91
Bint Jbeil, 179
biopower, 130, 212n13, 216n11
Biqa' Valley, 5, 68, 128, 132, 178, 204n23
birth rates during famine, 45
black bread, 67, 68
Bliss, Frederick: on charitable and relief work, 169, 170; declensionist discourse of, 110, 114; modern student engagement with text of, 185–86; trauma of famine in narrative of, 83–85, 90, 91, 95–98, 100, 102, 103
Bliss, Howard, 35, 45, 152, 153, 154, 156, 216n6
blockade of Ottoman ports by Entente powers, 3, 13, 30, 34, 35, 54, 91, 129, 196n1
Bou Najm, 17
Bourj al-Barajneh, 131
Bourj Hammoud, 131, 137, 212n11
Boyer, Benoit, 131, 137
bread, symbolic quality of, 67–68
Britain: coal imports from, 6; diaspora fund transfers, freezing of, 4; trade embargo (1915), 3; WWII, occupation of Lebanon during, 194n32
Brown, Charlotte, 145
Brummana, 24, 91, 150–51, 154, 163, 169
bubonic plague, 129, 131, 134, 136, 212nn7–8, 215n80
Bustani, Wadih, 67
Butler, Judith, 48, 115, 165
Byblos (Jbeil), 132, 137
Byerly, Robert, 23–24, 111, 165

USS *Caesar* ("Calpurnia's husband"), 156
camels, rumor about slaughter of, 123
Camporesi, Piero, 118–19

cannibalism and necrophagy, 61, 111–13, 118, 122, 203n72, 209nn36–37
Cavell, Stanley, 210n56
Cavid Bey, 193n7
Chakra, 62
charitable aid and relief programs, 147–73; American humanitarian aid during WWI, 151–60; American Mission, 149, 152, 153, 154–60, 163; American Relief Committee, 158, 164; Beirut, relief work banned in, 8, 153; corruption and embezzlement, accusations of, 157–60, 217n28; costs of, 158, 163, 216n2; effectiveness of, 159–60; France, famine relief from, 11, 152; illicit aid, 154–58; loans and lending, 155, 206n84; local programs and support networks, 150–51; memories of, 158–60; Near East Relief, 11, 42, 122, 152, 216n2; Nickoley on, 100–101; pastoral work/proselytization and, 160–62; patronage systems, 80–81; Red Crescent, 80, 153; Red Cross, 80, 83, 149, 152–54, 158, 163; religious institutions providing, 81, 151, 152, 160–62, 219n72; remittance smuggling, 154–58; shifting attitudes of aid workers, 147–49; soup kitchens, 24, 33, 91, 97, 150, 154, 159, 163, 168, 217n21; Syrian Protestant College, 148, 152, 154; trauma and burnout of aid workers, 167, 168–72; triage power and moralization of worthiness, 149–50, 163–67, 169–71; typhus, vulnerability of medical professionals to, 143–44; urban versus rural availability of, 75–76; workshops and shelters, conjunction of, 166–67
children: as beggars, xii; birth rates during famine, 45; dying in famine, 47, 49, 52, 57, 202n44; on famine diets, 69; trauma of observing suffering of, 96–97; triage by aid workers, 164, 165, 169; vulnerability to famine, 25, 26

cholera: funerary practices affected by, 54–55; outbreaks of, during famine, 129, 130, 133, 135, 140, 212n8; poverty and, 135; typhus compared, 136; vulnerability to famine and, 18, 22, 25, 127, 133
Choueifat, 177
the Chouf, 31, 41, 141, 163
Christianity/Christian populations: conscription of Christians, 193n5; death rates, 201n18; declensionist famine discourse, religious allusion in, 117; establishment of Lebanon as Christian-dominated state, 13, 58; in French censuses (1921 and 1932), 43–44; funerary practices/body disposal, 50, 141; Greek Orthodox, 32, 219n72; Hoyek's famine memorial, 175; Maronite Catholics, 12, 13, 36, 58, 85, 152, 174, 195–96n50; Ottoman punishment/genocide, famine perceived as, 10–11, 26; religious faith and famine, 160–62
Chtoura, 68
cleanliness. See hygiene
common community of sufferers, creation of, 123–24, 211n94
compassion fatigue, xii, 57, 95–102, 145, 146
conscription in WWI, 2, 23, 27–28, 34, 39, 123, 193n5, 193n7, 200n1
constructs: in declensionist discourse of poverty and suffering, 107, 113–14, 115, 117, 119, 125; diseases as, 128, 141–46, 212n5; famine redefining, 16, 172; moral triage by aid workers and, 149, 150
coping strategies. See surviving and coping
Cortas family, 150
COVID-19 pandemic, 185, 207n35
crime, increase in, 108–9
currency, Ottoman, collapse of, 7, 27, 28, 35, 65, 66, 73, 75, 80, 158, 199n83
cutaneous diphtheria, 130

Dakdouk family, 179–80, 183
Dale, Mary, 96, 110, 121, 156
Damascus, 6, 15, 62, 73, 74, 80, 123, 181, 219n72
Damour, 112, 131, 134, 209–10n41
Dana, Charles, 33, 34, 90, 155, 156, 158–59
Darwaza, Muhammad ʿIzzat, 73, 77
Daʿuq, ʿUmar, 81, 144, 150
Dawkins, Richard, 211n86
The Dawn of a New Era in Syria (McGilvary), 122
Dayr al-Qamar, 32, 67, 79, 137, 141
de Waal, Alex, 159, 212n95
death and the dead, 38–60; anonymizing of, 47–48; burial of dying woman alive, 38–40, 48; cannibalism and necrophagy, 61, 111–13, 118, 122, 203n72, 209nn36–37; causes of death in famine, 22–23, 44–45; CFRs (case fatality rates) for disease, 130, 138, 141, 212n12, 214n65, 215n77; economy of, 54; funerary practice/body disposal, 50–55, 203n63; grave robbing, 54, 122, 209n36; meaning, literary ascriptions of, 55–58; number/percentage of deaths in famine, 12, 14, 40–46, 58–59, 194n19, 200–201n18; in postwar political discourse, 58; relationship to overall understanding of famine, 58–60; sex and gender roles affecting, 23–25; social and psychological impacts of, 39–40, 46–49; Syria, death from famine in, 197–98n33; typhus, number of deaths from, 138–41; as "ungrievable," 48, 50; war dead, 44, 48
declensionist famine discourse, 105–26; cannibalism and necrophagy, 61, 111–13, 118, 122, 203n72, 209nn36–37; class elements of, 107; common community of sufferers, creation of, 123–24, 211n94; crime, increase in, 108–9; dehumanization of sufferers via, 117–19, 125–26; documentation, framing, and construction of, 113–19; evidence of decline, 107–13; food taboos, breaking, 110–13, 118; historical narrative and, 125–26, 212n95; (mis)information, acquisition and transmission of, 119–24, 211n82, 211n84; *inhitat*, 105–6, 208n3; intent and consequences of, 106–7; memories of the famine and, 174–75; poverty and, 106–7, 116, 119, 126; prostitution and sexual misconduct, 108–10; religious allusion, use of, 116–17
dental surgery for Ottoman notable wounded in attempt on life of Jamal Pasha, 154
Dhahir, Sulayman, 108, 112, 118, 125
Dhahr al-Baydar pass, 181
diaspora Lebanese: after civil war of 1860, 44, 201n19; freezing of remittances from, 4, 10, 78; smuggling of remittances by American Mission, 154–58, 160
diet. *See* food
diphtheria, 129, 130
disease and famine, 127–46; CFRs (case fatality rates), 130, 138, 141, 212n12, 214n65, 215n77; construct, disease as, 128, 141–46, 212n5; funerary practice/body disposal and, 52–55; hygiene and, 128, 134–35, 136; malnutrition and nutritional diseases, 9, 23, 45, 116, 117, 127, 132–34; migration and troop movements affecting, 130, 134, 136, 137, 214n56; modern versus traditional medical care, 69, 129–30, 140; nursing care, access to, 134; outbreaks of disease during famine, 129–35; poverty and, 134–35, 136; vulnerability to disease in famines, 22–23, 26, 127–28, 132–34. *See also* cholera, malaria, typhus, *and other specific diseases*
displaced persons. *See* migration
Dodge, Bayard, 42, 46, 51, 97, 99, 106, 107–8, 154, 163, 168–69

Dodge, Cleveland, 154, 216n2
Doolittle, George: on charitable aid and relief programs, 148, 153, 157–59, 168, 170; declension discourse of, 108, 110, 111, 117; on disease and famine, 127, 130, 144; on empty/emptied houses, 72; on foodstuffs, 65, 68, 70; on funerary practices, 52, 54–55; on loans and lending, 80; on meaning of death, 56; on migration to towns, 77; on number of famine deaths, 41, 46; on social/psychological effects of famine deaths, 39, 41, 46, 48, 49, 52; trauma, on experience of, 96, 102; variability of famine experience and, 31, 33, 199n68
doomscrolling, 211n84
dramaturgy, concept of, 211n82
Dray, Arthur, 91, 154, 163, 169–70
Druze, 8, 14, 27, 31, 36, 153, 163
dynamic events, famines as, 19
dysentery, 9, 22, 23, 24, 25, 127, 128, 129, 133, 135, 212n8

Ebola, 142, 215n77
economic assets and vulnerabilities, 17–18, 20–22
economic crisis, famine/WWI as, 6–7, 27, 31–32
elderly: conscription as agricultural laborers, 38; triage by aid workers, 164, 165; vulnerability factor, age as, 25–26
emotional trauma. *See* trauma, experience of
empathetic hedonism, 121
employment. *See* work and wages
Entente powers: archival sources of, xiv–xv; blockade of Ottoman ports, 3, 13, 30, 34, 35, 54, 91, 196n1; espionage, Ottoman fears of, 155–56; occupation of Syria-Lebanon (1918), 3; Ottoman closure of transfers of funds through, 4; remittances from abroad, freezing of, 4, 10, 78
Enver Pasha, 76, 194n9, 204n23

epidemic disease. *See* disease and famine
Erdman, Paul, 33, 157, 158, 162

Fahmy, Khaled, 213n15
Fairuz, 175–76, 177
fallaha, 35, 199n87
famine in Lebanon. *See* Lebanese famine of World War I
famine system theory, 17, 196n5
Fassin, Didier, 113
Fayadh, Aneese, 162
Faysal ibn Husayn, 11, 27
festivals and holidays, celebration of, 91
films about Lebanese famine, 175–78, 179, 183, 196n1
flour. *See* grain and grain production
fodder and animal foods, 68–69, 204n33
food: alternative types and preparations, 61, 62–63, 64–70; cannibalism and necrophagy, 61, 111–13, 118, 122, 203n72, 209nn36–37; charitable programs favoring food over cash relief, 164, 165; fodder and animal foods, 69, 204n33; luxury goods and indulgences, 67–68, 91, 171; malnutrition and nutritional diseases, 9, 23, 45, 116, 117, 127, 132–34; price of, 65, 66–68, 72–73; quality and quantity of, 23, 63, 64–65; seasonal foods, 70; taboo-breaking, declensionist discourse about, 110–13, 118; wild herbs and roots, 69–70. *See also* agriculture and animal husbandry; grain and grain production; starvation; *specific types*
Foster, Zachary, 196n1, 201n18
Foucault, Michel, 216n11
Fowler, Arthur, 160–63, 166
France: censuses of Greater Lebanon (1921 and 1932), 43–44; Christian Arab ties with, 10, 13; diaspora fund transfers, freezing of, 4; famine relief from, 11, 152; WWII, occupation of Lebanon during, 194n32

fuel shortages, 6
ful (fava beans), 70
funerary practice/body disposal, 50–55, 203n63
Furayha, Anis, 1–2, 17, 71, 77, 180, 182

gender. *See* sex and gender roles
genocide: Armenian genocide, 11, 147, 216n2; famine and conscription perceived as, 10–11, 123, 196n1
Gerard Institute, Sidon, 145
Germany: humanitarian aid from, 151; Ottoman bombardment of Crimean ports using cruisers from, 193n8
Gharb region, 71
Ghassayni, Shahin, 36
grain and grain production: alternative types and preparations, 63, 65–70; Druze shayks of Hawran, 14, 27; fixing of grain prices, 7, 28; flour shortages and flour cartels, 4–5, 75, 93, 205n60; locust plagues (1915) and, 6, 28; price of grain and flour, 66–67; profiteering, speculation, and hoarding, 4–5, 6–7, 8, 11, 27, 35–36; regional variation in, 4, 8, 29–30; reserves, limitations of, 6; shortages of agricultural workers, 8, 28; war requisitioning and control of, 4, 6
granular conjunctivitis (trachoma), 26, 129, 131, 135
grave robbing, 54, 122, 209n36
Greater Lebanon. *See* Lebanon
Greater Syria. *See* Syria
Greek Orthodox, 32, 219n72

Hadath, 154, 217n28
Haddad, Gregorios, 219n72
al-Hakim, Yusuf, 33
Halba, 28
Halbwachs, Maurice, 183
Halwani, Yazan, 174
Hamlin Sanatorium, 34, 67, 159

Harris, Ira, 23, 69, 143–44
Hawran, Druze shayks of, 8, 14, 27, 31, 36, 181
Hayes, J. N., 128
Herman, Judith, 97
Hertz, Robert, 51
hindbeh, 69
Hitti, Joseph, 143, 144
Hitti, Philip, 201n18
holidays and festivals, celebration of, 91
Hollis, Stanley, 152
homelessness, 26, 76, 77, 105
horror, concept of, 116, 210n56
Hourani, Albert, 200n18
Howe, Paul, 196n5
Hoyek, Youssef, 175
humanitarian aid. *See* charitable aid and relief programs
Huwayek, Elias, 13
hygiene: declensionist famine discourse and, 119; dirt defined as matter out of place, 119; disease and, 127, 128, 134–35, 136, 143–46

Ibrahim Pasha, 213n15
Imagined Communities (Anderson), 211n94
Indian famine, 174
information/misinformation, acquisition and transmission of, 119–24, 211n82, 211n84
inhitat, 105–6, 208n3
intestinal parasites, 129, 133
Iran, 195n48
Iraq, 130, 206n14
Irish Famine, 174, 204n33
Italian conflicts with Ottoman Empire, pre-WWI, 1, 2

Jabal ʿAmil, 5, 24, 62, 70, 72, 130
Jalal Bey, 43–44
Jamal Pasha, Ahmed: Arslan and, 42; Beirut flour crisis and, 75, 93; chari-

table aid/relief programs and, 24, 151, 153, 154; dental surgery for Ottoman notable wounded in attempt on life of, 154; famine crisis, contributions to, 8, 10, 15, 123, 196n1; memories of the famine and, 173, 175, 177, 178; patronage systems and, 81, 93; political martyrs executed by, 175; in Qassim mythos, 178; rumors about, 123, 124; studies of, xiv; wartime rule of, 3, 76, 194n9
Jazzine, 137, 214n56
Jbeil (Byblos), 132, 137
Jessup, Anna, 34
Jessup, William, 148, 168, 170–71
jewelry, selling, 71, 72, 79
Johanniter Hospital, 151
Jounieh, 52, 131, 137

Kaiserman, Dr., 144
Kanaan, Ibrahim Naoum, 114–15
Kennedy Memorial Hospital, Tripoli, 23, 143–44
Keserwan, 31, 41, 77, 137
Khairallah, As'ad, 155, 159
Khalidi, Tarif, 178
al-Khalidi, Anbara Salam, 93, 118
Khiam, 38–39, 65, 110
al-Khuri, Istifan Ibrahim, 196n1, 201n18
Khuwayri, Butrus, 41
kibbeh, 68, 171
kwashiorkor, 116, 132

LaCapra, Dominick, 86, 121
LaGrange, Harriet, 47, 122, 144
land tenure and landlord servitude, 28–29, 72
Latron, Andre, 73
Law of the Method of Imposition of War Taxes, 2
Law on the Acquisition of Military Transport, 2
Lebanese famine of World War I, xi–xvi, 1–16; causal debates, 13, 17; deaths/death rates, 12, 14, 22–23, 194n19; as economic crisis, 6–7, 27, 31–32; end/consequences of, 11, 187–89; framing of, within historiography of WWI, 11–13; genocide, perceived as, 10–11, 196n1; historical parallels with current crises, xi–xiii, xvi; impact of WWI on Lebanon, 1–11; lived experiences of, focus on, xiii–xiv, 13–16; previous famine experiences, 20; sources for, xiv–xvi; timing and subfamines of, 8–10, 65, 88. *See also* charitable aid and relief programs; death and the dead; declensionist famine discourse; disease and famine; memories of the famine; surviving and coping; trauma, experience of; variability of famine experience
Lebanon: censuses of Greater Lebanon (1921 and 1932), 43–44; Christian-dominated state, famine and establishment of, 13, 58; civil war (1860), 44; impact of WWI on, 1–11; map, *xvii*; modern crises in, xi–xiii, 184–89, 207n35; terminological use of, ix
lemons, 66, 68
lending. *See* loans and lending
lice, as disease vectors, 18, 53, 128, 135, 136, 142–46, 215n80
Lisan al-Hal, 41
loans and lending, 7, 18, 28–29, 30, 35, 75, 80, 109, 155, 160, 187, 206n84
locust plagues (1915), 5–6, 13, 15, 19, 28, 122, 153, 173, 196n1
lollars, 188
Longrigg, Stephen, 200n18
luxury goods and indulgences, 67–68, 91, 171

Mabahith, 25, 43–44, 201n18, 201n21
al-Mahmassani, Muhammad, 175
Mahmoud, Hayat, 36, 67, 182, 183, 196n54

Mahmoud, Jammul, 14–15, 36–37, 181–82
malaria: different strains of, 132, 213n25; malnutrition and, 134; outbreaks of, during famine, 129, 130–32, 135, 146; quinine, access to, 212n9; transmission of, 131–32, 146; triage by aid workers, 164; troops afflicted by, 213n18; typhus and, 128, 135, 144; as vulnerability in famine, 9, 22, 23, 25, 127, 132
malnutrition, 9, 23, 45, 116, 117, 127, 132–34
Ma'louf, Mary Kfouri, 25, 26, 53
Mansourieh, 112
Maqasid foundation, Beirut, 151
al-Maqdisi, Jirjis Khuri: on death and the dead, 48; declensionist famine discourse and, 105, 108, 113, 117, 125; on disease and famine, 127; trauma, on experience of, 96, 98–100, 102; variability of famine experience and, 26
March family, 100, 153
Marjayoun, 201n21
Maronite Catholics, 12, 13, 36, 58, 85, 152, 174, 195–96n50
marqouq bread, 68
mass graves, 53, 203n63
Masterman, E. W. G., 49, 131, 132, 141, 142–43
the Matn, 137, 157, 212n11
Mazzacurati, Marino, 175
Mbembe, Achille, 216n11
McGilvary, Margaret: on charitable aid and relief work, 147–51, 156, 159, 160, 168, 169; on death and the dead, 53; declensionist discourse and, 109, 122, 125; on lending practices of American Mission, 206n84; trauma, experience of, 90, 97
measles, 129
memes, 211n86
memories of the famine, 173–89; centennial of WWI and, 174; charitable aid and relief programs, 158–60; as declensionist discourse, 174–75; familial versus collective, 183–84; in film, 175–78, 179, 183, 196n1; modern crisis in Lebanon and, 184–89; physical memorials, 174, 175; resistance and honor valorized over victimization, 174–84
Memory Tree (Halwani), 174
Mezher, Georges, 217n28
migration, 9, 73–78; adjustment of population statistics due to, 32; coastal urban areas affected by in-migration, 10; death, social and psychological impacts of, 47, 49; disease, spread of, 130, 134, 136, 137, 214n56; funerary practices and, 52–53; men more likely to undertake, 24, 25, 74; from Mount Lebanon region, 30–31, 38–39, 201n19; number of deaths from famine and, 43–44; poverty and, 74, 77; risks posed by, 21, 24, 74; rural-urban and smaller-larger community flow of, 74–77; support networks, loss of, 21, 24, 74, 81; as survival/coping strategy, 19, 21, 37, 62, 63, 73–78; by wealthy persons, 74; work/wages and, 24, 75, 76
Miller, William, 194n19
(mis)information, acquisition and transmission of, 119–24, 211n82, 211n84
Moawad, Yusuf, 196n1
moral decline. *See* declensionist famine discourse
moralization of worthiness/suffering, 149–50, 163–67, 169–71
Mount Lebanon: agricultural production in, 4, 29–30, 34, 71, 198n62; charitable aid and relief work in, 153; death from famine in, 41–43, 46, 123, 200–201n18; disease and famine in, 129–33, 137–38, 139; impact of WWI and famine on, 3–4, 10, 29–31, 34; map, *xvii*; migration from, 30–31, 38–39, 201n19; population of, 214n66; rumored

annexation by Damascus and Tripoli, 123; silk industry and sericulture in, 24–25, 34, 198n62; summer retreat to, availability of, 91–92; terminological use of, ix
"the mountain." *See* Mount Lebanon
Mounzer, Lina, 186
Muhieddine, Husni Bey, 25, 45, 139, 212n8, 212n11, 214n65
muleteers, 27, 36, 37, 92, 176, 180
Munif Bey, 'Ali, 5, 153
Muslim populations: agricultural laborers, salaries of, 32; in French censuses (1921 and 1932), 44; funerary practices, 50; Hoyek's famine memorial, 175; Shi'i population, 38, 62, 179, 200n1; Sunni population, 44, 93, 151
mutasarrifiyya of Mount Lebanon. *See* Mount Lebanon

Nabatieh, 62, 72, 112, 118, 137
Nablus, 140
Nabye, 157
Nakhul, John, 201n18
Naqqash, Albert, 32, 43–44
Near East Relief, 11, 42, 122, 152, 216n2
Nebite, 157
necrophagy. *See* cannibalism and necrophagy
Nelson, W. S., 90, 96, 108, 155–56, 157–58, 159
New York Corn Bank, 155
Nickoley, Edward: on charitable and relief work, 168; on death and the dead, 38, 50, 51, 54, 56–58, 59; declensionist discourse of, 106, 111–13, 115–18, 121–23, 208n5; on speculation and profiteering, 36; summer retreat to mountain, 92; on trauma of observing suffering, 95, 99–102, 103, 104, 186; on typhus, 144–45, 146
Nimeh, William, 90
Nogales, Rafael de, 93

O'Grada, Cormac, 197n27
ophthalmia, 26, 127
oranges, 65, 68, 204n27
Ottoman Empire: American neutrality with, during WWI, 151–52, 194n12; archival sources of, xiv–xv; blockade of Ottoman ports by Entente powers, 3, 13, 30, 34, 35, 54, 91, 196n1; bombardment of Crimean ports by, 3, 193n8; charitable aid and relief programs funded by, 151; currency collapse, 7, 27, 28, 35, 65, 66, 80, 158, 199n83; Entente espionage, fears of, 155–56; famine crisis, contributions to, 7–8, 10–11; genocide, famine and conscription perceived as, 10–11, 123, 196n1; grain reserves, limitations of, 6; impact of WWI on Lebanon via, 1–11; information, acquisition and transmission of, 120; length(s) of wartime experience in, 88, 206n14; patronage systems in, 81; in *Safar Barlik* (film, 1968), 175–78, 196n1; smallpox vaccination campaign, 129–30, 212n11; transfers of funds through Entente financial institutions, closure of, 4; WWI and dissolution of, 12
Ozdemir, Hikmet, 130

Palestine: body lice, perception of, 142–43; death, social and psychological impacts of, 49; deaths from famine in, 42; length of wartime experience in, 206n14; malaria, prevalence of, 130–31, 132; as regional breadbasket, 4, 30; typhus in, 137
Palestine Exploration Fund, 49, 83
Palestine Exploration Quarterly, 142–43
parasites: intestinal, 129, 133; lice, as disease vectors, 18, 128, 135, 136, 142–43, 215n80; mosquitoes, and transmission of malaria, 131–32, 146
Paris Peace Conference, 11

Passion des Chrétiens du Liban, 196n1
patronage systems, 21, 29, 78, 80–81, 150, 151
photographic documentation of famine, 114–15
Pitts, Graham, 196n1, 201n18
plague. *See* bubonic plague
pneumonia, 135
poverty: charitable aid, urban versus rural availability of, 75–76; constructs of, 107, 113–14, 115, 117, 119, 125; death, social and psychological impacts of, 47, 49; declensionist famine discourse about, 106–7, 116, 119, 126; disease and, 134–35, 136, 137, 143–46; funerary practices and, 52–53, 55; migration and, 74, 77; moral triage by aid workers and, 164–67; as most significant vulnerability in famine experience, 9, 20–23; typhus and, 128; urban poverty in Sidon, Tripoli, and Tyre, 30
Presbyterian American Mission. *See specific entries at* American Mission
Presbyterian Board of Foreign Missions, 147, 156, 158, 159, 160, 170
profiteering, speculation, and hoarding, 6–7, 8, 11, 27, 35–36, 109
prostitution, 25, 61, 108–10, 130
ptomaine poisoning, 111, 209n30

Qabl an ansa (Furayha), 1–2
Qajars, 12
Qassim, Milhem, 178–79, 180, 182
al-Qattan, Najwa, 118, 183
Quatre ans de misère (Yammine), 41

Rahbani brothers, 175
Rantisi, Rima, 173, 188
Ras al-Matn, 1–2, 77
Red Crescent, 80, 153
Red Cross, 80, 83, 149, 152–54, 158, 163
refugees: Armenians/Armenian refugees, 11, 12, 137, 147, 212n11, 216n2; in Lebanese famine (*See* migration); Syrian refugees in modern Lebanon, xi–xiii, 184–87, 207n35
regional differences in famine experience, 5, 9–10, 19–20, 26–31
relief programs. *See* charitable aid and relief programs
religious allusion in declensionist famine discourse, 116–17
religious faith and famine, 160–62
religious institutions: charitable aid provided by, 81, 151, 152, 160–62, 219n72; funerary practices/body disposal, 50, 141; pastoral work/proselytization and aid work, 160–62. *See also specific institutions*
remittances: American Mission's smuggling of, 154–58, 160; foreign, loss of, 4, 10, 78
requisitioning of food and commodities, 2–3, 4
Riyashi, Liza, 68, 205n46
Rockefeller, John D., 155, 216n2
Rosenberg, Charles, 211n82
Rufayil, Yusuf, 105–6, 108, 110
rumor and fact, acquisition and transmission of, 119–24, 211n82, 211n84
rural areas. *See* urban versus rural areas
Russia ports in Crimea, Ottoman bombardment of, 3, 193n8

Sabaʿ, Affeffi, 34, 159
"al-safalat al-fiziologiyya" (physiological baseness), as cause of death, 22
Safar Barlik (film, 1968), 175–78, 179, 183, 196n1
safar barlik (Ottoman mobilization campaign), 2
saj-style *marqouq* bread, 68
sale of possessions, 72–73, 170
Salibi, Kamal, 159
Salibi, Salwa, 85
Saʿab, Mahmud Khalil, 79–80
scabies, 129, 135
Scherer, George, 160

Schumann, Christoph, 196n1
secondhand suffering, 94–102
Sen, Amartya, 198n46
sericulture. *See* silk industry
sex and gender roles: conscription of women and elderly as agricultural laborers, 38; death, social and psychological impacts of, 47; employment for women, 24–25, 28, 34; feminization of famine victims, 115, 175; masculine cultural obligations, 175, 180; memorials to famine and, 175; migration, men more likely to undertake, 24, 25, 74; prostitution, 25, 61, 108–10, 130; vulnerability to famine and, 23–25
shelters and workshops set up as relief programs, conjunction of, 166–67
Shimlan, 159
Shweir, 92, 154
Sidon: charitable aid and relief programs in, 76, 156–58, 160, 161, 165; death from famine in, 46, 48–49; food alternatives in, 68; landlord servitude in, 29; malaria, prevalence of, 131; population estimates for, 201n21; Presbyterian missionaries in, 145; sex and mortality in, 23–24; trauma, secondhand experience of, 99; typhus, prevalence of, 137, 144, 145; urban poverty in, 30
Sidon Girls' School, 99
Sidon Seminary, 145
silk industry, 4, 5, 13, 24, 27, 29–30, 34, 77, 194n14, 198n62
Slovic, Paul, 100–101
smallpox, 22, 38, 127, 129–30, 132, 133, 134, 212n11
smugglers, valorization of, 27, 36, 176, 180–82
social assets and vulnerabilities, 17–18, 20–22. *See also* poverty; wealthy and middle classes
social constructs. *See* constructs
social decline. *See* declensionist famine discourse

social distancing practices, 145
Sorokin, Pitirim, 20, 108, 121, 211n77
soup kitchens, 24, 33, 91, 97, 150, 154, 159, 163, 168, 217n21
Spears, Edward, 194n32
Standard Oil Company, 155
starvation, 22, 47, 48–49, 94, 116, 164
A Story of Our Syria Mission (Presbyterian Board of Foreign Missions), 147
sufferers and suffering: common community, creation of, 123–24, 211n94; constructs of, in declensionist discourse, 107, 113–14, 115, 117, 119, 125; moralization of worthiness and, 149–50, 163–67, 169–71; secondhand suffering, 94–102. *See also* trauma, experience of
Sukarieh, Mayssun, 178
support networks: declension discourse about familial breakdown, 105, 110–11; local relief programs, 150–51; migration and loss of, 21, 24, 74, 81; patronage systems, 80–81, 151; as survival/coping strategy, 78–81. *See also* charitable aid and relief programs
Suq al-Gharb, 33, 97, 154, 159
Sursuq family, 5, 81, 93, 175
surviving and coping, 61–82; as agency, 82; agriculture and animal husbandry, 62, 71–72; compassion fatigue, xii, 57, 95–102, 145, 146; food alternatives, 61, 62–63, 64–70; food prices, finding money for, 65, 66–68, 72–73; food quantity and quality, 23, 63, 64–65; leisure activities and vacations, 91–94; loans and lending, 18, 28–29, 35, 75, 80, 109, 155, 160, 187, 206n84; migration, as coping strategy, 19, 21, 37, 62, 63, 73–78; proactive and reactive methods, 63; as rational cost-benefit assessments, 62, 64, 78; sale of possessions, 72–73; as series of adaptive strategies, 61–62, 64; successes and failures of, 64; support networks, 78–81; variability and individuality of, 63

syphilis, 25, 110, 130, 134, 164, 213n15
Syria: death from famine in, 41, 43, 197–98n33; food prices in, 66; Greater Syria, defined, 193n4; interior regions, local food production in, 27; length of wartime experience in, 206n14; migration from 1881–1914, 201n19; refugees in modern Lebanon, xi–xiii, 184–87, 207n35; as regional breadbasket, 4; typhus in, 137; WWI, effects of, 3
Syrian Protestant College, 81, 83, 100, 108, 144–45, 148, 152, 154, 158. *See also specific associated persons*

taboos and taboo breaking: cannibalism and necrophagy, 61, 111–13, 118, 122, 203n72, 209nn36–37; food taboos, 110–13, 118; interest in information about, 122; prostitution and sexual misconduct, 25, 61, 108–10, 130
Talaat Pasha, 194n9
Tamimi, Muhammad Rafiq, 32, 52, 53, 76, 77, 140
Tanielian, Melanie, 175, 201n18, 212n7
tannour ovens, 68, 177
Tannous, Afif, 67, 71, 79, 157, 182
Tannous, Nachle, 157
Taylor, Timothy, 55
Thompson, Elizabeth, 196n1, 201n18
Tilly, Charles, 184
time: blandness, despondence, and monotony of daily routines, 89–91; festivals and holidays, celebration of, 91; Lebanese famine, timing and subfamines of, 8–10, 65, 88; problem of filling, 89–94; subjective experience of, 86–89; vacations and leisure activities, 92–94
Traboulsi, Fawwaz, 201n18
trachoma (granular conjunctivitis), 26, 129, 131, 135
trauma, experience of, 83–104; challenges of writing about, 84–86; charitable aid and relief workers, trauma and burnout of, 167, 168–72; consequences of, 102–4; historical significance of, 86; hopelessness and demoralization, 96; hunger and starvation, 94; (mis)information, acquisition and transmission of, 121; as intergenerational and ongoing, 187–89; leisure activities and vacations, 91–94; monotony of daily routines and means of filling time, 89–94; normalization, desensitization, and compassion fatigue, xii, 57, 95–102, 145, 146; observation of suffering as, 94–102; subjective experience of time and, 86–89
triage performed by aid workers, 149–50, 163–67, 169–71
Tripoli: charitable aid and relief programs, 76, 160–62, 163; deaths from famine in, 47; declensionist famine discourse from, 108, 113; funerary practice/body disposal in, 53, 54–55, 203n63; landlord servitude in, 29; malaria, prevalence of, 131; migration to, 74, 76, 77; Mount Lebanon, rumored annexation of, 123; poor food quality and food alternatives in, 23, 69; population estimates for, 201n21; Presbyterian Mission in, 108; typhus, prevalence of, 137, 143–44; urban poverty in, 30
Tripoli Girls' School, 47, 122
triumvirate, 3, 194n9
tuberculosis, xii, 9, 25, 34, 45, 84, 129, 133, 134, 135, 136, 187
Turjeman, Ihsan, 109
Turks/Turkey. *See* Ottoman Empire
turmus, 68
typhoid, 22, 23, 25, 127, 129, 134, 135, 212n8
typhus, 135–46; areas most affected by, 137–38; cholera compared, 136; conditions amplifying spread of, xii, 134–35; conscripts succumbing to,

23; as construct, 141–46; as endemic disease, 135–36, 214n52; epidemics during WWI, xii, 47, 127, 128, 135–41; funerary practice and, 52, 53; immunity of survivors, 215n67; in Khiam, 38; louse-based etiology of, 18, 128, 135, 136, 142–43, 215n80; malaria and, 128, 135, 144; medical professionals' vulnerability to, 143–44; migration and troop movements spreading, 130, 136, 137; number of deaths/death rates from, 138–41, 214n65; poverty and hygiene, relationship to, 134–35, 136, 137, 138, 143–46; refugees and, xii; reporting on, 138–41; sex/gender and vulnerability to, 24, 25; social segregation to avoid, 99; social/psychological impacts of death from, 47; triage by aid workers, 164; vulnerability to famine and, 23, 24, 25, 37, 127, 134, 137–38

Tyre: charitable aid, availability of, 75; funerary practice in, 52, 53; landlord servitude in, 29; malaria, prevalence of, 131; migration to, 76; population estimates for, 201n21; ratio of unmarried women to men in, 24; typhus, prevalence of, 137, 140; urban poverty in, 30

United Kingdom. *See* Britain
Université Saint-Joseph, Beirut, 151
urban versus rural areas: charitable aid, availability of, 75–76; coastal urban areas affected by in-migration, 10; migration, rural-to-urban and smaller-to-larger community flow of, 74–77; poverty, urban, 30
Utidjian, Dikran, 154

Van Zandt, Philomela, 144–45
variability of famine experience, 17–37; age as vulnerability factor, 25–26; death, causes of, 22–23; disease, as vulnerability, 22–23, 26 (*See also specific diseases*); dynamic events, famines as, 19; food, quality and quantity of, 23; food prices, 66; luck, effects of, 18; multiplicity of factors affecting, 19–20; poverty as most significant vulnerability, 9, 20–23; regional differences in, 5, 9–10, 19–20, 26–31; sex and gender roles, 23–25; social/economic assets and vulnerabilities, 17–18, 20–22; starvation, 22; survival/coping strategies, 63; vulnerability and resiliency factors, 19–26; work and wages, 31–36

vicarious suffering, 94–102
villages/communities: lost to famine, 46, 77; as support networks, 78–81

Walker, Dennis, 196n1
wasta, 21, 197n8
wealthy and middle classes: compassion fatigue of, 99; leisure activities, resentment of, 92–93; migration by, 74; moral triage by aid workers and, 165; profiteering by, 109; social/economic assets available to, 17–18, 20–22; summer retreat to mountain by, 91–92; typhus, social fear of, 144–46
winter conditions during famine years, 21, 57, 70, 99, 181, 197n10
women. *See* sex and gender roles
work and wages, 31–36; conscription and worker shortages, 27–28, 38; Entente blockade affecting, 54; migrating to obtain, 24, 75, 76; women's employment, 24–25, 28, 34. *See also* agricultural labor
workshops and shelters set up as relief programs, conjunction of, 166–67
World War I: American humanitarian aid during, 151–60; American neutrality with Ottomans during, 151–52,

World War I (*cont.*)
194n12; centennial of, 174; conscription in, 2, 23, 27–28, 34, 39, 123, 193n5, 193n7, 200n1; as economic crisis, 6–7, 27, 31–32; famine during, 12, 195n48 (*See also* Lebanese famine of World War I); framing of Lebanese famine within historiography of, 11–13; impact on Lebanon, 1–11; Ottoman Empire, dissolution of, 12; typhus epidemics during, xii, 47, 127, 128, 135–41
World War II, occupation of Lebanon during, 194n32

Yalman, Ahmed Emin, 32, 33
Yammine, Antun: accusations against Ottoman officials by, 196n1, 204n23, 217n28; on death and the dead, 41, 46; declensionist famine discourse of, 109, 112, 118, 125; on disease and famine, 127, 139, 141; on documentation of famine, 1
Yuhanna Maroun Monastery, 67

Zahle, 68, 72, 74, 76–77, 131, 137, 138, 144, 157–58, 161
za'atar, 70
Zeine, Iskander, 144
Ziadeh, Nicola, 80
Zinsser, Hans, 135–36, 214n52, 215n80

The authorized representative in the EU for product safety and compliance is:
Mare Nostrum Group
B.V Doelen 72
4831 GR Breda
The Netherlands

www.ingramcontent.com/pod-product-compliance
Lightning Source LLC
Chambersburg PA
CBHW031804220426
43662CB00007B/517